Mixed Emotions

Mixed Emotions

Beyond Fear and Hatred in International Conflict

ANDREW A. G. ROSS

The University of Chicago Press
Chicago and London

Andrew A. G. Ross is assistant professor in the Department of Political Science and affiliated faculty with the Center for Law, Justice, and Culture at Ohio University.

The University of Chicago Press, Chicago 60637
The University of Chicago Press, Ltd., London
© 2014 by The University of Chicago
All rights reserved. Published 2014.
Printed in the United States of America

23 22 21 20 19 18 17 16 15 14   1 2 3 4 5

ISBN-13: 978-0-226-07739-0 (cloth)
ISBN-13: 978-0-226-07742-0 (paper)
ISBN-13: 978-0-226-07756-7 (e-book)
DOI: 10.7208/chicago/9780226077567.001.0001

Library of Congress Cataloging-in-Publication Data

Ross, Andrew A. G. author.
    Mixed emotions : beyond fear and hatred in international conflict / Andrew A. G. Ross.
        pages cm
    Includes bibliographical references and index.
    ISBN 978-0-226-07739-0 (cloth : alkaline paper) — ISBN 978-0-226-07742-0 (paperback : alkaline paper) — ISBN 978-0-226-07756-7 (e-book)
1. Emotions—Political aspects. 2. International relations—Pyschological aspects. 3. World politics—Psychological aspects. 4. Terrorism—Public opinion—Psychological aspects. 5. Ethnic conflict—Public opinion—Psychological aspects.   I. Title.
    JZ1249.R67 2014
    327.1'6019—dc23
                                                            2013007996

♾ This paper meets the requirements of ANSI/NISO Z39.48-1992 (Permanence of Paper).

CONTENTS

Preface and Acknowledgments / vii

Introduction / 1

ONE / Circulations of Affect in Global Politics / 15

TWO / Contagion and the Creativity of Affect / 39

THREE / The Affective Politics of Terror / 67

FOUR / Emotions and Ethnic Conflict / 93

FIVE / Justice beyond Hatred / 123

Conclusion / 151

Notes / 163
Bibliography / 191
Index / 209

This book is about the emotions connecting ordinary people to the world of politics. It dispenses with the still-commonplace notion that emotions affect only a marginal population of especially zealous political actors. In the post-Enlightenment West, we generally treat emotions as among the least reliable and most expendable human capabilities—merely private states with no proper place in intellectual deliberation over politics. We associate emotional conduct with people different from ourselves and, perhaps, places far away from our own. Resisting these assumptions, the theories and cases discussed in this book depict emotions as by-products of everyday social interaction and constitutive elements of political action. As people receive messages through mass media and participate in other rituals of public life, they accumulate repertoires of emotional expression. These circulations of affect are contagious, but not in the negative sense of that word: expectations, hopes, fears, and other socially transmitted responses are integral to the way people—both elites and ordinary citizens—inhabit cultural and political communities. Far from a corrupting force, emotions lie at the heart of political practice in the modern world.

This effort to redignify emotion stems from a long-standing curiosity about the emotional lives of ordinary people and the impact they have on political contestation. There is more than a small dose of personal soul-searching embedded in the project—a fact that took me an embarrassing number of years to recognize. The project is undeniably a product of some deep, inarticulate need to understand why, in a world of emotional intensity, I often felt left out in the cold, as it were. I am happy that my work on the book has provided some insight on this introspective level, even as a proclivity for doing theory insulated me from intimate contact with actual, emoting people (the irony is not lost on me). The book also grew out of critical engagement with various scholarly literatures invested in intellectualist conceptions of human agency. As a one-time student of political theory, I felt tremendous disappointment in neo-Kantian philosophies privileging reflective forms of reason and celebrating the promise of deliberative democracy. I then rebelled, somewhat haphazardly, against a broad spectrum of rationalist and state-centric approaches to international relations, all of which seemed overly detached and artificially cleansed of the complex motivations and commitments that make human actors behave the way they do. The book is an attempt to capitalize on these hesitations by developing an alternative framework better suited to the affective intensity of global politics—and to the profound complexity of affect itself.

This book's progress toward publication has been long and circuitous, and I hope never to travel that exact path again. One minor consolation is the thought that perhaps such a confounding subject matter somehow deserved an especially long period of gestation. I can also say that the final product is better poised than earlier versions to deliver an unconventional theorization of emotion to a broad audience. In retrospect, the project almost certainly would have progressed more quickly had I reached out for more feedback along the way. I am very grateful to Janice Gross Stein and Neta Crawford, both of whom endured reading a bumpy manuscript and offered provocative challenges and generous suggestions for smoothing it out, and to David Pervin, who took a leap of faith in shepherding the project along at the University of Chicago Press. I am also grateful to Christie Henry and Shenny Wu at the Press for their help in David's absence, and to Therese Boyd for her very thorough copyediting work.

I sincerely hope the book still bears some traces of the vibrant intellectual community from which it once sprang: the Political Science Department at Johns Hopkins University. I owe a great debt to Siba Grovogui, both for his keen insight and intellectual provocations as a supervisor and for his good humor and support as a friend. I am grateful also to Bill Connolly for his guidance and still regard his seminars as unrivaled machines for intellectual creativity. I only hope Sibagro and Bill can find traces of their influence somewhere in these pages. I also thank the many other faculty members who provided feedback and guidance at different stages, especially Jane Bennett, Mark Blyth, Jennifer Culbert, Dan Deudney, Niloofar Haeri, and Ruby Lal. I am grateful also to the many fabulous grad students with whom I shared ideas, hopes, and fears (and drinks) while in Baltimore: Erin Ackerman, Jen Baggot, Kelly Barry, Jacquie Best, Blake Ethridge, Harry

Gould, Dan Levine, Matt Moore, Patrick Peel, Smita Rahman, Indira Ravindran, Nick Tampio, and Lars Tønder.

The book is largely a product of my career in the great swing state of Ohio. I was fortunate to spend 2007–8 as a postdoctoral fellow at the Mershon Center for International Security Studies at Ohio State University. I am still grateful that Alex Wendt read an article I had written as a graduate student, had the intellectual generosity to look past its inexperienced bravado, and signed off on an invitation to Mershon. While the postdoc did not, alas, lead imminently to the book's publication, that year offered an invaluable opportunity to do much of its necessary groundwork. During my stay in Columbus, Rick Herrmann, Ted Hopf, Jennifer Mitzen, and John Mueller all provided advice, feedback, and/or support; Srdjan Vucetic offered some excellent comments on an earlier draft of chapter 4; and Anja Jetschke and Zach Zwald supplied an extraordinarily engaging cohort of fellow fellows. I owe a very large debt to my colleagues down the road in Athens. The Department of Political Science at Ohio University has been a wonderful home, and I am grateful to my colleagues for their good humor, generosity, and professionalism. John Gilliom offered sage advice during the external review process at Chicago, and Deena Proffitt and Nina Sharpe have provided outstanding administrative support at every stage. Rob Briscoe, Susan Burgess, Maria Fanis, Judith Grant, Jim Mosher, Kathleen Sullivan, Taka Suzuki, Myra Waterbury, Patty Weitsman, and Julie White have also variously provided friendship, conversation, and professional guidance along the way.

The book has benefited from the many panels, talks, conversations, and e-mails shared with friends and colleagues in the broader academic community. For ongoing advice, encouragement, and substantive challenges, I thank Janice Bially Mattern; I only hope the book does justice to the support and insight Janice has generously shared. I am also especially grateful to Todd Hall; my collaborations with him, albeit works in progress, have had more impact on me than he might think. I consider myself fortunate to have crossed intellectual paths with Ian McNeely—or, more accurately, that he took the initiative and had the extradisciplinary reach to cross over to my wobbly path at several stages to offer invaluable feedback. Maria Fanis has been a great friend, mentor, and interlocutor, and I hope the book, which she has not yet read, might lead to many more conversations to come. I am also thankful to the many scholars I have met at talks, workshops, and conferences, some of whom have even pushed through my reserved awkwardness with professional networking: Jean-Marc Coicaud, François Debrix,

Jenny Edkins, Tuomas Forsberg, Nick Onuf, Brent Sasley, Brent Steele, Mira Sucharov, Geoff Whitehall, Wes Widmaier, and Maja Zehfuss.

The book would not have been possible without the consistent support of friends and family, some of whom have spent years waiting patiently for rare news of its progress. I will always be indebted to my parents, Graham and Susan Ross, for their encouragement and support; they have been re- markably tolerant of my gradual "Americanization" and all the inconve- niences and sacrifices it has incurred for them. I am grateful also to Cheryl and Rich Rowe, who have on many, many occasions offered their (almost) tireless care for their grandchildren in my absence; my professional life would likely be very different were it not for their generosity. I am deeply thankful for the enjoyment and intensity that my two little boys, Daniel and James Rowe, have brought to my life. It is humbling to discover that parenting a child can provide more schooling on the mysteries of emotion than years of scholarly research. And then there's the person who holds us all together: my wife, partner, and best friend, Erin Rowe. Her intellect and love pervade the space around her and benefit those of us fortunate enough to share it; I am daily grateful to her for allowing me to embed myself in such a rich and finely tuned emotional life. I dedicate the book to her.

INTRODUCTION

From casual observers to trained experts, people care about challenges such as terrorism, violent conflict, and humanitarian crises. These are not just technical problems demanding solutions but also matters possessing emotional gravity. Political problems acquire emotional significance when they involve human suffering, moral controversy, and other qualities of pressing moral concern. But, as the theories and cases presented here suggest, emotional intensity is also shaped by the events, communicative practices, and social interactions through which people experience political contestation. This book studies affective dimensions of global politics by investigating the way social interactions intensify, harmonize, and blend the emotional responses of those who participate in them. I begin with on-the-ground events such as protests, speeches, and commemoration rituals and trace the emotions they evoke among coparticipants—both elites and ordinary people, both near and far. Revisiting well-studied civil conflicts from the 1990s, as well as the war on terror from the 2000s, the book finds sites and types of emotional impact missed by research trained on identities, institutions, or interests. By reconceptualizing the social genesis of emotion, the book offers a fresh account of both where to look for emotions and how they matter for the study of global conflict.

At the core of my analysis is the idea that studying legal and political dimensions of emotion requires understanding how they are transmitted socially. What I term "circulations of affect" are conscious and unconscious exchanges of emotion within a social environment. People acting in concert develop shared repertoires of emotion. While participants in a social interaction do not become emotional carbon copies, they are exposed to a stock of emotion-generating objects and to the emotional expressions of coparticipants. Through both social and neural processes, people imbibe the emotions around them; together, these mechanisms of emotional exchange comprise a process of contagion. As our brains mirror the emotions of others, often without conscious awareness, we internalize common forms of emotional expression. People exposed to similar patterns of emotional stimulation harmonize their respective habits of affective response. Studying emotions outside the laboratory requires tracing the social interactions and events contributing to this affective contagion.

A central aim of the book is to account for the political significance of emotions without cleansing away the distinctive properties that make them elusive as topics of study. As emotions are transmitted from one individual to another and from one social setting into others, opportunities abound for surprising expressions and creative combinations. Because the associations we develop between emotional responses and their eliciting objects are often loose and pliable, emotions have a propensity to migrate across social fields; underlying excitations are sustained even as their cognitive meaning shifts. Fear of terrorism can migrate into fear of chemical weapons, for example, and economic grievances easily mutate into ethnic resentments. Emotions are not logical propositions; they can exit one environment and install themselves in another in ways that defy cognitive categories and scientific expectations. One of my principal aims here is to study affective dynamics in a way that preserves their capacity for surprise. In the late nineteenth and early twentieth centuries, philosophers such as William James and Henri Bergson regarded emotions as vital sources of creativity. I embrace this sensibility and treat emotion as a source of novelty in international law and politics.

A central contention in the book is that standard emotion categories—such as hatred, anger, fear, joy, and empathy—are of limited usefulness when studying real-world social environments. In the late nineteenth century, James argued that psychologists were becoming overly fixated on emotion categories, which he considered inadequate for describing the richness of affective experience. More recent research in neuroscience has confirmed that each emotion is generated by a constellation of interlocking neural processes rather than by its own control center in the mind. Moreover, research in social psychology and cultural theory suggests that emotions are flexible and shifting responses that intersect with and blend into one another. Fear, for example, is not generally confined to one eliciting object but migrates contagiously across to others. And emotional responses are interconnected, as when fear intensifies resentment or betrayal of trust sparks anger. The book is therefore not about any one or two emotions, let alone about predicting the causal role these might have; rarely are single emotions stable enough in social settings to have such uniform effects. Rather than add emotions alongside traditional causal variables, then, my approach assumes that emotions shape political agency through shifting patterns of co- and multi-causality.

To make sense of the social properties of emotion, I draw especially from two literatures well beyond international relations (IR). From research in the sociology of emotion, I derive an account of how emotions both generate and are generated by social interactions. Microsociology, the study of small-scale interpersonal interactions, has never featured large in the grand study of international politics. And yet theories in this tradition can offer an account of how emotions propagate, through microlevel interactions, into social patterns of affect. Sociologies of communication extend this account into situations involving technologically mediated interaction. The second literature is neuroscience. Although research on the brain offers no clear theories of political behavior, it has quickly become a key resource for conceptualizing the role of emotion in human agency. The science of the brain reveals, for example, that large parts of our emotional lives are nonconscious, that the brain facilitates emotional recognition by simulating the emotions of others, and that the neural and somatic systems involved in generating emotions are deeply affected by socialization. Even by scanning only the brains of individual human subjects, neuroscientists are confirming what sociologists have long believed: emotions play an indispensable role in regulating social interaction. As these disciplines uncover the depth and importance of affect for human judgment and decisionmaking, scholars of politics face both an obligation and an opportunity to take its political impact seriously.

I learn from these extradisciplinary resources without purporting to be an expert in them. The book does not contain an exhaustive account of scholarly contributions in microsociology, neuroscience, or the emerging field of social neuroscience. Nor do I expect my empirical claims to be fully consistent with all available clinical evidence. My aim is not to glean fixed laws of emotional politics but instead to float synthetic, experimental, and contestable accounts of affective processes based on complementary theories and conceptual resources. IR scholars are unlikely to keep up with multidimensional problems such as social networking or global protest movements without making bold, fallible steps into unfamiliar disciplinary environments. I offer one possible route through two or three such environments, extracting from them new insights about emerging forms of political agency in global politics. The book is not intended to be the last word on emotion in IR but a step toward further conversation in a different, less intellectualist, key.

My reconceptualization of emotion is applicable to many cases in global politics. The social processes at its core—the generation of affect through interactions, its contagious transmission, and its diffusion through communications technologies—are implicated in various issue-areas and at national, subnational, and transnational levels. In this book, I revisit several now-textbook cases from the last two decades whose emotional impact has been overlooked or misunderstood. Each illustrates how emotional forms of agency can affect political outcomes, sometimes in surprising ways. Focusing on the former Yugoslavia and Rwanda, I offer a critical reassessment of the emotions involved in so-called ethnic conflict and postconflict recovery. I also investigate popular responses to the terrorist attacks of September 11, 2001, with a brief comparison to the Madrid bombings of 2004. Although in other ways very different, each of these cases provides insight into how emotions are generated and circulated across different geographic locations and cultural contexts. By assembling together cases normally farmed out to specialists in foreign policy analysis, security studies, and transitional justice, I extract new insights into the genesis of emotion in social interactions, their circulation through communications technologies, and their reciprocal and sometimes unexpected effects on political processes.

Social interactions can produce and circulate emotions in various ways, depending on the case under consideration: these may be organized social practices with formal standards of competence, such as a legal trial, but they may also be more episodic social phenomena, such as media events or political demonstrations. What these interactions share is not a formal structure but three looser attributes: coparticipation, a focus of attention on a common object or activity, and concentrations of public communication. In the case of Yugoslavia, I focus on protests, speeches, and commemoration rituals, paying specific attention to Milošević's "meetings of truth" in 1988 and a series of reburial rituals in 1990 and 1991. In the Rwandan case, I examine especially political speeches and radio broadcasts, which involve engagement between speaker and audience but also among audience members. In both cases, UN tribunals, local courts, and commemorative rituals served as dramaturgical spectacles that shifted popular reactions to atrocities of the past. Amid American responses to September 11, less visible forms of social interaction—racial profiling and hate crimes—became crucial to public internalization of the new terrorist enemy. At different scales and through diverse modes of communication, these interactions create, augment, or alter affective circulations in politically significant ways.

My case studies highlight the material context behind the global politics of affect, including the importance of communications technologies in facilitating exchanges of emotion. A common assumption in some sociological studies is that emotions are displayed and/or transmitted in face-to-face interactions such as social dyads, small gatherings, or crowds. The deeper penetration of modern technologies into everyday life is in many cases rendering these assumptions obsolete. In global politics, emotionally significant social interactions are increasingly involving dispersed participants connected through communications technologies such as radio, television, cell phones, electronic mail, social networking—and often many of these together. Few Americans were directly exposed to the 9/11 attacks, and yet most had continual access to the barrage of images, symbols, and memories circulated in a frenzy of national media coverage. In each case, I find evidence that communications technologies intensify the communication of affect across individuals, expand the reach of political speech to dispersed audiences, and heighten the sensitivity of elites to popular emotion. More than simply human responses, circulations of affect are often induced, enhanced, and altered by technology.

Combining local interactions with extralocal processes of reproduction, the book follows transmissions of affect across conventional levels of analysis. In the former Yugoslavia, political protests and other crowd activities generated popular emotions in specific locations, but these reverberated throughout the republic with the help of televised news broadcasts. In Rwanda, emotions elicited during political speeches and everyday social gatherings were echoed and intensified by a "drumbeat" of radio broadcasting in the months before and during the mass killings. In the wake of 9/11, covert practices of racial profiling and local hate crimes were made nationally visible by digital communications and cable news coverage. Each case involves communications technologies capable of delivering social interactions to various scales of activity: local interactions can expand to the national or global level, and national and global developments can trigger reactions at the local level. In different ways and through different channels, each case demonstrates the special capacity for emotions to sustain a range of multiscalar interactions.

Resisting the idea that elites are somehow immune to affect, the book examines the interplay between the emotional interactions of ordinary people and those populated by political and cultural elites. State officials and decisionmakers are involved across these cases, as illustrated by the flurry of diplomacy in the wake of 9/11, and by the mobilization efforts of nationalist elites in the Balkans and the Great Lakes Region of Africa.

My account assumes these actors are inspired, shaped, and legitimized by social displays and exchanges of emotion; political elites apply their expertise to problems laden with emotional significance. Elite communications are received by multiple audiences sensitive to the narratives, symbols, and tones they employ. In situations where elites are themselves participants in emotion-inducing social interactions, a strict separation between elite and mass obscures reciprocal sensitivities. Satellite television, blogging, social networking, and other communications technologies have made these political environments not just interconnected but interpenetrating and mutually constitutive. As social settings become linked as never before, affective circulations create feedbacks and synergies among actors with differing degrees of formal authority.

My selection of cases warrants two points of clarification. First, since these conflicts are commonly associated with emotional phenomena, some readers may consider them "easy cases" that, selected for the presence of emotions, cannot unto themselves accomplish much in the way of theory-building. While it may be true that terrorism and ethnic conflict have become poster children for emotional politics in common parlance, the easy case dismissal is fitting only for a study whose goal lies either in proving that emotions matter or in specifying which ones matter most. My objective is instead to reconceptualize the kinds of emotional processes that might be operating across a range of political and legal issue areas. Studying the direct causal origins of hatred in ethnic conflict would warrant including both cases where hatred was expected to play a significant role and cases selected for its alleged absence. But my concern lies in tracing indirect and diffuse effects that cannot be tested in this manner. The conflicts in Rwanda and Yugoslavia are often cited as exemplary spectacles of hatred, whether that emotion is seen as stemming from primordial origins or modern processes of social construction. I revisit these cases in order to highlight the analytical benefits of pursuing an alternative account of the emotional processes involved. The book is an agenda-setting project dependent less on tight case selection than fine-grained, ethnographically informed studies attuned to the complexity of affective processes. Each case becomes, in the end, less "easy" than it first appears.

A related hesitation is that these cases represent apples and oranges, mixing phenomena of very different levels—internal conflicts, transnational terrorism, and interstate wars—and political and cultural environments—Africa, Southeastern Europe, and North America. These points of difference provide, however, an empirical breadth that helps to illuminate the genre of emotionally charged political events from varying perspectives. My aim is not to distill divergent cases into a universal theory but, instead, to map the fluidity with which different shared emotions find their way into several kinds of political phenomena with global dimensions. The generalizable processes I find are open-ended tendencies, such as the propensity for creativity in emotional politics, rather than fixed causal linkages. It is true that the cases I discuss involve very different environments in terms of culture, legal and political institutions, and communications technologies. And yet, some common elements—such as political speeches, crowd activities, and media communications—offer a preliminary reason to assemble these cases together to see what might be discovered about how emotions combine and intersect in real-world social environments. Incorporating cases from different regions and cultural contexts also safeguards against dubious presuppositions that emotions are somehow confined to traditional cultures or less developed political systems.

By bringing extradisciplinary resources to bear on familiar cases, the book offers a timely challenge to some conventional assumptions in IR theory. To begin with, I show how emotions have political effects across traditional levels of analysis. By approaching affect as socially generated and transmitted, we can step back from familiar worries regarding a misapplication of psychological characteristics to states and other corporate actors. Emotions become not private feelings but public expressions that circulate in and through a variety of social actors in global political events. Protestors and activists are inspired by powerful convictions, but so too are leaders and diplomats. Institutions, identities, values, and norms all routinely acquire affective significance. I study patterns of emotional interaction that both affect decisionmaking within the state and inspire new configurations of collective agency beyond it. The book is not about opening the black box of the emotional individual but about tracing flows of affect seeping across his or her porous and expressive edges.

The book also offers a rejoinder to theories of identity in IR. Both the ethnic conflicts of the 1990s and the sometimes Manichean endorsements of the war on terror have been treated by many constructivists and cultural studies scholars as clear instances of identity politics. Elites, ordinary citizens, and the authors of popular culture—all are cited as complicit in framing such conflicts through the reductive categories of ethnic, racial, or religious identity. The constructivist analysis of identity has not stopped with these particular topics, and now many aspects of international politics—from routine diplomacy to the diffusion of human rights norms—are said to be filtered through identities and their standards of appropriate behavior. All of this work has achieved remarkable new insights in a field traditionally skewed in favor of more tangible measures of economic and military power. Moreover, there is some reason to suppose that many of the phenomena discussed by identity theories—for example, nationalism, religious recognition, citizenship, or foreign policy discourse—are steeped in affective significance. When George Bush spoke about the war on terror in the aftermath of 9/11, for example, he often evoked pride in freedom, democracy, and other values deemed central to American identity. Similarly, ethnic mobilization in the former Yugoslavia relied on pride associated with the Serb identity—as well as fear for its erosion. Many identities become invested with affective significance and consequently serve as focal points for emotional mobilization.

Nevertheless, there is reason to pause before privileging identity as a starting point for the study of emotion. While the emotional dimension of identity seems undeniable, the cases I consider here suggest that not all patterns of collective emotion bear a one-to-one correspondence with a well-established cultural identity. My account shows that shared emotions emerge from lived social interactions rather than from abstract cultural identities. Over time, some patterns of emotional response may become concentrated among populations who also adhere to or celebrate a group identity, and emotions may give new energy to cultural identities. But in a world of unconscious, overlapping, and sometimes fleeting emotional responses, such connections cannot be assumed in advance. The case studies in this book therefore trace the emergence of new forms of collective agency, sometimes prior to the adoption or celebration of a cultural identity. I argue, for example, that we cannot understand the complex genesis of the Arab/Muslim/Middle Eastern enemy in America's war on terror by starting out with the assumption of a coherent, identity-based process of cultural and political categorization. On the flip side, where I investigate cases with well-rehearsed and familiar identity categories, such as those in Rwanda or Yugoslavia, I regard social circulations of affect as one more reason to treat those categories skeptically—as political abstractions but not ethnographically sufficient representations of everyday life. One of my objectives in these cases is to trace the emotional genesis of cultural identities and symbols rather than presume them as pre-existing objects of political manipulation.

Because the association between emotion and identity has proven to be so resilient, I devote time throughout the book to dismantling some of the discursive constructions sustaining it. Some targets are obvious but still needing further interrogation, such as the notion of "ancient hatreds." Commonly invoked during the 1990s to make sense of conflict in the Balkans, this trope has been poked and prodded from all directions over the past fifteen years. Indeed, the idea retains little scholarly credibility. And yet its successor theories, while dispensing with elements of primordiality, have all too often preserved the notion that *hatreds* are prevalent in ethnic conflict and/or that collective emotions are generally aimed at clearly recognizable cultural out-groups. By opening up the complexity of emotional exchanges involved in an "ethnic" conflict, I go a step further—displacing not only the "ancient" but also the "hatred." Other targets seem more innocuous and yet reflect a no less limiting conceptualization of emotion. The much-discussed phenomenon of anti-Americanism, for example, aggregates attitudes and motivations to foreign populations and presumes "America" as their uniform object of elicitation. To move beyond hatred, and to open up a looser connection between identity and emotion generally, later chapters work back and forth between critically interrogating emotional tropes and putting more nuanced theoretical propositions in their place.

My theorization of emotion as a creative source of collective agency can help make sense of the emotional events of the early twenty-first century. From terrorism, war, and revolution to advocacy and social networking, we now inhabit a world where the passions of ordinary people can achieve global impact. Where new communications technologies facilitate global waves of protest, transnational social movements, and Wiki-leaked diplomatic conversations, emotional exchanges sustain communities of otherwise dispersed participants. Where a local event is delivered to global audiences, scale no longer serves as a reliable predictor of political impact. The protests of Tahrir Square, for example, began as local gatherings but, greased by television news and social networking technologies, generated a cascade of revolutionary sentiment across North Africa and the Middle East. More recently, jitters from risky investment schemes in the American real estate market escalated into the worst global financial crisis since the 1930s. In a different vein, after intensive campaigns tapping social networking technologies, genocide in Darfur sparked an unprecedented degree of humanitarian concern among American college students. Where technologies of communication modulate the volume and reach of popular emotion, collective actions at the global level can change profoundly. The conceptualizations and propositions I advance here can inform future research into this elusive and shifting terrain of emotional politics.

The first two chapters launch this effort by assembling a multidimensional theory of emotions as neurosocial phenomena with distinctive psychological properties and political potentials. Chapter 1 defines the idea of "circulations of affect" and explains how emotion circulates in and through individuals in the context of social interaction. Drawing from microsociological theories, I show that emotions are not just psychological feeling-states but also expressive social displays and contagious transmissions. Emotions, in this view, connect individuals who participate together in social interactions of various kinds—from small, face-to-face social groups to more diffuse interactions mediated by communications technologies. To understand how emotions become shared in these social situations, I tap neuroscientific research showing that the brain generates emotions through a process of simulation and that many emotions occur when one person mirrors the affective displays of others. The result is emotional contagion: the unconscious and unintentional transmission of emotion through a process of social display and imitation. Eschewing its commonplace association with the spread of infectious disease or social malady, I draw from work in social psychology and microsociology that treats emotional contagion as a key element of human behavior in the social world. The first chapter lingers on the ontological consequences of contagion, questioning the traditional assumption that the intentional and autonomous individual lies at the heart of human agency. Since emotions are connective tissues bringing individuals together in social collectivities, my account contests the notion that individuals occupy a distinct level of analysis. Rather than psychological attributes whose application to social phenomena represents fuzzy thinking, emotions become key elements underpinning social constructs—such as beliefs, norms, identities, and symbols—already familiar to scholars of global politics.

Chapter 2 demonstrates that emotional circulations endow these social phenomena with special properties, especially ambiguity and flexibility. Supplementing research in psychology and social psychology with conceptualizations in social and cultural theory, I argue that emotions lie at the center of a human capacity for creativity. Social displays and simulations of affect entail unexpected migrations of emotion through time and across social settings. As contagious circulations of affect accumulate over time, social actors are exposed to new combinations of emotion and emotional memory. Emotions are decoupled from their original circumstances of elicitation and migrate to new objects and actors. As a result, emotions not only underpin processes of socialization but also give rise to moments of rupture and renewal. This creative tendency of emotions to migrate and interpenetrate gives them a special capacity to affect political behavior through relations of co- and multi-causality. I also outline here the method I use in later chapters to study these emergent and complex processes empirically.

The chapter's conceptualization of affective processes promises a better analytical grip on protest movements, media frenzies, transnational networks, and grassroots organizing for justice—the various impassioned and volatile social interactions discussed in later chapters.

The remaining chapters explore the political effects of affect in cases of terrorism, ethnic conflict, and transitional justice. Refusing methodological conventions that discount emotions, I appeal to interdisciplinary tools appropriate to their distinctive qualities. I draw from journalistic sources, microhistorical research, and ethnographic studies to make sense of the many ways loyalty, memory, and sentiment shape and are shaped by social contexts. My case studies identify emotionally charged local events such as political speeches, protests, and legal trials and then trace the memories they activate and the collective sentiments they engender. I modify the techniques of interpretivist social science to trace powerful currents of evocative political discourse. Where collective emotions are not fully explained by the linguistic content of political discourse, I construct plausible inferences about the paralinguistic elements also present. The result is an account that begins not with settled identities but with the dynamic emotions that make global politics both multiscalar and unpredictable.

Chapter 3 investigates the powerful emotions associated with terrorist violence after September 11. By tracing the emotional expressions circulating through popular media and political speeches, I show that familiar emotions such as fear and anger were not generic responses but adaptive ones—affected by prior normative commitments, evolving social practices, and available memories. Rather than purport to offer a comprehensive theory of how emotions prepared elites and ordinary Americans for war, the chapter concentrates on specific emotional processes, especially those contributing to the social construction of the terrorist enemy. Drawing from research in cultural studies and evidence gathered by public interest groups, I show that government-sponsored acts of racial profiling helped to invent the terrorist enemy as a racialized synthesis of Arab, Muslim, and Middle Eastern phenotypic and cultural stereotypes. The resulting constructions had, I argue, a subtle but important impact on public tolerance for the use of force. The chapter also uses a comparison to the Madrid bombings of March 2004 to sharpen the contention the emotions evoked by terrorist violence are shaped by the normative commitments, social practices, and emotional sensitivities present in a given context. Amplified by public acts of protest, popular emotions adapted to evolving political developments: initially mixed reactions developed into anger directed at the governing party, seen as having provoked the attack by supporting the US war in Iraq. Whereas the attacks of 9/11 mobilized popular support for war, the 3/11 bombings reactivated antiwar sentiment and sparked anger toward the Spanish government. The chapter shows that emotions such as fear and anger are not fixed psychological responses but shifting composites of contagious affect.

Chapter 4 studies the circulations of affect involved in ethnic conflict, focusing on the early stages of nationalist mobilization in Serbia and Kosovo between 1987 and 1991, and the incitement of genocide in Rwanda between late 1990 and 1994. Critiques of the "ancient hatreds" hypothesis have successfully shown that hatreds are socially constructed rather than primordial. I take these arguments a step further, positing the category "hatred" as an abstraction that obscures the complex emotional processes involved in violent conflict. I show how political speeches, crowd activities, and reburial rituals created environments in which diverse sentiments and memories were creatively blended into the emotional politics of violence. These cases involved wide-reaching and multidimensional processes of mobilization that theories of identity construction, elite manipulation, and symbolic politics have yet to appreciate. Because so much of the existing scholarship on ethnic conflict proceeds with a simplistic image of emotion, the accounts we have of recent conflicts remain one-sided, with many focused on the guiding role of identity. And so this chapter returns to cases well rehearsed in IR but whose emotional aspects remain poorly understood.

Misunderstanding the emotional genesis of conflict has concrete implications for the way we approach security, peace, and justice in conflicted societies. Those who expect endemic "cycles of hatred" worry about the re-emergence of repetitive emotional expressions and consequently miss the originality of emotional responses to violent conflict—and their potential to fuel innovative solutions to it. In chapter 5 I turn to the emotional politics of justice, reconciliation, and social repair. With an empirical focus on Rwanda and, to a lesser extent, South Africa, I examine the role of emotions in juridical and quasi-juridical institutions. My concern is not to offer new institutional solutions to ethnic conflict but to show how existing approaches to transitional justice—tribunals, truth commissions, community-based courts, and grassroots initiatives—can benefit from increased concern for the emotional contexts in which they operate. I show that quasi-juridical institutions such as truth commissions have permitted an emotionally engaged form of justice, but have often also limited this through insistence on "forgiveness," "national unity," and other forms of identity-based reconciliation. Rwanda's experiment with local courts illustrates both the potential and fragility of participatory models of justice. The process of lived participation can generate trust among coparticipants, but is readily undermined by political campaigns promoting unity.

Chapters 3–5 realize a key ambition developed earlier in the book: to assess the political impact of affect without assuming in advance its coordination or coherence. Tracing these effects empirically requires leaving aside familiar expectations dictating intentionality as a cornerstone of political agency. Emotions have specific properties that change the way human beings act in social and political settings. A circulation of affect does more than sustain identities, institutions, and norms; it also shifts the basis of legitimacy behind these things by coupling them with new sources of symbolic inspiration and performative energy. Following these affective dynamics helps us understand some enduring mysteries in global politics—how, for example, new political movements emerge, how cultural identities absorb support from adjacent social and economic grievances, and how events and memories from the past continue to shape interactions in the present. Far from a repetitive affliction, affect is integral to the way human actors navigate a shifting terrain of social interaction.

ONE

Circulations of Affect in Global Politics

Global politics is awash in public expressions of emotion: after eighteen "days of rage" forced Hosni Mubarak from office in 2011, the popular agitation migrated to Yemen, Bahrain, Iraq, and Libya. A decade earlier, the terrorist attacks of September 11, 2001, triggered waves of fear and anger—in the United States and around the world. During the early 1990s, nationalist sentiment contagiously filled political and cultural voids in post–Cold War Eastern and Central Europe. In each of these events, emotions were not momentary pathologies of a few ill-informed actors but broadly shared responses inflecting a wide range of social and political relationships. The emotions involved were not just private feelings but contagious patterns of human responsiveness that disrupted settled norms and relations and inspired new movements, networks, policies, and institutions. From revolutionary moods and collective memories to moral outrage and communities of fear, emotions shape the way people act in public settings. Somehow this human capability we normally impute to individual actors takes on a social existence as well.

And yet, while pundits, experts, and even some scholars routinely use terms such as "national pride," "bearish markets," or "climates of fear," the phenomena described by these terms often drop out at precisely the point where the science of politics begins. Disciplined studies of international relations generally adopt frameworks and methodologies that conceal social dimensions of emotion that otherwise seem intuitively plausible. For example, while public debate over 9/11 has been quite comfortable citing the fear, anger, and hatred that affected American public culture, scholarly investigations have gravitated instead to measuring individual attitudes or exploring the psychology of neoconservative elites. Research on ethnic conflict has become a showcase for the alleged risks associated with collective emotion as an analytical category, with much of the scholarly work on this topic attempting to discredit primordialist accounts that treat emotions as having ancient, cultural origins. As an object of study within the social sciences, the idea of shared emotions continues to lack credibility.

This chapter seeks to remedy these deficits by theorizing emotions as "circulations of affect"—conscious and unconscious exchanges of emotion occurring in and through the process of social interaction.[1] Reaching well beyond international relations (IR) for extradisciplinary tools, I treat these affective circulations as products of both social and biological processes. As theories in the sociology of emotion suggest, people who participate in social activities together generate shared affective responses. I tap this literature to explain how the many interactions of social life—such as protests, political speeches, commemoration rituals, and legal events—spark not only psychological responses but also circulations of affect. Those circulations acquire political significance especially as communications technologies distribute social interactions to spatially dispersed audiences. I also draw from recent research in neuroscience, which helps to explain what is happening in the brain as people coparticipate in emotion-inducing interactions. While clinical findings are unlikely to offer IR scholars research-ready hypotheses, they do confirm that our brains recognize the emotions of others by simulating those expressions ourselves—and that the neural systems involved in simulation are deeply affected by socialization.[2] Neuroscientists are thus confirming what sociologists have long believed: that emotions play an important role in regulating social behavior.[3] They are psychological feeling-states but also biosocial phenomena constituting and circulating through minds, brains, and social environments.

Reconceptualizing emotions in this way generates some clues about their role in the social world of politics. Rather than treating emotions as idiosyncratic feeling-states with isolated impact on select, vulnerable individuals, we are positioned to look for a broader spectrum of emotional politics. I argue in this chapter that emotions play an important role in sustaining the processes of socialization familiar to constructivist IR theory. Circulations of affect supply the conscious and unconscious tissue from which social beliefs, norms, and identities are forged. Emotions are not confined to the individual level of analysis but extend out to social phenomena—norms, collective actors, and even institutions—seemingly lodged at different levels. This chapter seeks to establish the sociality of emotion and outline its ontological and political consequences. This preliminary step is necessary for the second chapter, where I show that circulations of affect possess special properties that can also inspire moments of creativity and change. Emotions, it turns out, are not simply stable habits and dispositions but adaptive and fluid capabilities central to the way social actors navigate political environments. Whether upholding settled norms or serving as first responders at moments of alarm, emotions have a profound impact on the composition and intensity of collective agency and the cultural material available for collective political action.

Mixed Emotions

The emotions present in social settings are composite phenomena that consist of biological and social dimensions but also encompass the various emotion types familiar to the psychology of emotion. Focusing on single emotions misses the complex and multifaceted circulations of affect associated with political protest, national mobilization, transnational advocacy, and other activities common in an age of global communication. Emotions have psychological dimensions that can and should be studied in clinical settings where it is possible to isolate discrete psychological responses. But in a field such as global politics, where many objects of study involve historical processes and culturally mediated communications, we also need to account for both the way emotions circulate socially and the tendency for such exchanges to involve shifting mixtures of affect rather than stable and uniform emotion categories. The social world of global politics is too messy for an off-the-shelf application of categories from psychology.

Yet, by enumerating clear and distinct emotion types, the modern psychology of emotion pushed in the opposite direction for much of the second half of the twentieth century. Psychological research has contended that emotions are undervalued largely because their cognitive profiles have not been adequately elucidated. Prior to the modern science of emotions, the term "passion" was often used to refer indiscriminately to intense human responses exceeding the control of reason.[4] Beginning in the nineteenth century, attention turned from fearing passion as such to locating its specific physiological origins. William James developed one of the most influential theories of emotion as a product of the body. But, as the psychology of emotion developed during the twentieth century, the Jamesian view fell from favor, and scholars turned instead to mapping the cognitive makeup of each emotion.[5] Human emotions seemed too diverse to attribute all to physiological responses—then seen as primitive and uniform. The result was a cognitivist turn that tried to hold each emotion sufficiently still to locate behind it a signature belief structure.[6] From psychology to analytic philosophy, the cognitivist assumption that emotions come in tidy, individually wrapped packages formed the baseline for several generations of research on the subject.

My contention is not that psychological categories are dispensable but that, used in isolation, they lack the analytical leverage needed for the historically layered and culturally diverse social environments involved in global politics. Topics confronted by IR scholars are unlikely to involve clear and distinct emotion types over time. For example, realism often regards security dilemmas as products of fear. But what exactly do realists mean by "fear" in this context? By emphasizing the negative impact of fear on perception—its role, for example, in sustaining the cult of the offensive—the realist approach tells us little about its peculiar qualities as an emotion. Social actors experiencing insecurity often know very little about the origins of fear, and that ambiguity becomes integral to the emotion. As Neta Crawford notes, a person may assimilate diverse things as objects of fear even where they have little or no real connection.[7] Fear often manifests itself less as "fear of X" and more as an unsettling anxiety whose opacity permits latitude and flexibility in how "X" is imagined. In the months prior to Rwanda's genocide, for example, extremists succeeded in broadening the category "Tutsi" to include a larger and larger class of enemies: Rwandans believed to have assisted Tutsis, Rwandans of mixed marriage, women viewed as sexually depraved, and so on. Where the source of fear is difficult to discern, the work of emotional creativity begins.

Similar problems apply to hatred, perhaps the paradigmatic emotion in culturally oriented studies of global conflict. While social constructivists have rightly challenged the notion that hatreds are of primordial origin, many retain the assumption that "hatred" is nevertheless a useful way to describe the social construction of enmity. Empirical evidence often reveals a more complex story. The ethnographic research discussed in chapter 4, for example, points to relatively low levels of hatred in Rwandan society, even among those who perpetrated the genocide. Studies of the former Yugoslavia—often cited as a hotbed for this particular emotion—give equal reason to pause: where conflicting parties do describe hatreds, these descriptions function as shorthand for more complex emotions. Even in cases we often consider "textbook" illustrations of identity-based hatreds, therefore, conflict has more varied emotional roots—extending out to an array of collective memories, social insecurities, and evocative rituals. Setting out to study "hatred" in such cases prefigures the emotional landscape of a conflict by assuming, first, that recognizable social groups are the salient containers of emotion and, second, that emotions commonly involve recurring feelings of dislike directed at an opposing group. Even legal scholars presume "cycles of hatred" as the baseline against which to pursue transitional justice. The category thus shapes the way we think about the people involved in a conflict—as political neophytes mired in perpetual enmity—and their accordingly grim prospects for social recovery.

Adding more emotion categories affords only a partial solution to these problems. The psychology of emotion has long been a cottage industry of taxonomizing. Contributions variously offer lists of two, five, ten, or some other number of primary or basic emotions. Cognitivist approaches focus on the logical connections and patterns among emotion categories, often regarding a set of basic emotions as logical building blocks for more complex ones.[8] Grief, for example, is rooted in some composite of sadness and love for the object lost. Resentment incorporates anger and humiliation. Each combination of basic emotions yields a more multifaceted response. But psychological accounts presume that the resulting emotions—grief, resentment, pride, and so on—are themselves isolated responses provoked by discrete objects. Inventing new emotion types only preserves the hope that for each stimulus we might find a distinct, corresponding response. This ambition underestimates the density and ambiguity of emotional experience. As phenomenological and neurological research has demonstrated, real emotions often blend together and mutate during the process of social interaction. Sometimes component emotions are no longer individually detectable in the resulting mixtures.[9] The more we look for emotions that correspond to clear and distinct emotion objects, the less we see the linkages connecting one emotion to its many collaborators.

There is thus no straightforward answer to the questions "Which emotions matter in politics?" or "Which emotions matter in IR?" Although psychological categories have conditioned us into believing that behind each emotion lies a clear object and moment of elicitation, affective interactions are rarely so neat and tidy. Emotion categories are artificial handles later added to the organic situations of lived experience. As Dewey argues, we only think we have "anger," for example, because some outside observer—in an attempt to establish responsibility for an action—describes our conduct in that way.[10] James registers a similar complaint when, in *The Principles of Psychology*, he worries that psychology had reified each emotion with an essential logic. When James writes that "the trouble with the emotions in psychology is that they are regarded too much as absolutely individual things," he does not mean what critics have often alleged: that all emotions are the product of the same, simple biological trigger.[11] He is concerned instead that psychological categories treating emotions as self-contained "things" cannot capture the complexity and fluidity of embodied experience. What James calls "pure experience" in his writings on "radical empiricism" has been confirmed by neuroscience and phenomenological psychology:[12] people often do not know how they feel, do not know what makes them feel the way they do, experience mixed emotions, and/or transfer emotions from one interaction to the next. "Hatred" and other familiar emotion types thus serve as invitations to closer empirical investigation, but not adequate categories for social and political theory.

In this book, I employ "affect" and "emotion" interchangeably and as umbrella terms encompassing various emotion types.[13] I treat emotion/affect as a multidimensional capability that consists of activations of the insular cortex and limbic system, employs maps of the body, and sometimes generates feelings.[14] Because affect can be transmitted through publicly available expressions and coproduced through social interactions, I regard social circulations as one of its common manifestations. My neurosociological approach deliberately avoids placing "feelings," the subjectively perceptible experiences of emotional response, at the center of emotional politics. As the "mental expressions" of emotion, feelings are a possible but not necessary component of an affective circulation.[15] By insisting on the centrality of subjective reflection to emotional response, cognitive approaches have tended to blur the lines between emotions and feelings. Neuroscience has helped to once again disaggregate emotion from its felt dimension, uncovering the many affective processes—from unconscious desires and moods to implicit memories—that, while detectable through neuroimaging, are too quick or habitual to generate subjective feelings. I do not deny that subjective feelings are a dimension of emotion or that they become politically significant where subject to public discussion—for example, testimony at a truth commission, the personal reflections of a leader, or confessions from a public intellectual. My investigation considers these subjective feelings where they occur but does not conflate them with emotion.

Confirming the Jamesian view, research in neuroscience has shown that what we commonly describe as emotions are a diverse array of responses and states with varying degrees of conscious awareness and intentional control. Not only do some emotions never develop into feelings, but also the feelings we do experience are often connected to multiple, cross-cutting emotional processes. Moreover, some emotions are not discrete responses but "diffuse" moods that apply to multiple objects and linger over time.[16] One way to make sense of this plurality of emotion is to posit a pattern of "nesting." In such an account, enthusiasm, malaise, and other "background emotions" exist within "basic emotions" such as anger and fear, and both types are nested within complex "social emotions," such as pride, envy, and guilt.[17] The subjective feelings we have of emotional experience incorporate still more complex composites of all three types. These findings compel us to consider the interplay among not only different emotion types (fear, hatred, anger, and hope) but also varieties of affect (feelings, emotions, implicit memories, and moods). This diversity is not an exceptional characteristic that can be set aside in the interests of parsimonious theory; it is the default setting in a complex world of affective politics.

Circulations of Affect

This book opens up a rich field of socially constructed and politically charged emotions that I term "circulations of affect." A circulation of affect is a conscious or unconscious transmission of emotion within a social environment.[18] When human beings participate together in social interactions, they are exposed to a common stock of emotion-eliciting encounters. These social interactions can take a variety of forms, encompassing the many actions that bring human beings into contact with one another, whether directly or mediated by communications technologies.[19] Diplomatic meetings, legal trials, religious rituals, commemorative events, protests, rallies, and political speeches—all are social interactions with the potential to expose participants to emotion-inducing stories, symbols, and practices. They also supply venues of coparticipation at which individuals gain access to the emotional expressions of others; seeing others display an emotional response can engender homologous responses from coparticipants. These social interactions generate not identical emotional profiles within all participants but threads of shared emotion that exist notwithstanding the many dispositions, sentiments, and memories that continue to differ.

Emotions are located in individual persons but also extend beyond and between them.[20] Folk psychology encourages us to view emotions as private experiences—deep, inner feelings that only rarely become intelligible to others. And yet, as Darwin suggested in his classic but lesser-known study *The Expression of Emotions in Man and Animals*, emotions, manifest in facial expressions, are capabilities that communicate states of being to a world of concerned others. That our emotions acquire special significance to us as private feelings does not change the fact that they are also social. Building on these assumptions, theories in microsociology—the study of everyday social interaction—treat emotions as relational capabilities that facilitate communication and social interaction. Combining seminal work by

Durkheim and Goffman, Randall Collins shows that emotions, norms, and other social phenomena are products of "interaction rituals." For Collins, most social encounters—from the highly formalized down to the episodic and experimental—can meaningfully be studied as interaction rituals. The latter are social events involving the presence of two or more people in one place (copresence), some recognizable delineation of participants from nonparticipants, shared attention toward an object or activity, and collective emotional experience.[21] With this framework, Collins traces the emotional exchanges coursing through social networks, workplace environments, and other situations in which individuals sustain unmediated contact with others.[22] Repeated or widely shared interactions can shape the emotions of a community. Emotions are thus intimate, private, and subjectively vivid, but also transsubjective properties of the social world.

Collins's sociology of emotions offers some clues as to how emotions are shared in the context of interaction. Participants in a common activity develop parallel emotions through a process of "rhythmic entrainment." As coparticipants become focused on a common object, they develop common expectations, conscious or unconscious, of which emotions others are likely to express. In an attempt—again, conscious or not—to "coordinate" with those expectations, individuals enact similar responses within themselves. Collins describes the process as "smoothly role-taking in the ongoing flow of the interaction."[23] The development of common emotions is not simply a psychological disposition of certain chameleon-like actors but a product of most social interactions. The contagious transfer of emotion is, moreover, not necessarily conscious. It rests instead on a process of embodied interactions, in which actors are exposed to the expressive displays of others. As Charles Taylor explains, "bodily styles" express affect publicly before "the framing of all intentions to communicate anything."[24] As actors are somatically exposed to the expressive displays of others, these provide the basis for emotional contagion.

Circulations of affect are thus sustained by a psychosocial process of contagion. I define "emotional contagion" as the nonintentional transfer of an emotion or mood from one individual or group to another. As various social psychologists have argued, expressive displays of emotion can be "caught" by others in social settings.[25] Emotional contagion involves what Gabriel Tarde presciently described as "reciprocal impregnations of affective states" and "inter-cerebral action at a distance."[26] Contagion occurs between individuals but also permeates the associations and groups in which they participate. It can be studied through clinical observation of individual subjects but also sociologically, through analysis of the rituals, events, and mediated exchanges giving rise to emotional transmission. As recent research in neuroimaging suggests, emotional contagion is an automatic, nonintentional process; when emotions are transmitted from one person or setting to another, the transmission is therefore less willful than a diffusion of ideas or a convergence of policy.[27] Even without trying, we routinely soak up and replicate the affective expressions around us.

The term "contagion" carries unfortunate baggage, having long denoted the communication of pathogen and disease.[28] Studies of contagion in political contexts generally use the term metaphorically to describe alarming tides of corruption or dysfunction. As Kantian instincts counsel us to attribute truth, peace, and other historic achievements to reason and will, it seems natural to connect anomie with disease and relegate both as the vestigial work of contagion. And yet a strain of sociological inquiry since Tarde has rightly preserved a place for contagion as a legitimate genre of social interaction, for which these normative evaluations are ill suited. To associate contagion with social pathology is, after all, to overlook the commonplace idea that laughter, faith, and joy can all spread contagiously.[29] Emotional contagion is an ordinary feature of social life, with no specific normative or political valence. What makes contagion distinctive is the modality of transmission involved rather than the moral desirability of the object transmitted.

How exactly does contagion work? One explanation for emotional contagion focuses on subjective appraisals of emotional conduct. In this view, emotions are transmitted when a person emulates the emotional response of another; those emotions form part of that person's appraisal of her or his situation. When others are angry, for example, we have a reasonable basis for supposing that some stimulus warranting anger is present. Social psychologists call this mechanism "inferential" because actors are inferring objective characteristics of an environment from the emotional displays of others.[30] Such inferences are then used to devise socially acceptable and strategically beneficial behavioral responses. For example, actors may seek to emulate the emotions deemed appropriate in a given situation in order to ingratiate others.[31] When participants in a group engage in this kind of intentional copying, they develop shared patterns of emotional conduct.

The inferential appraisal view captures some cases of shared emotion but misses others. An assumption behind this approach is that social actors are aware of the emotional displays of coparticipants. Others feel fear, for example, and manifest it through emotional expressions; I then recognize their expressive displays and reflect on an appropriate and advantageous response of my own. If a person seems to be feeling sad, I might emulate that emotion in order to convey solidarity. Alternatively, I might display sympathy, a complementary response that social norms deem appropriate under the circumstances.[32] Either way, awareness of available emotional displays generates patterns of emotional matching and coordination. The inferential mechanism is not irrelevant, but it does seem unable to capture instances where emotions are shared in the absence of such awareness. In some environments, actors emulate a socially circulating emotion without consciously deciding to do so. The question is: how?

To account for nonintentional transmissions of emotion, a second approach in social psychology describes a process of "primitive emotional contagion"—a form of emotional communication, akin to Collins's "rhythmic entrainment," occurring without an intermediary process of cognitive appraisal. Rather than recognizing an emotional display and choosing a suitable response, actors "catch" the emotions of others through nonconscious channels. A seminal study defines primitive emotional contagion as "the tendency to automatically mimic and synchronize facial expressions, vocalizations, postures, and movements with those of another person and, consequently, to converge emotionally."[33] As actors sense the embodied emotional displays of others, they unwittingly adopt congruent responses. The social psychology of contagion has offered no definitive list of the subsidiary mechanisms sustaining contagion: some of the available research studies facial expressions and tone of voice, while many scholars are simply concerned with verifying the occurrence of contagion rather than testing for its precise vehicles.

Unlike convergence through inference, primitive emotional contagion occurs in the absence of cognitive appraisals. We can mimic the emotions and moods of others even without conscious awareness of them. One study shows that "mood contagion" occurs even without any intention to emulate the emotions of another person. After listening to a philosophical text read aloud, participants recorded moods congruent with the "happy," "sad," and "neutral" tones in which the reading was conducted. Another study finds evidence of contagion associated not only with generalized moods, the subject of early research, but also specific emotional objects. As participants navigated everyday decisions and events, they recorded their own emotions and those of a partner. The researchers find evidence of emotional convergence even after controlling for conscious appraisals.[34] While its exact workings are as yet unclear within social psychology, evidence of a form of emotional contagion not rooted in conscious appraisal seems compelling.

Research in neuroscience has recently confirmed a neural basis for this "primitive emotional contagion." This work suggests that, while some emotions may be deliberately emulated, many are replicated nonconsciously within the brain. A key question in the study of emotions has centered on the process of emotional recognition: how exactly do human beings recognize emotional expressions in others? One response from psychology treats emotional recognition as an element of perception, and emotions as pieces of information associated with certain emotion-generating objects. Part of our cognitive understanding of certain objects or facial expressions, in this view, is information about their emotional significance. Recent research in neuroscience suggests, however, that emotions are triggered not only below the level of conscious awareness but also through an indirect activation of pre-existing associations between emotions and the objects previously eliciting them.[35] The brain uses shortcuts, or "tricks," that combine emotional objects or displays with previously internalized but implicit stores of knowledge about "emotionally competent stimuli."[36]

One thread within the neuroscience of emotion has further postulated the importance of simulation in emotional recognition. Earlier work by Antonio Damasio pointed to the important role of the body in emotion. Resuscitating James's much older theory, Damasio argues that emotions involve continuous status reports on the face, skin, blood, and other sensory instruments of the body. Unlike James, however, Damasio thinks the exact mechanisms through which the body is surveyed are flexible and varied: not all emotions involve reports on the *actual* state of the body.[37] He proposes instead that these embodied surveys often involve hypothetical images of the body, "as-if" constructions, which are sufficient to generate a subjective awareness of an emotion—a feeling. Damasio's account treats the brain as a malleable collection of capabilities that invents emotional repertoires over time, rather than a computer preloaded with software. In some cases, synthetic constructions are not triggered by an actual emotional object but instead by memory or an empathic interaction with others expressing an emotion. In these cases, the brain "previews" a body map as a way of registering internally the emotions of another person.[38] The result is a form of empathic simulation.

The idea of sharing emotion through simulation is supported by the recent discovery of "mirror neurons." These neurons in parts of the premotor cortex operate both when a person performs an action and when he or she observes that action performed by another. First identified by an Italian lab studying motor control in macaque monkeys, similar processes have since been identified in the human brain using fMRI technology.[39] Moreover, previously confined to the study of actions, there is now evidence that mirror neurons may play a role in shared emotions, as the brain creates simulations of an emotion perceived in others.[40] One early study exposed participants, first, to foul odors expected to generate disgust and, second, to short video clips of actors exposed to such smells and responding accordingly with expressions indicative of disgust. The result was heightened activation of neurons in the same part of the insular cortex in both direct and perceived emotional experiences.[41] Mirror neurons make possible a rapid and nonconscious process of simulation that may or may not involve the overt bodily changes associated with the emotion being simulated. The involvement of mirror neurons in simulating emotional response helps to explain not only how a person understands the emotions of others but also how emotional states become "synchronized" among members of a group.[42]

The discovery of mirror neurons is at once controversial, incomplete, and extraordinarily enticing. Cognitive psychologists, philosophers of mind, and others invested in intentional theories of interpersonal recognition (including the "theory theory" of the mind) have variously challenged the extension of macaque findings to humans, disputed the claim that neural mirroring is a sufficient condition for imitation, and denied the importance of simulation for intersubjective understanding.[43] Even among themselves, neuroscientists disagree on what conclusions can be drawn from the available evidence—although to the nonspecialist these disagreements may seem like instances of the proverbial glass half-empty.[44] Nevertheless, while mirror neurons are unlikely to be sufficient conditions for empathy as such, they do appear to play a role in emotional simulation. And the role they play endows simulation with a degree of automaticity. As one scholar writes: "This simulation process is not an effortful, deliberate pretense of being in somebody else's shoes. It is an *effortless*, automatic and unconscious inner mirroring."[45] The capacity for this automatic simulation challenges the idea that the connection between the human brain and body is a strictly private affair. We possess a neural capacity to replicate within us the emotions of others: mirror systems create what one neuroscientist describes as "invisible strings of shared circuits [that] tie our minds together, creating the fabric of an organic system that goes beyond the individual."[46]

That the brain facilitates an "automatic" form of emotional contagion does not mean that all brains automatically reproduce all emotions. Evidence from neuroimaging suggests that empathy is not a unified emotional response system but a "mosaic" of different processes in different regions of the brain. This composite quality may, as one team of authors notes, help to explain why "people's reactions to other people's emotions may be expected to differ in fine-grained ways." Each of the many components contributing to emotional simulation represents an opportunity for individuals or local communities of individuals to develop idiosyncratic styles of empathic performance. Indeed, the entire mirror neuron system has been widely recognized to involve a dimension of socialization. Monkeys in the Italian lab, initially unfamiliar with motor movements involving human instruments and lab equipment, developed the necessary familiarity over time—they acquired mirror responses through learning. Although it remains unclear how training might affect empathy, mirror systems do reveal a "plastic" quality, suggesting they may be sensitive to situational and possibly cultural differences.[47]

This evidence from neuroscience is thus validating some of James's seminal insights.[48] Although his contribution became widely discredited during much of the twentieth century, James was essentially correct to regard the body as a social window to a world of emotional connections. Brain scans conducted while research subjects are exposed to displays of emotion and emotionally significant stimuli confirm that we understand others' emotions by mapping them onto our own bodies.[49] The body's emotional capabilities can be activated even in the absence of a willful effort or conscious perception of others' emotions, as so-called mirror neurons send signals to the insular cortex and limbic system to emulate those emotional expressions. Offending our deepest intuitions about the separateness of one human body from another, fMRI research is uncovering evidence that circuits within our very own brains are shared with those around us. Echoing James, neuroscience now regards the body as less a property of a person than a malleable interface between coordinated concentrations of energy.

Mediated Interactions

Research on emotional contagion has tended to focus on small-scale interactions rather than large social groups. Constraints associated with brain-scanning equipment have confined scholars in neuroscience to individual subjects and their mediated interaction with actors displayed on a video screen. Scholars in social psychology have addressed emotional convergence between parent and child, patient and therapist, college roommates, pairs of consumers, and other social dyads. Some research explores the effects of mood and shared emotion on sports teams, and scholars of business management have studied emotional contagion as a quality of effective workplace environments and leadership styles.[50] However, the modern field of social psychology has generally been confined to those controlled groups that can be accommodated in clinical research. Methodological norms and protections for human research subjects have meant that empirical work in the field retreats from consideration of real-world emotional transmissions.[51]

Even a cursory survey of passionate protests, election upsets, and humanitarian crises suggests, however, that emotional contagion is alive and well beyond the laboratory walls. Wherever people are exposed to the emotions of others, directly or through communications technologies, contagion has the potential to shape collective agency. Microsociology supplies additional resources to make sense of emotional contagion in social environments. Microsociologies of emotion investigate the context of social interaction and how it affects the diffusion of emotion. Whereas much of the scholarly attention in psychology has focused on why certain individuals are more disposed to emotional expressiveness and contagion, sociologists assess the situational characteristics that heighten the intensity of emotional contagion.[52] By investigating factors such as the degree of shared attention and the prior emotions associated with an interaction, we can better understand the intensity and significance of emotional transmissions.[53] For the microsociology of emotional contagion, the unit of analysis is not interacting individuals but the situation of interaction itself.

Instances of contagion cannot be abstracted from the interactional situation because its properties affect the transmission of emotion. Collins argues, for example, that emotional contagion is more intense where a differential of power exists, although he regards social stratification as itself the product of the "emotional energy" of an actor rather than her or his material capabilities.[54] Emotional transmission is also contingent upon the memories and expectations participants bring to an interaction. Disappointment, anger, or other negative emotions become more likely when prior expectations are not met in actual experience.[55] Scheff finds that interactions involving the severing of social bonds generate shame, while those affirming such bonds generate pride.[56] Emotional contagion or "entrainment" is neither a strange affliction of weak personalities nor a necessary feature of all interpersonal interactions. In the sociological account, interactions become sites of contagion where certain conditions exist: copresence, mutual attention, and strong background emotions (what Collins calls "high emotional energy"). Understanding emotional contagion requires not only psychological surveys but also sociological investigation of interactional contexts.

The microsociology of emotion is less helpful, however, when it comes to interactions mediated by communications technologies. Inspired by Goffmann's "presentations of self," microsociologists argue that social interactions involving copresence are inherently more capable of engendering emotional contagion. Face-to-face interactions are presumed special because they take place through an overtly embodied process of entrainment. Extending themes first considered by Wittgenstein, the microsociology of interaction regards the body's movements as expressions that make public internal states not exposed in written and spoken communications.[57] Because actors become affectively attuned through facial gestures, bodily comportment, and other physiological displays, this literature links communication to physical proximity. In short, interaction requires copresence. Collins notes that interaction rituals occur when "human bodies come close enough to each other so that their nervous systems become mutually attuned." "Bodily presence makes it easier," he argues, "for human beings to monitor each other's signals and bodily expressions; to get into shared rhythm, caught up in each other's motions and emotions." Turner makes an even stronger case, emphasizing the evolutionary dominance of visual contact; human beings are, he argues, "programmed to read emotions visually first, then process them through speech."[58] The interactionist approach assumes that, while spoken and written communication may take mediated forms, the bodily expression of affect must be direct. As a result, interactions mediated through telephone, television, or electronic media are inherently weaker.[59]

And yet there is strong evidence to suggest that emotional contagion can and does operate in the absence of copresence. Research in social psychology suggests that contagion can occur even in the absence of actual displays of emotion. One study of "anticipatory mood matching" finds that participants only had to imagine the prospect of interacting with another person to begin sharing that person's mood.[60] If emotional contagion is possible even without interaction of any type, it should be possible in situations of mediated interaction. Neuroscientists have shown that emotional simulation is a multimodal process involving not only facial expressions but also smells, sounds, and tones of voice. One author observes: "in a physical encounter, evidence from visual, auditory, and tactile senses can add together to form a more intense sharing in face to face situations." Other studies confirm that direct exposure to facial expressions generates more intense brain activity when compared to emotionally evocative images.[61] But it is unclear how these findings might change in social settings hosting multiple modes of concurrent emotional stimulation, environmental sources of knowledge that might intensify an affective experience, or repeated exposure over time. As one neuroscientist has speculated, for example, it is conceivable that the accumulation of repeated exposure to media violence over time may generate simulated actions and emotions.[62]

These preliminary findings and speculations confirm what scholars in media studies have long argued: that emotions can be activated through exposure to provocative radio and television broadcasts.[63] Mediated communications may lack the repertoire of embodied expressions that come with direct interaction, but they employ others. A televised broadcast might, for example, overlay visual images of a person with sad music to create a multimodal interaction with a different kind of emotional potential than a face-to-face encounter. Mediated interactions are unlikely, moreover, to involve isolated modes of emotional stimulation, since we often consume television, Internet, and other media in situations that expose us simultaneously to the reactions of others. For these reasons, we cannot afford to assume that mediated interactions are inherently weak sources of affective stimulation.

Moreover, technological changes have enhanced the viability of mediated contagion. Collins's argument that mediated interactions preclude "get[ting] into shared rhythm" may well apply in contexts where radio and television involve sporadic exposure and extended news cycles. As technologies of communication extend and accelerate mediated interactions, however, the argument becomes less tenable. Indeed, this shift was noted by Tarde already at the turn of the twentieth century. Through the advent of the newspaper and other communication technologies, he surmised, the actually assembled crowd had given way to "the public" as the most salient manifestation of collective sentiment.[64] A public emerges wherever ideas and sentiments are shared within a dispersed audience whose members have a sense (*conscience*) of those others implicated in the association. Moreover, the public is inherently more complex than a crowd. The absence of proximity, which he describes as "contagion without contact," means that each individual inhabits multiple publics.[65] As communications technologies increase the potential for dispersed contagion, Tarde's insights are all the more applicable.

In the age of the twenty-four-hour news cycle, streaming video, and social networking, "contagion without contact" has become ubiquitous. Following the attacks of September 11, Americans were connected by a frenzy of national media coverage. As the US military entered Afghanistan, and later Iraq, al-Jazeera coverage generated circulations of anger and outrage across dispersed and diverse audiences.[66] In Egypt and other recent cases, social networking technologies have forged politically consequential connections among previously isolated citizens. From print media and television news to twenty-four-hour news channels, the blogosphere, and SMS/text messaging, communications technologies are facilitating diffuse but emotionally significant forms of social interaction. One contribution to the sociology of mass media conceptualizes these mediated settings as "quasi-interactions"; another treats mediated interactions as simply another mode of interaction centered on "watching" others rather than experiencing with them.[67] Both recognize that by altering the material context of social interaction new media technologies broaden the scope of emotional exchange.

Shared emotions can also result from interactions involving serial participation. That is, actors need not participate in a social activity simultaneously to be similarly affected by it. Over 30 million people have experienced the United States Holocaust Memorial Museum since it opened in 1993. Many of these have surely left with a shared stock of emotional experiences, even though very few exchanged emotions face to face.[68] In this way, institutions, buildings, and other settings can allow for convergent emotional experiences through the serial exposure people have to them. My discussion of violence in Rwanda and the former Yugoslavia involve this kind of non-copresent emotional impact. Ethnic cleansing in Bosnia was practiced in a piecemeal fashion, spreading from one village to the next. Yet even those exposed to different incidents accumulated blocks of diachronically shared anxiety and fear. By dispensing with the assumption that emotions are locked up in the hearts and minds of individuals, we can begin to trace the many ways in which they are both cogenerated and transmitted.

Social discourse, too, is an important site of affective transmission. Discursive media of various kinds—news media, political speeches, literature, film, and so on—transmit symbols, identities, narratives, and other emotionally significant constructions. Such discursive content is often socially recognized as having emotional resonance. Interpreting the cultural meanings behind emotional discourse is the traditional concern of hermeneutic scholarship across the social sciences, although that tradition has tended to conceptualize the ideas, norms, and values reproduced through discourse in a way that omits their emotional significance.[69] Communicative interactions convey emotionally significant meaning through various paralinguistic channels. For example, narratives of racial hatred in Rwanda were effective not just because they reproduced racialized narratives but also because they did so through relentless and seductive radio broadcasts. In this and several other cases, I focus on tone of speech (or "prosody"), since it has attracted special attention in the literature on emotion, but sociolinguists are also generating provocative accounts of the importance of hand gestures and other embodied modalities of communication.[70] By elucidating some of these expressive dimensions of discourse, we can access layers of socialization not fully captured by standard hermeneutic inquiry.

I should note that the social circulation of affect neither negates the individuality of social actors nor entails a loss of human agency. While emotions are shared by the brain and generated through social interaction, those exposed to emotional contagion do not somehow become affective carbon copies. Individuals may resist socially transmitted affects or interpret them through different cognitive frameworks. And, since a person launches those subjective efforts against an accumulated history of prior interactions, differences also emerge in less intentional ways. Emotions are often malleable responses whose profile changes through the process of circulation—a process theorized in the next chapter.[71] Because it results from many diffuse acts of simulation, emotional contagion is often a site of ambiguity and change rather than an exact replication. A person may therefore emulate socially available emotions imperfectly or against a different baseline of pre-existing affective experiences. Agency involves not transcending social circulations of affect but internalizing them against the particularities of personal experience. As individuals, we participate in a multiplicity of intersecting and overlapping circulations of affect; what makes me different from others are the goals and preferences I hold but also the specific constellations of affect coursing through each of us. Investigating these circulations demands, as the next chapter suggests, a radically new conceptualization of the central role of emotion in human agency.

Affect as a Vehicle of Socialization

Once we recognize that emotions can be shared, we can begin to consider the variety of ways they affect social and political relations. Circulations of affect are, after all, embedded in local interactions with great moral and political significance, from protests and rallies to commemorative events and legal trials. Some emotional byproducts of these interactions are likely to be so subtle that they go unnoticed, while others are dramatic and fuel more visible political outcomes. As Collins explains, interaction rituals give rise to emotions of differing intensities, ranging from those with low "emotional energy" to those with high. Both can have political impact. A dramatic rise of fear, for example, can affect foreign policy, as it did in post-9/11 America. On the other hand, a lack of popular enthusiasm can engender its own political effects, as when public boredom with the UN tribunal for Yugoslavia affected its reputation as an institution. Circulations of affect contribute to political outcomes in complex and compound ways. Because they shift and mix together, emotions seldom function as simple causal forces directly responsible for discrete policies or signal actions.

The political impact of emotion stems from its genesis in social interaction. People who participate together in social events and practices develop shared emotional repertoires. Durkheim famously argued that such interaction rituals engender a process of "collective effervescence" in which co-participants internalize social norms through shared emotional rituals.[72] These shared emotions are not merely fleeting reactions but evaluative orientations people assign to elements of the social world—from beliefs, norms, and identities to actors, symbols, and institutions. Participation in a circulation of affect thus facilitates the socialization of actors into the norms and identities of a community. Identification with a group is more than just an intellectual belief in one's suitability for membership, or an ideological commitment to the values it espouses. Shared identity is rooted in affective affinities, such as trust, solidarity, or pride, and these are generated also through embodied, affectively attuned participation in a community's rituals. Whereas constructivist models of socialization often assume an element of willful adherence to social roles or rules, a parallel process of affective assimilation prepares actors to want these things in the first place.

Acquiring patterns of emotional response socializes people into the identities, beliefs, norms, institutions, and other social structures they inhabit. For example, where national and other collective identities take hold, they often have powerful affective roots; an identity is not only a social category but also a lived, visceral connection to a community of others. As Jonathan Mercer has recently shown, many beliefs are not just cold calculations but inspired, sometimes unquestioned, beliefs.[73] Social norms can also have an emotional impetus, where members of a community become attached to a code of conduct and react to those who transgress it. As Talcott Parsons suggests, social norms have value because members of a society experience them as desirable.[74] Even institutions have affective significance—eliciting, for example, trust, hope, or resentment. The United Nations, to take the most obvious international example, has historically galvanized the faith and hope of liberal internationalists. On a more local level, the South African Truth and Reconciliation Commission came to embody the trust and magnanimity it sought to cultivate. By inspiring norms, identities, and institutions, emotions tether us to familiar and socially sanctioned modes of behavior.[75]

Stereotypes notwithstanding, it is impossible—and imprudent—to classify the political impact of emotion as either automatically good or bad. Consider, for example, the emotions associated with the United Nations. The organization is sometimes celebrated as the institutional embodiment of liberal hopes for international peace and the rule of law.[76] And yet because of those very ideals, the UN provokes antipathy among conservatives in America: for Glenn Beck or John Bolton, for instance, the institution is a prelude to "One World Government" and therefore a harbinger of fear. Many cherished international norms spring from emotional roots. The prohibition against torture, for example, is rooted in the disgust that practice eventually provoked in the societies of early modern Europe.[77] And yet arguably more destructive norms also stem from affective processes—such as the principle that ethnic homogeneity should form the proper basis for national self-determination. In the former Yugoslavia between 1987 and 1992, emotional investments were displaced from one norm, multiethnic federalism, onto its chauvinist competitor. Normative ambivalence is also reflected in the emotional politics of identity. National and transnational identities have historically served as desirable vehicles of resistance and solidarity. But so too have they contributed to violent and protracted conflict. The resentment and humiliation associated with the Palestinian Intifada, for example, have congealed over time into relatively stable features of that conflict.[78] In such cases, circulations of affect become properties of a social environment, infusing the many interactions hosted therein.

Emotions function differently than other forms of socialization. We often speak of ideas, beliefs, and norms as social forces affecting political behavior. As intellectual constructions, these vehicles of socialization become explicit topics of deliberation and strategic choice; they are also often objects of social discourse, as leaders and institutions incorporate them into political speech. Research in neuroscience has revealed, however, that large parts of our psychological and social lives take place without summoning conscious attention. From voting behavior to elite bargaining, many actions in the world of politics are unlikely to be subject to prior evaluation by the intellect. Emotions allow actors to absorb socially relevant expectations without these commitments registering in explicit statements and public discourses. This implicit, unobservable quality does not make affect any less significant as a vehicle of socialization, although it does ensure that its effects are more difficult to detect and trace empirically. We cannot begin to address these empirical challenges until we relax the assumption that emotions affect only our innermost psychic lives and recognize their role in communicating social norms and constituting social actors.

Levels, Units, and Identities

In a discipline encompassing both individual and corporate actors, IR scholars have long worried about misapplying psychological attributes to states and other groups. On what grounds, we ask ourselves, can beliefs or feelings be applied to states and other corporate entities? Following Gabriel Tarde's seminal conceptualization of "sociological psychology," I argue that these worries are generally misplaced:[79] once we recognize that emotions have a social reality, they are already something more than "psychological attributes." Emotions are part of the social tissue connecting individuals near and far. A state, for example, consists of courts, parliaments, agencies, and other political substructures but also constellations of emotion and belief distributed across its various participants. Political actors are not individuals first and citizens later; they are a mélange of attachments and repulsions, each secured through constellations of shared emotions, memories, beliefs, and (sometimes) identities. In treating emotions as embodied and communicable responses rather than individual feeling-states, we can legitimately speak of circulations of affect that constitute a range of collectivities in global politics. Rather than worry about a fraudulent attribution of psychological traits to the state, I move on to investigate the diverse forms of collective agency emotions engender.

My theorization of affect thus resists compartmentalizing levels of analysis. Rather than attribute emotions to leaders, voters, and other individuals in a way that separates these social actors from states and other corporate units, my sociological approach treats emotions from the outset as interactive processes with social properties. Studying the social properties of emotion does not require "scaling up" from individual to collective, since circulations of affect are already a connective tissue constituting social collectivities.[80] As Tarde contended over a century ago, persons are no more sites of a distinctly "individual" level of analysis than they are expressions of corporate agency in its various forms. Contemporary microsociologists concur, suggesting that all structures at the macro-level involve micro-level patterns of action.[81] Skeptical of the levels distinction, I study emotions as interactive and connective tissues cutting across actors and entities typically compartmentalized into levels. As I investigate empirical cases normally kept separate—for example, nationalist leaders, protest movements and grassroots organizations, and cultural dimensions of foreign policy—I do so out of a conscious effort to capture affective dynamics likely to elude a standard typology of levels.

Emotions thus help to sustain many familiar corporate entities in global politics. States, for example, benefit from the emotional support of their citizens. Without the loyalties we normally describe as patriotism, the state would be only a cold, legal apparatus for solving collective action problems. Intergovernmental organizations, too, depend upon some degree of enthusiasm and trust among the citizenry of member states. The UN enjoys legitimacy among the leaders and populations of the member-states whose voice the organization guarantees. Very different emotional dispositions likely exist in states such as Israel, which feels its sovereignty violated by UN resolutions, compared to European members, who have historically demonstrated greater enthusiasm for institutional delegation. While mediated through diverse contexts, the legitimacy wielded by IGOs is a product of not only cognitive beliefs but also trust, hope, and other constituent emotions.

Circulations of affect do more than unite formal and familiar entities such as states and institutions, however. In an age of social networks, terrorist organizations, and transnational human rights campaigns, emotions also give rise to informal types of collective agency. Members of a terrorist organization, for example, may share resentments and anxieties even though they are geographically dispersed, in sporadic communication, and only loosely united by a common identity. Consider also the constellation of organizations, individuals, and norms comprising international regimes. Where regimes have low levels of coordination and low degrees of awareness of themselves as institutions, emotional connections to an event or campaign are integral components of the collective agency involved. Finally, the waves of global protest—in response to the provocative statements of Salman Rushdie, Pope Benedict, or US president George W. Bush—are sustained by similarly affective circulations. The individuals involved may belong to a group that can be objectively identified according to a "Muslim" identity, but this abstract criterion is not what explains the intensity and impact of their protest. In each of these cases, we find emotional attachments—what Collins calls "pockets of solidarity"—rather than institutionalized connections.[82]

Understanding emotion as a vehicle of socialization requires reassessing the ubiquity of identity in IR theory. Identity has arguably become the most important lens through which to view the actions of social groups in international politics: no longer the special province of critical theory or constructivism, it has become an analytical reference point for both realist and institutionalist theories. And the category is now being applied well beyond race, ethnicity, gender, and other areas commonly associated with identity politics. States with strong humanitarian commitments, for example, have been described as "good samaritan" states, and regional IGOs such as ASEAN are said to embody distinctive identities associated with the procedural norms they employ.[83] While the concern over identity has sparked fascinating research agendas, we need to think twice about whether it is well suited for conceptualizing the specific properties of affective socialization.

Emotions can have social effects even in the absence of identity. There is a tacit assumption in the literature on identity that where people are found acting together they are bound to have an idea of themselves as a group.[84] And yet global politics involves protest movements, social networks, and other social practices for which participants hold no explicit idea of themselves as a group. As identity theories posit elaborate systems of cultural coding, they abstract identity from lived reality. Scholars of social practices are telling us that many activities in international relations involve more doing than thinking.[85] Where actions are routinized or informal, socialization may operate less through identity and other ideational constructs and more through habit, memory, and emotion. By shifting the focus onto circulations of affect, we can supplement knowledge of well-defined, identity-owning groups with some understanding of associations with lower levels of self-awareness. Ad-hoc and implicit forms of collective agency are vital elements of ethnic conflict, transitional justice, and terrorism; in a world of accelerated communication and global sensitivity, these are key players.

The limits of identity can be seen across a variety of topics and cases. In ethnic conflict—often seen as a paradigmatic instance of identity politics—identity in fact captures only one dimension of collective agency. As Straus has shown, perpetrators in Rwanda were not universally united by an explicit identity that tightly structured their conduct. Some studies suggest instead that contagious circulations of fear worked as temporary connective tissues, bringing otherwise loosely affiliated individuals and communities into association.[86] Fear created virtual communities of perpetrator and victim. It is relatively easy for outside observers to imagine after the fact that violence has well-defined targets. Those on the ground, however, tend to experience it through the multiple allegiances of everyday life. To take another example, the attacks of 9/11 immediately sparked a global outpouring of emotion in response to America's loss. Todd Hall has shown that Russia and China, states not generally supportive of US foreign policy, nevertheless responded with obligatory expressions of sympathy.[87] The "community" created by the attacks was not, as identity theories would have us believe, contiguous with "the West" or some other cultural or geopolitical entity. The event of 9/11 created a temporary constituency outraged by the senseless violence of terrorism; short-term emotions became conjoined in a way that affected collective political agency.

Conclusion

Recognizing that emotions are not locked in the hearts and minds of individual actors allows us to begin studying them as social processes. What I am calling circulations of affect are mixtures of emotion that come to define social climates and sustain certain social norms, identities, and beliefs. They are rooted in neural processes of simulation that create "shared circuits" within the brains of seemingly autonomous actors. As people participate in social interaction, they are thus affected and constituted by the emotions of others. Circulations of affect create blocks of emotion—such as trust, fear, or hope—that contribute to who social actors are as they approach political deliberation and action. Emotions help social actors navigate a complex world of competing and overlapping norms and values. As I argue in the next chapter, emotions also signal moments of change and serve as sources of adaptation, synergy, and resistance in relation to those same social norms and values.

TWO

Contagion and the Creativity of Affect

A core contention in this book is that a political theory of affect needs to account for its elusive, ephemeral, and unpredictable effects. IR scholars have tapped various frameworks to understand how foreign policies, institutional innovations, and legal norms travel in an interconnected world—for example, through learning, path dependency, and moral argument. As significant as these social mechanisms are, none captures the fluidity of emotional interaction in cases of concern in global politics, such as those involving large crowds, intense communications, and culturally contested topics. For example, workers' strikes in the former Yugoslavia during the late 1980s combined synergistically with the politics of ethnic nationalism. And, across the Middle East, North Africa, and parts of South Asia, contagious acts of political resistance have repeatedly followed the provocative speeches and gestures of Western authorities. These cases involve mixtures of interconnected and flexible emotions—such as anger, fear, humiliation, and sympathy—readily transmitted across borders and among actors. My objective in this chapter is to investigate how the transmission of affect through contagion sustains the fluidity and volatility evident in such cases.

Emotions both facilitate and block processes of socialization. The previous chapter demonstrates that emotions have a social dimension: transmitted in and through social interaction, circulations of affect become integral to socialization. Over time, affective orientations crystallize into the deeply held commitments we hold as members of a society—from national identities and religious beliefs to cultural taboos and founding documents. It is not surprising that we often qualify social standards and institutions as "cherished," "sacred," or "powerful." Even as emotions supply a society with some of its normative glue, however, they also inspire acts of resistance and change. Much of what is surprising in the behavior of others results from their emotional capabilities. This unpredictability has historically led scholars in the West to denigrate emotions as epistemologically and morally unreliable; prior to the nineteenth century, emotions were more frequently termed "passions" and treated as unfortunate impulses beyond a person's control. While some emotional disruptions surely pose real problems—contributing even to enmity, violence, and war—the instability of emotion is rooted in an element of creativity with no necessary moral or political valence. Understood as social circulations, surprising emotions can serve as vehicles of change: when compassion fuels humanitarian generosity, for example, or when trust enables the peaceful settlement of conflict, the fluidity of affect becomes notably more beneficial to the practice of politics.

This chapter takes stock of the specific psychological, neurological, and social properties of contagion as a mechanism of emotional transmission. Research in both neuroscience and social psychology has shown that contagion can occur in the absence of intentional or strategic appraisals—we "catch" the emotions of others without even trying. An emotion or mood can travel contagiously even when recipients are not exposed to its eliciting event or when they merely imagine or anticipate the emotion in question. As these contagious processes occur over time, emotions can become attached to memories shared by those with no personal exposure to a remembered event. These findings warrant close attention especially for research on topics involving complex histories, interactions across cultural milieus, or intense forms of political contestation. As emotions and moods travel from one social context to another, the source of affect may be ambiguous or multiple; the range of actors to whom a given emotion is transmitted is likely to be porous and flexible. Contagious circulations of affect follow chains of social interaction rather than abstract constructions of identity or cultural membership. The result is that emotions, far from rote impulses, are creative forces with potential to disrupt business as usual in the world of politics.

I show here that circulations of affect involve something more than a simple diffusion of uniform emotional states. Writing well before the advent of cognitive psychology in the mid-twentieth century, philosopher-social theorists such as William James, Henri Bergson, and Théodule Ribot appreciated the creativity of emotional exchange. They understood that, in the process of transmission, affect changes intensity, switches objects, and forges new symbols. In facilitating these dynamics, circulations of affect alter the social relations of those participating in them. Contagion occurs in and through processes that are neural and embodied, but it would be mistaken to suppose that biological roots entail hardwired formulas of emotional replication. On the contrary, as some neuroscientists have begun to suggest, the brain's mechanisms of emotional simulation permit ambiguity in the social expression and exchange of emotion. The creativity of emotional contagion is not only compatible with its biological genesis but may also be partly explained by it. Contrary to common images of it as a pathological phenomenon, contagion has no necessary ethicopolitical status; what is distinctive about contagion is not the desirability of its object but the kind of process through which it spreads.

Properties of Emotional Contagion

The previous chapter explained that emotions are shared socially. Statements such as "the group was overcome with melancholy" or "a feeling of hope is in the air" capture situations in which a mood or emotion pervades social space. Such descriptions are all too familiar, and yet they betray our most fundamental assumptions about emotions as subjective feelings owned by individuals. Even where we tacitly endorse the idea of emotions as internal feeling-states, it is hard not to recognize the ubiquity of emotion in social settings. Whether or not they enter conscious awareness, emotions are by-products of the many interactions we inhabit—from casual conversations to polished political speeches and from local rituals to global media spectacles. In each of these situations, the emotional responses of participants become focused on common circulations of affect. Those shared emotions may be fleeting, and they may be inflected with diverse meanings and degrees of significance among participants. And yet coparticipation in an emotional interaction generates a baseline of affective experience against which a person registers modifications, personal styles, and acts of resistance.

My concern in this chapter is to return to some of the theoretical resources previously discussed in order to specify the properties of emotional contagion. A recent contribution to the literature on social practices has noted some of these peculiar qualities. Drawing on work by philosopher and social theorist Theodore Schatzki, Janice Bially Mattern shows that social practices involve embodied displays of emotion. Emotions, in her account, are not internal states that achieve outward expression but "emotional practices" that occupy the nexus between something internal and something external. She also emphasizes that emotions endow human beings with agency capable of not only conforming to but also creatively adapting social structures.[1] Bially Mattern takes us well beyond standard psychologies of emotion as feeling states, and she points to their central role in human adaptivity and innovation. Her account raises a series of important questions about how exactly emotional transmissions generate creativity and what specific effects this creativity has on social and political agency. To answer these questions, we need to explore further the peculiar neuro-psycho-social properties of emotional contagion.

These properties are elusive in part because, while sharing emotions is a common experience, the precise mechanisms of affective exchange are relatively inconspicuous. This invisibility does not solely derive from the fact that something unobservable is being communicated. After all, we regularly acknowledge the communication of values, beliefs, and other intangible mental constructions. Indeed, it seems absurd to treat identities, norms, or ideologies as somehow trapped in the mind of an individual; probably it does not even occur to us to suppose that they might *not* exist as properties of a social relation. With these phenomena, however, we can readily observe their social transmission also in various kinds of observable communication, such as speech, narrative, and argument. Such public mechanisms of transmission are visible to participants and observers alike. Even if norms, identities, and beliefs are also exchanged through less directly observable channels of communication—cultural rituals, perhaps, or embodied social practices—their credibility as objects of study is established by those other more observable mechanisms often involved.

In the case of emotional contagion, the precise mechanisms of circulation are generally invisible. Emotions are often exchanged without becoming overt topics of conversation. Social actors do talk about emotions from time to time: we can observe discourse about emotion in public discussion over the fears affecting a presidential candidacy, or the powerful anger connected with the 9/11 attacks; it is manifest also in the familiar emotional tropes—from "ancient hatreds" to "anti-Americanism" and "Islamic rage"—shaping public debates over foreign affairs. And yet in some situations, a social transmission of affect can occur in the absence of any discourse *about* it: fear can be in the air before social actors declare its presence. In such instances, it may be especially difficult to assess the properties of emotional contagion and their effects on social interaction. Nevertheless, the resources discussed in the previous chapter, along with research in social psychology, provide some important clues.

One distinctive dimension of emotional contagion relates to its durability over time. It may seem tempting to assume that the more widely emotions spread, the more temporary or fleeting they must be. A common objection to the study of emotion in political contexts is the contention that, while emotions may prevail in the moment, they soon fizzle—in the light of day, affective responses must surely yield to the calm voice of reason. It is true that emotions may dissipate quickly in some circumstances. In situations where cultural and political authorities may seek to curb the expression of public sentiment, institutions and other initiatives may succeed in suppressing collective emotional responses. In post-apartheid South Africa, for example, Nelson Mandela's government aggressively promoted national unity as a surrogate for resentment and anger. Circulations of affect may also fade in situations where distant events fail to sustain the attention of public officials and journalists. As studies of "compassion fatigue" suggest, humanitarian crises and natural disasters often trigger waves of well-intentioned but short-lived empathy. The hasty dissipation of collective affect may in fact be the default position in a world where many emotion-generating interactions fail to capture the attention of participants and, as such, never coalesce into a contagious circulation.

Nevertheless, there are good reasons to pause before dismissing too quickly the temporal durability of emotional contagion. Research in psychology has found that even acute or short-term emotions carry over into subsequent perceptions and judgments. An early study suggested that the cognitive significance attributed to an emotion could become severed from the situation of initial arousal. Experimental evidence showed that research subjects whose emotional response is generated artificially by injections of adrenalin describe their experience with cognitive framings supplied by the researchers during a contrived questionnaire procedure. The results thus indicated a gap between emotional excitation, on the one hand, and the meaning a person gives it, on the other. The latter bears no necessary connection to the physiological stimulation experienced and, moreover, is influenced by socially available cues and standards.[2] The study also suggested an interconnected process of emotional experience, in which the underlying energy of emotional arousal could shift into subsequent emotions. Exploring the effects of "affective priming," another study contended that "nonconscious affect can 'spill over' onto unrelated stimuli." Research in psychology continues to explore these processes, seeking to specify which emotions are most susceptible to transfer and how their "spillover" affects subsequent judgments and beliefs of various kinds.[3] Even before their social transmission, emotions have a footloose quality and a migratory potential.

The process of affective transfer becomes more complex as we consider real-world social settings in which a variety of emotion-inducing interactions are at play. Early research in social psychology recognized, for example, that the residual effects of multiple emotions can combine in a process of "emotional escalation." An emotion, in this view, is not a discrete event but an episode in an ongoing process of "excitation transfer." In the layered, sequential reality of everyday experience, "admixtures of emo-tions . . . appear to be the rule, not the exception."[4] Zillmann's model sug-gests that emotions are best understood not as fixed and discrete things but as modular bits of energy that can be plugged into a variety of successive objects and experiences. In the case of long-term emotions or moods, there may be even greater latitude in the range of possible experiences and objects to which a mood could transfer. As Frijda explains, moods are not "centered around an object or event," but "in a fleeting manner attach now to this object, then to that." As a mood stretches across successive interactions, an element of ambiguity enables connections to a variety of potential objects.[5] Emotions can be fleeting, but so too can they endure by flowing into sub-sequent interactions.

Studying emotions in social settings therefore requires looking for in-stances where seemingly dissipating responses are actually morphing into some alternate form. Collins's account of social interaction represents one attempt to do just this. In his framework, an emotion is not a fixed entity but a malleable response that mutates in and through interaction. Through repeated interaction rituals, he argues, the disruptive responses associated with specific eliciting events can be prolonged into longer-term emotional dispositions, such as enthusiasm, pride, or trust. Building on Durkheim's theory of "collective effervescence," Collins suggests that repeated interac-tions capture emotional energy accrued through short-term emotions and preserve it in the form of symbols. A symbol for Collins is a concentration of emotional energy from the embodied process of interaction.[6] Where in-teractions are sufficiently repetitive and focused on a shared emotion, then, otherwise fleeting responses can crystallize into a more lasting sentiment. Where multiple participants share some of the same interaction rituals, those more durable sentiments become elements of a social environment.

Recent work in cultural theory offers a complementary resource for an-ticipating the social and cultural manifestations psychological tendencies might have. Sara Ahmed notes, for example, that affect frequently moves "sideways," as fear of one object later becomes attached to another. Affect, in her account, possesses a "sticky" quality that endows certain objects and signs with emotional significance. Hate crimes in Britain, she argues, are products of pain and fear that have mutated into hatred toward certain populations. Through a process of repetition, the term "Paki" has absorbed a repertoire of resentments and fears associated with immigration and multi-culturalism.[7] Building on Deleuze's conceptualization of affect, Massumi attributes an "autonomy" to affect because he recognizes its capacity to over-flow the boundaries of a particular body. For Massumi, specific communicative events can "transduce" affect from one social field to another. When incidents of domestic violence increase on Super Bowl Sunday, he argues, it is because televised media transmissions transduce affective potential from a highly charged sports event to a domestic setting.[8] These contributions to cultural theory offer plausible accounts of how social transmissions of affect change the social environments in which they occur.

Because of these peculiar exchanges across time and space, the emotions generated in one social setting or at one event can seep into subsequent interactions. Especially in environments where communications technologies are active in serializing emotional responses over time, the power of these transfers of excitation should not be underestimated. Where emotional responses are cultivated through institutional practices, memorialization rituals, or social movement campaigns, they may even become constitutive of social climates. Emotions with different temporal qualities expand and contract in ways that defy simple causal relations: short-term responses can accumulate into lasting sentiments and memories, and the latter can become baselines for surges down the road. Appreciating the social and political role of affect in international conflict requires investigating these interconnected modalities of affective circulation.

Contagion and Creativity

Affect flows through social interaction, and its form and content change along the way. When actors apply a memory from one event to make sense of another, they relive the emotions associated with that memory. But every repetition comes with a difference—or, as Tarde stated in his seminal study of imitation: "All repetition . . . springs from some innovation."[9] When an emotional response or state is being repeated across different contexts, an element of creativity is involved. This means that when we study, for example, the Serb nationalists who applied memories of 1942 to 1992, identifying the underlying innovation sustaining that replication becomes an important analytical objective. Or, in approaching the cultural aftermath of 9/11 in America, we need to consider not only the impact of pre-existing stereotypes regarding Muslims but also how these creatively combined to constitute the "Islamic terrorist" as a new social category. Social interactions generate synthetic combinations, as affective responses flow through time and migrate across actors and environments. Each synthesis is an opportunity for change: new movements may succeed while established ones fail; distant memories can revive a cultural symbol in decline; or an institution might resonate with popular expectations in ways its architects never anticipated. The ambiguity and flexibility of emotional contagion possesses a capacity for change that I call "creativity."

The idea of creativity warrants several qualifications. First, creative acts should not be equated with heroic gestures of transcendence. While it is tempting to associate the term "creativity" with acts that magically step outside prevailing social structures, I apply it instead to selections, transfers, mixtures, and mutations of already-existing emotions and emotional phenomena. Rooted in the peculiar properties of contagion, creativity is the product of affective transmissions across otherwise disparate objects, experiences, or actors. Second, to say that an action exhibits a creative dimension is not to say it is either morally good or politically desirable. The creativity of emotions is part of what makes them enticing resources for a wide spectrum of social movements and political projects. Creative circulations of affect are distinctive not because they are inherently good or just but because they engender thoughts or actions that are unexpected. Finally, in associating contagious circulations of affect with creativity, I am not suggesting that some emotions are inherently disruptive while others are necessarily stable. One influential framework in neuropsychology identifies two "affective subsystems": a "disposition" system, which sustains habitual behaviors through responses such as elation and enthusiasm, and a "surveillance" system, in which anxiety or fear triggers behavioral adjustments.[10] Without denying the value of this approach, I locate creativity in the process of interaction, where emotions of various kinds intersect and mutate. In real-world social environments, circulations of affect continually give rise to expectations and emotional baselines that alter subsequent responses.

Prior to the cognitivist revolution, studies on emotion often cited creativity as one of its most noteworthy qualities. By the early decades of the twentieth century, the idea that emotions fueled innovation or creativity had been variously endorsed by William James, Théodule Ribot, and Henri Bergson. Placing emotions squarely at the heart of the "creative imagination," Ribot attributes to them both the impetus behind innovation and its raw material: by uniting disparate experiences sharing the same "emotional stamp," he argues, affect "offers an almost unlimited field for novel combinations." Bergson echoes this view when he announces that "it is emotion above all which vivifies, or rather vitalizes, the intellectual elements with which it is destined to unite."[11] Ribot and Bergson recognized that emotions sustain both durable habits and creative innovations. As the social theorist Hans Joas explains, while actors are guided by habit, habitual behavior invariably encounters liminal situations in which the creativity of action must take over. For James, emotions are integral to the way human beings apprehend the flux of lived experience. He views the world as a "field of possibilities in which something new can evolve." Drawing together themes from James, Dewey, and Mead, Joas establishes creativity— "the liberation of the capacity for new actions"—as an essential component of action in a social world.[12]

The creativity of affect emerges from the peculiar features of contagion as its mechanism of transmission. From research across several disciplines, I distill three interconnected sources of creativity. The first is that emotions are prone to surge in circumstances where public events intensify interaction among large numbers of people.[13] Surges of emotion have the potential to inspire movements, campaigns, and deliberative efforts to alter settled norms. As noted in the previous chapter, emotions can sustain durable patterns of conduct and social structures. By inspiring identities and beliefs, they help to sustain both entrenched conflicts and reliable channels of cooperation: fear and humiliation, for example, have calcified into stable habits in the intractable conflict over Palestine, and trust has created durable habits of reciprocal support between historical allies such as Israel and the United States.[14] These stable emotional commitments are important aspects of emotional politics, and they confirm what Durkheim, Parsons, and later social theorists tell us about the potential for emotions to uphold social norms. But emotions are not always attached to steady routines and institutionalized practices. As Collins says of an interaction ritual, it "can be repetitive and conservatizing, but . . . also provides the occasions on which changes break through."[15] Where dramatic events and media spectacles assemble and focus the attention of an audience, shifting patterns of emotional energy redirect social interaction.

What makes an event into a public spectacle is in part its capacity to activate popular emotion. Such events trigger bursts of affective energy that cannot be fully predicted in advance: for example, the bipartisan swell of national solidarity in the United States following the 9/11 attacks; the surge of anger following the Danish cartoon affair; or the circulations of hope in the aftermath of the Rwandan genocide. Collins and other social theorists following Durkheim suggest that public events become emotionally significant because they intensify social interaction and concentrate emotional energy across an audience of coparticipants. The resulting "collective effervescence" contains potential for invention, as new emotional responses trigger shifts in social norms and institutions.[16] In Collins's account, interaction rituals generate in particular new symbols, and the transmutation of emotion into symbol is, he argues, a fundamentally creative process. By inspiring new symbols and norms, an emotional event has the potential to modify a social environment.

The second source of emotional creativity lies in the flexibility and ambiguity inherent in the process of contagion. Various studies of social interaction suggest that skills, ideas, norms, and emotions can jump from one setting or object to another. As noted above, emotions can carry over from one situation or object to another. Research in psychology also suggests that unconscious, automatic responses generated by some situational feature of a person's social environment are likely to be activated by other environments containing analogous features; indeed, part of what such automatic responses do is help us adapt to new surroundings.[17] This neurological and psychological flexibility is reflected in social theories emphasizing the adaptability of social actors to new projects and settings. For example, recognizing that social practices can intersect, Adler and Pouliot note that multiple practices may "combine and form a new type of competent performance." This process of "hybridization" is, they explain, sustained by "innovative associations and as such is often equated with creation."[18] Adler and Pouliot provide as an example the convergence of Christian religious organizations and campaigns for humanitarian intervention. The readiness with which commitment to one social project can in such cases seep into another can be explained in part by the ambiguity of the underlying emotional circulations. A variety of social and cultural theories attuned to the complexity of emotional experience suggest that the severability of an emotion's social meaning from its underlying affective energy allows for greater migration across objects and settings. Emotions are thus especially prone to the sort of "innovative associations" Adler and Pouliot describe; indeed, the ubiquity of emotion in the world of politics may in fact make the phenomenon of "hybridization" the rule rather than the exception.

The mechanism of contagion is thus more complex than a simple repetition. Admittedly, one conceivable rendering of contagion could treat it as a closed circuit of emotional transfer; as Ahmed worries, affect in this view becomes "something that one has, and can then pass on, as if what passes on is the same thing."[19] And yet contagious transmissions of affect involve more complex and creative processes than such an image suggests. As emotions move laterally across objects and settings, they can fuel unexpected challenges to settled social structures. The identity of the "Islamic terrorist," for example, was not reinforced by post-9/11 fears but forged by it: new practices of racial profiling helped to fuse certain racial, cultural, and religious markers with the social category of the terrorist. The conflict in Darfur, to use another example, did more than spark humanitarian concern among Americans—according to Mamdani, it also created a powerful but silent association between anti-Arab prejudice and moral outrage over genocide.[20] As affect circulates through contagion, the process of excitation transfer and ritual entrainment ensure that it does so as a dynamic potentiality rather than a thing. Where emotions readily detach from their original circumstances of elicitation, creative agency follows.

Finally, creativity arises when the flow of emotional experience affords temporal syntheses across successive social interactions. As theories of microsociology tell us, social interactions are enacted not on a blank slate but against an ongoing backdrop of lived experience. As one study puts it, human agency is best conceptualized as "a temporally embedded process of social engagement" with connections to past, present, and future.[21] In the context of ongoing interaction, emotions are not discrete events but flexible states and responses that reach backward and forward in time. Theories of emotional carryover and excitation transfer suggest that arousal from one interaction can spill over into later ones. Each instance of transfer involves a creative shift of "emotional energy" from its original moment of elicitation to some later event. Social interactions act as hinges, allowing energy from one temporal context to flow creatively into another.

This flow of emotional experience is borne out in human memory, where emotional memories are continually recalled and injected into the present. Folk psychology presumes that a memory's availability to consciousness is determined by its proximity to the present: the more distant an experience becomes, the less intense is our memory of it. But neuropsychological research suggests instead that memory recall is closely connected to the moods and emotions present at the time of retrieval. Extending Bergson's insight that distant memories may retain their emotional significance and appear in cognitively unrelated contexts, Schacter calls this phenomenon "mood-congruent retrieval."[22] Where the emotional interactions in the present stimulate recall of distant memories, a combinative or synthetic process is taking place. Notwithstanding cognitive dissonances between them, objects are united by the emotional qualities—what Ribot called the "emotional stamp"—they share. Research in neuroscience is confirming what Bergson and an earlier generation of theorists understood: that memory retrieval is a flexible and creative process.

Neuroscience offers insight into what is happening in the brain at these moments of creativity. Scientific research on emotion often uses cases of neural damage or psychological disorder in order to establish a baseline of normal brain activity. Nevertheless, there is reason to suppose that even the ostensibly normal functioning of emotional simulation and expression allows for variation and flexibility. Research in psychology and neuroscience generally classifies such effects as forms of "bias." For example, studies have shown that the amygdala supplies implicit emotional associations that can fuel racial stereotypes. These automatic discriminations are not failings of the brain; rather, they are inherent in "the ordinary mechanisms of everyday emotional learning and memory."[23] The amygdala internalizes racialized emotional associations over time and applies these in the flow of social experience to a variety of incoming objects. Because these responses are automatic, we have minimal latitude to influence the range of objects to which they are applied.[24] Far from hard-wired, the brain accumulates emotional associations from experience and sometimes applies these expansively to objects and situations to which they may not fit by cognitive standards.

Damasio helps to confirm the brain's creativity when he recognizes that the process of emotional elicitation through body maps routinely confronts opportunities for slippage. A constructed body map can attach itself to an object or expression in a way that "may be unexpected and sometimes unwelcome." These "juxtapositions," he argues, "affirm the relative autonomy of the neural machinery behind the emotions" and supplies evidence of "a vast domain of nonconscious processes, some part of which is amenable to psychological explanation and some part of which is not."[25] Damasio's speculations echo James's insights on the creativity of emotional experience. Creativity lay at the center of the philosophy James called "radical empiricism," which studied the flux of experience before it is mediated by concepts and categories. James could justifiably say very little about this flux, calling it only "a subconscious more." For him, emotions are unencumbered by intellectual abstractions and therefore offer momentary glimpses of "pure experience."[26] James was arguably the first to appreciate that emotions, first responders in the flux of everyday life, creatively adapt to a world of surprising experiences.

The potential for emotional creativity is likely to increase in social settings, where many forms of interaction overlap and serve to connect dispersed populations. Research in social neuroscience still reveals relatively little about how the processes of affective simulation discussed in the previous chapter are altered in environments populated by diverse actors and multiple emotional processes. In an artificial laboratory environment with discrete stimuli and small numbers of research subjects, simulation may exhibit regularity and coherence. But in real-world social settings, that process is likely subject to more creative juxtapositions of the sort Damasio anticipates. Where digital technologies connect diverse and dispersed audiences, the opportunities for emotion to migrate from one topic or problem to another surely increase further still. And where social settings become dense with political protest and other expressive practices, new surges of affect are more likely to overflow the events and interactions originally eliciting them. Indeed, given the complexity and fluidity of everyday life, creativity may be the norm of affective transmission rather than the exception.

By tracing emotional interactions, we position ourselves to apprehend surprises and inventions that influence the course of global politics but go undetected in conventional theoretical framings. For example, following the resurgence of a historical humiliation can help us understand a person's pride in the present. Tracing circulations of fear or anxiety might help in detecting the rising salience of a cultural prejudice within a political community. Or, attending to the circulation of enthusiasm or hope within a social movement might shed light on the success of a campaign or protest. While circulations of affect may not cause specific outcomes, they lend urgency to new problems, threats, and solutions—and prolong interest in old ones. By infusing agency with creativity, emotions pluralize the field of possible responses and decouple action from a tight dependency on logics of symbolic resemblance, appropriateness, and strategic advantage.

Emotional Agency in Global Politics

Nonconscious neural processes engender surprising forms of affective simulation, across seemingly discrete human bodies. Because emotions utilize such a complex mechanism of transmission, they give rise to distinctive forms of social action, for which standard models of agency are not well equipped. Even when causal variables are social-structural (e.g., the balance of power) or cultural (e.g., nationalism) in nature, IR scholars tend to populate the world of international politics with individual persons. Whether these form a small number of specially qualified people making important decisions or a large number of ordinary people for whom such decisions are made, in both instances we tend to assume that garden-variety, intentional individuals lie at the heart of agency in global affairs. Studying contagious affect calls these assumptions into question. From heads of state and experts to celebrities and activists, individual actors are of course in no short supply, and yet social agency—the capacity to shape social interaction and its outcomes in global politics—is not exclusively confined to their willful efforts. Because emotions connect us to social norms, cultural groups, and political projects in many different degrees and combinations, we need an account of emotional agency refocused from complete persons to sub- and trans-personal affective capabilities.

Western philosophical traditions have generally resisted the notion that emotion might contribute to agency. Kant and other Enlightenment thinkers suggest just the opposite, treating emotions as a thinking person's least-reliable capabilities. Such presuppositions are reflected in the language historically used to describe human affect. Built into the term "passion" is the idea of invasiveness: its Greek root, *páthe*, contains the idea of pathology. The Greek term has several aspects: on the one hand, a passive suffering and, on the other, an action or perturbation exerted on the mind. Yet, while passions possess both passivity and activity, their active dimension tends to be of external origin—exerted on a self lacking the capacity for control.[27] The *OED* can thus define passion as a "fact or condition of being acted upon or affected by external agency."[28] "Emotions" come with similar baggage: they are agitations issuing from the mind, but a part of the mind external to the will. An emotion is an external contaminant from the body, and the job of the will is to resist its destructive calling. Each of these renderings treats emotions as impediments to meaningful action.

On the side of agency, conventional wisdom affirms its presumed discordance with emotion as well. In the modern social sciences, "agency" is generally defined as the intentional accomplishment of some desired end. Agency exists where an actor successfully achieves a goal-driven outcome. While *behavior* may spring from unconscious desires, *action* begins only with the intervention of a will that decides how and when a behavior might fulfill interests.[29] Most determinative for agency are the beliefs, ideas, and other willful elements that contribute to achieving a person's goals. A second dimension of agency concerns moral judgment. As Charles Taylor argues, utilitarian and other rationalist theories do not capture the evaluative work often associated with human action.[30] Human beings act within frameworks of personal esteem and moral worth; agency, in this view, is what Parsons calls the "effort" to apply such considerations to a field of possible actions.[31] Because this effortful process of evaluation places responsibility at the heart of agency, actors become centers of accountability for socially appropriate judgments and politically sanctioned conduct.[32]

These models capture important elements of human agency but miss the role played by emotions and other nonintentional forces. While many constructivists study the intentional forms of agency behind phenomena such as role-taking, rule-following, and deliberation, others have recognized important activities taking place at less willful levels. Already in the late 1980s,

Friedrich Kratochwil and Nicholas Onuf commented that rule-following operates partly through unspoken or tacit rules.[33] Only recently, with the literature on social practices, have IR theorists followed up on these ideas and challenged the presumed centrality of intentional forms of agency. Pouliot, Adler, and Hopf have persuasively shown that social actors cannot report on everything that leads them to act the way they do. Inarticulate forms of knowledge or "know-how" sustain deeply habitualized and institutionalized practices.[34] As social actors apply normative backgrounds, their effort is not always conscious. While these inarticulate social factors entail methodological obstacles, these have too often been invoked to write emotions out of the story of human action in global politics.[35]

Extending this work on the inarticulate underpinnings of social practice, I treat emotions as distinctive elements of agency. As historical and cultural prejudices are stripped away, emotions appear as capabilities alongside others: techniques, collaboratively deployed by mind and body, to help a living creature navigate a complex and changing environment. Research in neuroscience is demonstrating that even our most calculative decisions involve emotional processes. Without emotions to select from a broad array of possible problems and to highlight facts relevant to them, our actions and reflections lack motivation, focus, and urgency.[36] Affect influences momentous accomplishments but also the thousand little tasks and decisions that comprise everyday life. Marketing experts understand well, for example, that routine consumer behavior is infused with the emotional value of brand loyalties. Economists tell us that money management is partly a function of subtle feelings of economic security and confidence in the market. While emotions may not directly or exclusively determine an individual's course of action, they seem to have some influence—and one that is not strictly detrimental. Emotions are among the complex and interconnected capabilities shaping the outcome of social action, and the challenge for IR theory is to account for the degree and kind of effects they have.

Studying affect demands treating human bodies as contingently rather than foundationally connected to intentionality. Such an account of agency pushes at the limits of prevailing ontologies in social science. Constructivists in IR have notably drawn from the sociological theories of Bourdieu, Giddens, and Bhaskar an invaluable account of the co-constitution of agency and structure: social structures shape human agents, who in turn, through their decisions and actions, realize social structures. But as Wight argues, the agency-structure debate, for all its insights on the mechanisms of socialization, has said embarrassingly little about agency. Wendt is an exception, preserving a role for presocial dimensions of human nature but

declaring it secondary to socialization. Wight delineates a layered conception of agency that preserves the autonomy of human actors but allows for
social roles that differentially influence the access an agent has to do things
in the world. Each of these contributions wrestles with how to conceptualize units of agency in a world where socialization penetrates human life so
deeply. Both, however, treat the material, embodied dimensions of human
nature as the necessary beginnings of an intentional "self." Citing Bhaskar,
Wight explains the foundational importance of embodiment: "it is embodied intentionality which earths social life." The human body, in this view, is
a container for intentionality and the starting point for the layers of social
significance giving definition to a self.[37]

The neural and social mechanism of emotional contagion requires de-
voting attention below the level of complete persons to the affective capabilities that comprise them. In this vein, political theorist Diana Coole
advocates a focus on *"agentic capacities"* that are *"*only contingently, not
ontologically, identified with rational, individual *agents."*[38] Action results,
in Coole's view, not only from the intentions of agents but also from a
contingent collaboration among these agentic capacities. I view affect as being among such agentic capabilities: both responses located in individual
persons and tissues of social interaction connecting them to others. One
neuroscientist describes mirror neurons as "invisible strings of shared circuits [that] tie our minds together, creating the fabric of an organic system
that goes beyond the individual."[39] Once we accept that emotions are not
only feelings buried in the hearts and minds of autonomous individuals,
we must regard them as having some extrasubjective dimension. In Coole's
terminology, they are not personal but "transpersonal." Gabriel Tarde, in
adopting "desires and beliefs" rather than individuals as his primary ontological units, anticipates this transpersonal approach to social interaction.[40]
To switch from fully formed agents to agentic capacities, or from personal
feelings to transpersonal affects, does not mean that we cannot speak meaningfully about the familiar cast of characters—from leaders and bureaucrats
to activists and legal advocates—populating global politics. It means instead
that some of the outcomes we observe may result not from the intentional
actions of these individuals but from an invisible, shared, transpersonal,
and contagious circulation of affect.

Relocating agency in this way provides analytical leverage on, first, the
mediated and often transnational interactions increasingly affecting global
politics. In an age of instant communications, social networking, and the
twenty-four-hour news cycle, human interactions have become thoroughly
mediated by communications technology. Agency is now more than ever a

collaboration of human effort and technological power. To capture the convergence of human and material elements in agency, we have even greater reason to reach beyond conventional assumptions that locate agency in persons. As actor-network-theory suggests, an actor is simply something that "modifies other actors" in some observable way. Latour calls these "actants" in recognition that they may combine human and nonhuman elements. Jane Bennett even attributes agency—which, following Latour, she defines as the "power to make a difference"—to power grids and other material technologies.[41] Latour makes a provocative case for why scientific inquiry cannot afford to make assumptions in advance about the locations of agency. Circulations of affect are among those social processes that achieve effects without only the intentional effort of persons.

Decoupling agentic capacities or "actants" from actors also positions IR scholars to trace the impact of emergent actors in global politics. From socially networked protest movements to grassroots initiatives aimed at transitional justice, transnational criminal networks, and assemblages of humanitarian sympathy, circulations of affect are enabling unconventional forms of agency and surprising outcomes. Emotional circulations underpin forms of collective agency that do not display all the coherence and stability of established social or cultural groups. Because affect travels through contagion, we cannot afford to declare upfront which actors will be most effective in a given environment. As a result, the received wisdom of constructivism, regarding the importance of identity to social and political action, demands closer scrutiny. Theories of identity begin with relatively stable identities and then whisper an ostensibly minor caveat that people in real life have multiple identities and that, over time, those identities tend to change. The creativity of affect means that we cannot expect a one-to-one relationship between the connections it forges and the collective identities held by groups. Greased by technologies of communication, contagious emotions often fuel not only established actors but also invisible networks and temporary allegiances.[42]

This reformulation of affective agency highlights the slippery nature of emotional politics and the limited purchase instrumentalist accounts have on it. There is now a large and compelling literature on the way leaders cultivate popular emotion to achieve desired outcomes. This instrumental form of emotional agency can affect the formulation of foreign policy, as leaders express sympathy, pride, or fear toward other states and their policies. Diplomacy, in this view, is conducted within logics of appropriateness, where the latter is defined partly through standards of emotional conduct.[43] The use of emotion is more commonly recognized in domestic politics, where savvy leaders seize on emotional symbols and memories for public mobilization. The rich literature on ethnic conflict, for example, has demonstrated how leaders attuned to the need for public enthusiasm appropriate emotional symbols.[44] The argument in such studies is generally not that leaders invent emotions but that they recognize and appropriate extant patterns of emotional investment. Any given cultural milieu possesses emotional symbols—flags, historical events, or sacred sites—known to have special capacity to stimulate popular emotions. Through public speeches, campaign materials, and other forms of political communication, strategic actors appeal to these emotional stimulators to secure political support.

Instrumentalism presupposes a gap of reflection between the emotional entrepreneur and the emotion she or he wields. The intervention is instrumental precisely because elites are able to relate to an emotional sign *as a tool* for manipulating others rather than a force affecting them as well. Such situations are common in a world of deliberate and strategic actors. But the notion that leaders are inherently capable of rising above the emotions of the masses understates the ubiquity of emotional experience. Emotions often become elements of social interactions and environments inhabited by mass and elites alike. Preserving reflective distance between actor and emotion becomes especially difficult where emotions spread through contagion. A contagious circulation of affect is one that is transmitted unconsciously and thus without the stamp of recognizability held by established patterns of emotional conduct. Even the most strategic and reflective leaders are not immune from such circulations.

The relationship between elite intervention and popular emotion needs to be studied with greater attention to its contingency. Because successive emotional interactions are layered upon earlier ones, and because there is ambiguity in emotional experience, leaders exercise less control over emotional politics than commonly supposed. Emotional entrepreneurs cannot predict in advance the cascade of resonances that a symbol, ritual, or other act of mobilization engenders. As Deleuze and Guattari demonstrate, this approach offers a better grasp on especially intense moments of political mobilization, such as Germany's National Socialism. The movement succeeded, they argue, because of the multiple channels of affective support it received—many outside the party's propaganda machine. Nazism captured the emotions of anti-Semitism, but also those arising from economic deprivation and those induced by the state's deepening efforts at social control. Otherwise disconnected emotional interactions were folded into a flexible and creative process of mobilization.[45] Affects circulate across a community or population and begin to "resonate" as part of a movement. The potency of such a movement lies in its capacity to attract popular emotions before these have been fully articulated as part of a political program. By emphasizing the creativity of affect, IR theory can more effectively assess the potential and intensity of emerging actors in international politics—from nonstate security threats to social movements and institutional initiatives.

Investigating the creativity of emotional action requires attending to social and cultural processes often missed in the study of global politics. The science of international politics most often focuses on relationships in which variables are clearly defined: an independent variable x accounts for some observed event or change y. Some emotional interactions and processes indeed take such a form. For example, a pattern of popular emotion might initiate a shift in a state's foreign policy, or, as Petersen suggests in a study of ethnic conflict, "hatred" can produce violence against historically targeted groups.[46] Or, where a leader mobilizes public support through emotional appeals to nationalist symbols, we could describe one causal relation between agent and emotion and a second between that emotion and an outcome—popular support for nationalist policies. These accounts capture important dimensions of emotional interaction but also miss some of its puzzling elements. Emotions are often contagious social processes affecting leaders and publics alike. They are also temporally layered such that emotions in the present are affected by those preceding them and affect those that follow. Any effect we designate as an outcome for one causal process in turn feeds back into the emotional exchanges of another. Rather than disappear after contributing to a causal outcome, emotions tend to linger and reappear, in a new form, in subsequent interactions.

Part of the difficulty in studying emotions in international conflict and global politics is that they appear to influence outcomes through compound and indirect forms of causality. First, the creativity of affect ensures that emotional entrepreneurs do not fully control the emotions they deploy. In a complex world of overlapping and intersecting emotional interactions, creative syntheses may emerge unintentionally through the uncoordinated actions of dispersed participants or from the surge of emotional energy associated with historical events. The willful interventions of emotional entrepreneurs thus become contributory but not exclusive engines of emotional transmission. Second, the interconnectedness among emotional responses and states makes it difficult to parcel out discrete, individually packaged emotions. In the case of hatred, for example, not only does the emotion often thrive in environments of fear but what is commonly abbreviated as "hatred" in fact consists of diverse memories, sentiments, and grievances. The density of affective environments prevents us from isolating the discrete relations we would need to test for efficient causality. As James understood, our ideas and categories are never fully adequate to the flux of lived experience. His "radical empiricism" demands that emotional experiences be understood relationally rather than as isolated, efficient causes. For each of these reasons, we need a more complex conception of causality to accommodate the creative processes and mixtures that affect the politics of emotion.

One response is to agree with James's diagnosis of the complexity of emotional interaction, but then maintain that scientific study requires simplification in the interest of parsimonious theory-building. Only by setting aside the multitude of possible relationships are we able to test systematically for the efficient causality present in just a few. When such a causal relationship is found, investigation can return to the actual messiness of the world, to select and test additional interactions. Isolating relations from their complex environment is, from this perspective, not an ontological claim but a "methodological requirement."[47] As critics of standard science argue, however, methodological requirements too often translate into implicit ontologies. Connolly contends, for example, that "a particular orientation to method is apt to express a set of metaphysical commitments to which the method is deeply attached."[48] Methodological adjustments often compel ontological sacrifices—in this case, easing us into the assumption that the caricatured, discrete, and method-friendly emotions we engineer *really are* representative of the complex emotional processes involved in politics. A social theory of emotion needs instead a causal framework tailored to its distinctive properties.

Because emotions can work in temporally layered combinations, circulations of affect involve not closed circuits of a fixed emotion but transfers of emotional energy that can shift from one kind of emotional response to another. As the theory of excitation transfer suggests, the excitation associated with anger can be decoupled from its original object and plugged into fear, hatred, or some other subsequent response. Because emotional circulations come in composites, we need to avoid the temptation to isolate single emotions from the others that work with them: not "hatred" or "fear" but both mixed together. Social interaction involves interplay and reciprocal modification among emotional forces. Where fears are intense, we might see hatred normally directed to one group stretched and extended to others. The anxieties associated with an event such as 9/11, for example, allowed various race-, faith-, and ethnicity-based prejudices to become folded into a powerful new mix of anti-Muslim/anti-Arab sentiment. The composition of an emotion changes with each new circulation it enters. Emotions therefore signal a different kind of causal relation: rather than discrete units impacting one another directly, they involve reciprocally constitutive effects that continually reconfigure the composition of causal units.

The creative tendencies associated with emotional contagion require a modification of existing accounts of socialization. Constructivists seeking to offer an explanatory account of international relations—as opposed to those seeking a deeper "understanding"—generally adopt a version of "constitutive causality." In this view, a norm, identity, or other social structure does not affect action directly but, rather, constitutes actors more fundamentally by informing self-understandings and supplying standards of socially appropriate conduct. Such processes of socialization influence a range of social interactions, from traditional diplomacy and security policy to institutional commitments and compliance with international law. Nevertheless, studies of constitutive causality and its ancillary processes—socialization, norm internalization, learning—generally examine relatively stable patterns and extended horizons of socialization: a national identity that, over time, shapes a foreign policy of belligerence, or an international norm that is gradually internalized in ways that change domestic policy.

Emotions and emotional contagion involve a fluidity that cannot be reduced to direct or simple reproduction of social stuff. Theories of constitutive socialization often presuppose just such a process of replication. For example, John Searle, author of an influential philosophy of socialization, recognizes that actors become subliminally disposed to acting within systems of social rules. Everyday routines and habits bring us into conformity with institutional structures, even if we have no intentional awareness of following a rule. But because Searle describes these constitutive processes only abstractly as "unconscious dispositions and capacities," he falls back on a story of simple norm-following: even where the constitutive causes of an action are not consciously recognized, they nevertheless resemble the rules and institutions they come to support.[49] Based on this sort of reasoning, constructivists often imply a stable field of constitutive social processes: well-established social structures and institutions are replicated through the dissemination of beliefs, norms, and dispositions that support them.

But socialization is affected also by emotions whose creativity can interrupt normal patterns of social constitution. Bursts of emotion can diminish the weight of settled identities and give urgency to others. An environment of fear can bring heightened intensity to social and political movements favoring militancy. Enthusiasm for social recovery in conflicted societies can relocate popular energy from oppositional identities onto porous ones. Emotional responses help us to navigate a dynamic field of socialization, adjusting from one constitutive process to another. Something more is going on in these situations than a replication of social structures by units primed in advance to accept them. Where social interactions involve emergent beliefs, identities, and norms, they may permit new patterns of association to coalesce. Our causal model needs to accommodate, then, a subspecies of constitutive relations involving emergence, in which the outcomes of interaction cannot be gleaned in advance from the surface meaning of affective ingredients.[50] Emotional circulations may well give rise to a new identity, or support an existing identity, but there is no evidence within those emotions of a necessary relation they might have to any given identity. We cannot afford to assume, then, a correspondence between an emotion and the identities it supports or the units it affects.

Studying emergent interactions requires following an especially wide range of social and cultural processes. Explanations involving efficient causal relations, such as "actor A incites hatred" or "group B's hatred generates violence," capture some forms of emotional politics. Constructivist research focused on constitutive processes then broadens that focus to include instances in which emotions facilitate the replication of norms, identities, and other social structures. But circulations of affect also possess properties of ambiguity and flexibility that shape the kinds of effects they have in the world of politics. Outside the psychology lab and in the world of social interaction, we are more likely to observe shifting moods, re-emerging memories, and reciprocally entwined emotions than stand-alone feelings. Rather than looking for simple causes following from an emotion, we should instead immerse ourselves in the complexity of emotional circulation. Studying emotions requires respecting the particularities of these complex environments: their histories, the cultural norms they encompass, and the interactions, rituals, and practices used within them. Thick description, enhanced by evidence- and theory-driven reconceptualization, is indispensable in realizing these aims.

Method

The social world of emotion is a messy place. Emotions can fuel ordinary processes of socialization, but they can also surge, migrate, and blend in ways that disrupt business as usual. When Americans fixed on the collective memory of December 7, 1941, an element of moral confidence entered the debate on terrorism; and when unemployment intensified in the Yugoslavia of the late 1980s, the politics of ethnic nationalism absorbed some of the frustration it engendered. Often emotional connections do not make sense according to familiar categories and cognitive frameworks. The study of emotions in global politics thus needs to capture the full range of effects emotions can have—from the habituated and institutionalized to the fluid, ambiguous, and inchoate. Part of what set emotions apart from the beliefs, identities, and norms already studied in IR is the diverse forms they can take. We cannot afford to proceed by ignoring the most defiant aspects of affect and focusing on only those elements that can safely be assimilated into frameworks calibrated to choice, decisionmaking, or deliberation. My goal in subsequent chapters is to investigate contagious circulations of affect without tidying them up in advance to suit methodological imperatives.

Enlarging the study of emotion beyond psychological dimensions to encompass also neurosocial processes alters which investigative techniques might be most appropriate to apprehending them. Because emotions are often associated with private feeling-states, it is tempting to assume that we can access them empirically only by asking people how they feel. Surveys and interviews, for example, ask people to reflect on the salient feelings affecting their political conduct. And yet, when we consider both that many emotions remain unavailable to conscious awareness and that they are routinely transmitted through implicit processes of contagion, methods involving only subjective reports become insufficient. While affects may not be "repressed" by some portion of the psyche in the way Freud understood them to be, there is now wide consensus that much, if not most, of our everyday affective lives remains invisible to us. Unable to rely exclusively on what people say they feel, we must instead appeal to a more flexible patchwork of methods.

My first task is to interrogate popular discourses about emotion. These discourses consist of descriptions of emotional conduct ascribed by outsiders rather than reflexive descriptions or native codes of emotional conduct.[51] Before we can develop an account that captures the complexity and mutability of affect, we need to think critically about how emotions are conceptualized and narrated in specific social settings. Notions such as "ancient hatreds" and "cycles of hatred" have had a lasting impact on the study of ethnic conflict. And discussions of terrorism often take it for granted that "revenge" amounts to a natural response to violent attacks. As I argue elsewhere, the trope of "anti-American hatred" continues to inform American foreign policy toward the Middle East.[52] These discursive constructions underpin a normative orientation that regards emotions as sources of pathological behavior. More insidiously, they also shape prevailing understandings about which emotion categories are most useful and which emotions are most salient in global politics.

Beyond deconstructing these emotional stereotypes, I also seek ways to infer the existence of circulations of affect themselves. Here, the work faces steeper methodological and epistemological hurdles, although arguably no more so than those incurred by a strictly psychological conception of emotion. My account adds circulations of affect to the long list of intangibles—such as legitimacy, values, and informal norms—that, while never directly seen by the actors they affect, are nevertheless subjects of social and political research. Once we accept that emotions have a social reality, we can begin to study them by tracing outward from both the social expressions they engender and the social practices engendering them. While I am not able to point directly to the emotions generated therein, it is possible to assemble an empirical record of traces—in the form of emotional discourses, evocative symbols, and eliciting interactions—left behind. This process begins with events and practices whose peculiar sociopsychological qualities make them likely inducers of collective emotion: large numbers of people acting in concert, public expressions of grievance or aspiration, and/or intensifications of communication through mass media. While emotions are ubiquitous elements of social life, certain events nevertheless involve especially dense interactions and surges of emotional expression. From these moments of emotional upheaval, I move forward to capture the affects they generate, and then backward to consider those engendering them.

Emotions are not fleeting responses but *processes* of circulation. Milošević's "meetings of truth" in 1988 and the Madrid bombing of March 11, 2004, are moments of emotional upheaval. They are high-profile public events that can reasonably be expected to involve popular emotion and for which there is an accessible body of primary evidence and secondary research. From these key events, I trace outward to the circulations of affect they set in motion and the pre-existing emotional currents from which they draw. Emotionally significant events often supply moments of creativity that modify emotions from the past and reinject them into the present. While emotions often lose intensity after an evocative event, short-term emotions can fuel more durable moods and sentiments. I approach affect sensitive to the ways it can mutate through the process of circulation.

The book taps an array of sources from several disciplines to investigate a range of social interactions contributing to circulations of affect. Using studies from anthropology, sociology, and history, I reconstruct the emotional worlds inhabited by participants in interactions such as commemoration rituals or political rallies. Research conducted from the vantage point of everyday life makes it possible to assess the ebb and flow of emotional circulations.[53] I supplement these accounts with journalistic sources and other primary documents where doing so clarifies the ethnographic story. These complementary materials make it possible to construct plausible inferences about the source and impact of emotional circulations. My approach offers those inferences without relying on collective identities and other prior categories; these may be relevant if and where they are salient but I resist using them to prefigure the terrain of affective politics.

My case studies work back and forth from emotional discourse to social practices with nondiscursive dimensions. By "emotional discourse," I mean social communication that, whatever its substantive content, circulates affect among participants. The speeches of President Bush and other American officials in the wake of 9/11, for example, or the radio broadcasts inciting genocide in Rwanda serve as vehicles of shared affect. Discourses can reveal emotion by explicitly describing the emotions present in a given environment, by including content widely understood to have emotional significance, such as nationalist symbols or national security threats, and by employing paralinguistic elements, such as tones of urgency or excitement, that have emotional impact whether intended or not. Social constructivists have largely focused on the first two mechanisms of discursive socialization; I cast a wider net that considers also the expressive power of language.

Circulations of affect cannot be understood without contextualizing what social actors say with what they do in practice. Collective action can offer a valuable supplement to both the available discourses on emotion and the principles and grievances officially stated in public venues. Studying demonstrations, strikes, communal violence, and other behavior can serve as a litmus test for the truth and intensity of publicly stated convictions. In the case of Rwanda, for example, there was much talk about hatred, anger, and other emotions that might disrupt post-genocide recovery. And yet the enthusiasm for the government's experiment in community-based justice uncovers alternative dispositions toward hope and a sense of justice. In the United States following 9/11, while public officials often cited America's friendship with the Islamic world, the surge in anti-Muslim/anti-Arab hate crimes and airline passenger removals suggests that prejudices thrived nevertheless. By cross-referencing discursive evidence with observations of social conduct, we can assemble a more nuanced account of both reflective and unreflective dimensions of affect.

My approach is not entirely different from the inferential process used by other constructivist research. Constructivists infer the existence of identities from available discursive evidence: by studying how individuals and groups talk, they distill generalizations about the existence of norms, identities, and other nonobservable forces. My study of affective circulations embarks on a similar process, but with two principal differences. First, in considering discursive evidence, I include its expressive or paralinguistic dimension, especially prosody, in addition to its cognitive content and meaning. Second, I cross-reference public discourse with evidence of the lived social practices of ordinary people. My case studies draw from ethnographic and journalistic sources to assemble a record of how individuals and communities are acting over time. My approach departs from constructivist orthodoxy by suspending the assumption that an emotional circulation is a psychological property of "Serbs," "Americans," or some other identity group. While some collective emotional responses are tied to reflexive appraisals of membership in a state, nation, or other social group,[54] I focus instead on more emergent processes of affective harmonization. The book investigates emotional circulations without pre-established expectations about either their logical coherence or the identities they come to support.

Conclusion

Emotions are a ubiquitous and indispensable feature of social life. They shape the way individuals encounter one another, the way they come together into collectivities, and the way collectivities interact. Scholars of global politics—arguably the sphere of interacting collectivities par excellence—cannot afford to underestimate the impact of emotion. This book reconceptualizes emotions as social circulations of affect, underscores their creative potential, and then presents one possible approach for studying their impact on conflicts of international significance. Drawing from journalistic sources, microhistorical research, and ethnographic studies, I examine both discursive and behavioral evidence of emotion. The book works back and forth across three kinds of social phenomena: collective actions or practices with emotional significance; political speeches, media representations, and other emotional discourses that often surround those activities; and discourses about emotion, which tend to influence our very conceptualization of all affective phenomena. The result is not the only way to study emotion in global politics, but it is an approach capable of uncovering some of its creative and dynamic qualities.

The remainder of the book aims to illustrate, extend, and deepen the theoretical ideas presented in this and the previous chapter. Circulations of affect are products of social interaction fueled by both conscious forms of imitation and nonconscious forms of simulation, or contagion. The ambiguity and fluidity of emotional contagion endow these affective circulations with a capacity for creativity in the social world. The following chapters use and extend the theory to generate new insights into political problems and struggles formerly understood either through rationalist frameworks or constructivist approaches emphasizing identity, intentional agency, or both. Tracing social interactions whose participants range from ordinary people to cultural and political elites, I find creative circulations of affect integral to the processes of socialization, contestation, and collective agency involved in international conflicts.

THREE

The Affective Politics of Terror

The events of September 11, 2001, sparked an impressive outpouring of emotion. As a frenzy of media coverage replayed footage of the twin towers, Americans fixated on the pain of the 9/11 victims, the heroism of rescue workers, and the abhorrent specter of terrorism. However, while the presence of emotions seems clear, their genesis, content, and consequences are not. Critics on the left argued that a war-mongering elite was fomenting fear and anger and that such emotions were impeding constructive and measured debate.[1] Observers on the right regarded fear and anger as genuine and well-founded responses that ought to inspire a policy of retribution and just war.[2] Many Americans celebrated the patriotic solidarity and generosity the crisis had summoned.[3] Meanwhile, in describing the perpetrators of terrorism, talk-show hosts, bloggers, and public officials routinely noted their inexplicable rage and hatred. Amid this profusion of emotion-talk, there has been little agreement on what kind of emotions were sparked by 9/11, where they came from, how they adapted over time, and what political impact they had.

These lingering confusions highlight how little we know about the way emotions function in real-world political environments. There is now an array of important research on the causal role of one or two emotions: Did fear of terrorism, for example, cause the American public to overestimate the risk of terrorism or increase the desire to achieve certainty through decisive action? Was support for war rooted in anger and a desire for vengeance? Do higher levels of anxiety and threat perception increase public support for counterterrorism policies? Were the terrorist attacks caused by long-standing feelings of hatred toward the West?[4] However, by presupposing that fear had a stable and consistent object, that anger was continuously directed at a uniform target, or that fear, anger, or hatred can be isolated from adjacent emotions, these formulations too often miss the slippery quality of emotions circulating after 9/11. Single-emotion studies tend to overlook, for example, the way fear overlapped with and intensified hatred, or the way feelings of outrage hinged on the trust Americans felt in a secure homeland. Applying the categories of psychology in an abstract and static manner risks missing the many emotional processes at play in an event as multidimensional as 9/11. Challenging orthodox assumptions about the autonomy of individual emotions, this chapter traces the contagious and intersecting circulations of affect that followed the attacks.

Part of what makes September 11 distinctive as an emotional spectacle is the impressive plurality of emotions, actors, and cultural spheres involved. While many Americans felt anger toward the terrorists immediately responsible for the attacks, for example, a small minority felt that same emotion but attached it to perceived American injustices in the Middle East. Fear was arguably felt even more widely, but for a variety of reasons: because more airliners might be hijacked, because civil liberties were being eroded, or because investment portfolios could suffer. Followers of Reverend Jerry Falwell even feared the homosexuals and feminists whose secular values the 9/11 hijackers had allegedly targeted.[5] Fear was indeed a common response, but one that tended to shift readily from one object to another. The attacks were also said to be a result of hatred, and yet the uniformity of that sentiment and the coherence of its target were generally overstated.[6] Each of these emotional responses suggests, then, the need to investigate more closely the neuro-psycho-social processes that generated, combined, and circulated affective responses. In the wake of 9/11, emotions such as hatred, fear, and anger were altered by prior memories and prejudices, and by the many new social practices into which ordinary Americans were thrown. This chapter maps some of these emotional synergies, beginning with fear and anger but then stepping back to capture their interplay with ancillary affective responses.

In the aftermath of 9/11 affective responses did not occur on a blank slate but were shaped by the things people were doing before, during, and after the attacks. From late-night talk shows to grassroots memorials, Americans absorbed the emotional impact of these attacks in specific social settings.[7] The objects of popular fear shifted as the media frenzy gravitated from hijackers to anthrax letters, and from anthrax to Iraq. Emotional responses absorbed energy and meaning from the various social practices through which they were expressed. I highlight the analogy to Pearl Harbor—not because it was the product of emotion but because it brought with it politically significant emotions, such as courage and moral confidence, associated with America's "greatest generation." In the wake of 9/11, public fear interacted with a variety of affective circulations, adapting to changing social practices and resonating with available memories.

Focusing specifically on social interactions associated with racial profiling helps us to understand the implicit impact they had on both public fear for America's terrorist enemy and public acceptance of its counterterrorism policy. Practices of racial profiling invoked new ways of interacting that created Arab-Americans as a feared and implicitly racialized constituency within the United States. In a political context where ordinary Americans knew little about the perpetrators of terrorism, participation in these social practices supplied a credible mechanism for classifying "Arabs," "Muslims," and "Middle Easterners" as a group unified by cultural and phenotypic markers of identity. The affective dimension of this process was crucial in a "postracial" environment where overt racialization is proscribed. These covert, affectively imbued associations of the "Arab/Muslim/Middle Easterner" with terrorism made a small but important contribution to defining and legitimizing the legal and political exceptions associated with America's war on terror. As racialized security practices proliferated, the emotions they engendered heightened public support for counterterrorism policies that might otherwise have attracted greater resistance.

The affective genesis of the terrorist enemy signals the importance of social context for understanding how a dramatic event such as 9/11 engenders specific emotional responses. The attacks of 9/11 did not automatically spark anger or desire for retribution toward their author; they were instead an emotional work-in-progress—unexpected political acts whose emotional impact was shaped by prior normative commitments and changing social practices. Emotions siphon meaning and intensity from the cultural milieu in which they are expressed. A brief comparison to the Madrid bombings of March 11, 2004, at the end of the chapter helps to bring this complex genesis into focus. Whereas Americans tended to respond to 9/11 with fear and anger toward terrorist perpetrators, Spaniards mostly expressed anger and directed it at a conservative government seen as having provoked the 3/11 attack by supporting the US war in Iraq. And, whereas fear in the US case was fueled by the relentless frenzy of media coverage, antigovernment anger in Spain was fomented by escalating street demonstrations, as government officials sought to conceal information for political gain. The Spanish response emerged from a European national security culture in which terrorism was a familiar problem attributable to social tension, economic deprivation, and political provocation. The case helps to show that understanding the emotional impact of terrorist attacks requires tracing the normative commitments and the social vehicles of expression available in a given political environment.

Circulations of Affect after 9/11

As the events of September 11 triggered public emotions, these intersected with pre-existing emotional symbols, memories, and beliefs. Because this upheaval was an ongoing process, we cannot afford to study it only by sampling the momentary feelings of individuals. Public opinion data too often conceal the lived context of emotional politics: fluid processes of affective interaction become artificially freeze-framed. Emotions are not merely psychological states but participative byproducts of direct and mediated social interaction. By investigating the practices, rituals, and encounters of social life, we can glean a dynamic process of interplay among diverse emotions. To understand the emotions circulating in the post-9/11 period, I emphasize the temporal layering of emotional experience. Recognizing that no American was an emotional tabula rasa, I look backward to the precedents and contexts that shaped the receptivity of ordinary Americans to the event. And to appreciate the malleability of emotional responses, I also look ahead to the contagious effects the events of that day had in the weeks, months, and years that followed. Anger and fear likely fueled support for war in Afghanistan, but fear especially rippled out more broadly, migrating from domestic terrorism, via anthrax, to the threat posed by Iraq. The events of 9/11 sparked not single feelings or stable emotions but a creative and multidimensional process of emotional upheaval.

Circulations of affect are shaped by the participative rituals people engaged in following the attacks. Cultural studies of 9/11 and its aftermath have emphasized the way political speeches, news reports, popular culture, and other cultural media promoted certain ideas, beliefs, and identities.[8] These accounts need supplementary investigation of two sorts. First, we need to treat discursive media as sites of both intellectual exchange and expressive interaction. As the literature on "mediated discourse analysis" suggests, political speeches have live audiences near and far; newspapers are read together in public spaces; and television news and programming is received by dispersed audiences and families, friends, and coworkers assembled together.[9] Second, discursive media need to be understood alongside nondiscursive media such as memorialization practices, state security measures, and culturally targeted acts of harassment. To comprehend the emotional impact of 9/11, my account therefore examines not only what key actors were saying on the record but also how those narrativizations mingled, off the record, with lived experiences of the event.

Much of what Americans were doing after the attacks centered on remembering the events, searching together for their meaning, and speculating on which responses were feasible and just. Acts of terrorism are distinctive in achieving social and political outcomes through the communicative impact they engender. Many of these communications took place in and through news media coverage, transmitted through both conventional television and emerging digital networks; the news media had a profound and well-documented effect on public opinion in the weeks and months after the attacks.[10] This coverage both reported on and generated the fear, anger, and other responses associated with the event. Research in social psychology suggests that emotions do not diminish in intensity after some opportunity for cathartic expression; rather, they are intensified and prolonged by the process of "social sharing."[11] Moreover, media coverage served to enlarge the geographic range of affected populations, extending the trauma to Americans well beyond New York City, western Pennsylvania, and Washington, DC.[12] Had digital technologies and around-the-clock news coverage not been available to circulate images and narratives of this event, its emotional impact would have been less acute.

Participants in these social communications did not invent anew the symbols, identities, and beliefs used to make sense of the event. Rather, they activated sentiments and emotional symbols already existing within American culture. This creative process of adaptation is evident in the often-repeated analogy to Pearl Harbor. The immediate appeal to this analogy by news anchors, foreign policy experts, and political officials has been widely discussed. Together with their guests and correspondents, news anchors for the three main American broadcast television networks invoked "Pearl Harbor" fifty-eight times on the day of the attacks alone.[13] My concern is not to assess whether the analogy was appropriate, or whether it led to foreign policy misperceptions.[14] I am instead interested in the specific emotional memories and sentiments that accompanied the image of Pearl Harbor. As the literature on historical analogies in diplomatic history and foreign policy studies suggests, analogical reasoning is based on some characteristic two events are seen as having in common—in this case, a surprising, unprovoked foreign attack on American soil. The similarity on that one register then ushers in implicit equivalencies in other areas.[15] The appeal to Pearl Harbor thus helped to give meaning to the otherwise confounding events of 9/11, casting these as acts of aggression either warranting a military response or else likely to precipitate one.

In addition to such cognitive meanings, the analogy also supplied emotionally charged memories and convictions. By 2001 Pearl Harbor had become what one historian describes as "an emotion-laden icon."[16] Historical analogies and metaphors work not only by shaping objective assessments of an event but also by drawing observers into the subconscious emotional associations they evoke. An obvious example is when a comparison to the Holocaust not only classifies an event as a particular sort of international crime but also supplies the fear, guilt, anger, or disgust often associated with that signal case. Research on neuroscience confirms that these implicit attitudes or emotional associations become embedded within carrier symbols such as "the Holocaust."[17] When news anchors and commentators compared 9/11 to Pearl Harbor, then, they supplied information about the event but also charged it up with powerful normative and affective associations. Indeed, that event carried many such associations—from outrage and fear to courage, pride, and resilience. As commentators have suggested, the analogy was used to great political effect, as military virtues became crucial ingredients in selling the wars in Afghanistan and Iraq.

The analogy evoked not only specific emotions but also a general tone of confidence and righteousness. This moral tone has its roots in the nostalgic memorialization of Pearl Harbor and World War II during the decade prior to 2001. An aging cohort of World War II veterans had pushed for greater memorialization of the Japanese attacks, and a younger generation with no personal memory of that war had yearned for the national unity and moral clarity it offered. As historians and ethnographers have documented, the "memory boom" surrounding World War II gave rise to nonfiction bestsellers, Hollywood films, and beer commercials. Emily Rosenberg argues that these efforts climaxed during summer 2001 with the release of Jerry Bruckheimer's film *Pearl Harbor* (2001).[18] Political leaders and pundits contributed to this popular memorialization even before September 2001. Worried about losing the virtues associated with the World War II era, as early as 1999 George W. Bush invoked the moral authority of his father's generation, promising to "renew the bond of trust between the American president and the American military." World War II nostalgia thus reflected what Michael Valdez Moses calls "an unfulfilled epic desire on the part of a generation that felt itself diminished by comparison to the one that preceded it."[19] Pearl Harbor had become an emotional symbol of not only fear and outrage but also moral confidence, determination, and vigilance.

When the analogy to that event was invoked after September 11, these affective orientations came with it. John Mueller and others have noted that invoking Pearl Harbor helped to define the terrorist attacks as a "war" and delimit the conceivable foreign policy options accordingly. But the thriving analogy also injected public conversations with moral clarity borrowed nostalgically from America's "greatest generation." A defining feature of American narrativization of World War II was the moral certitude involved in that fight: unlike Vietnam and other later conflicts, this was a war in which good and evil were clearly demarcated in public consciousness. As Noon explains, the analogy supplied not analysis of terrorism on an intellectual level but a catalyst for national unity and a statement of confidence in the US government. Pearl Harbor offered "a compelling reaffirmation of national purpose" for Americans who had not fought in World War II but suddenly felt inspired by its moral purpose.[20] Pearl Harbor thus supplied emotional underpinnings for the credibility of the Bush administration and its emerging vision for national security policy.

If Pearl Harbor was important in shaping public responses to the terrorist attacks, the experience of 9/11 in turn affected the emotional significance of that memory. In other words, 9/11 formed a crucial phase in the lifecycle of this iconic political event. The emotions evoked by the terrorist attacks resonated with patriotic sentiments fueling the Pearl Harbor renaissance, and the already "emotion-laden icon" was charged up with even greater intensity. As the sociologist Randall Collins argues, symbols receive their affective significance from processes of social interaction. In his account, short-term emotions become preserved in the form of symbols, which are the medium through which emotional energy is sustained within a social environment. As repeated social interactions generate shared emotions, participants experiencing them can save these "fleeting feelings" by transforming them into symbols. These symbols, he argues, "are respected only to the extent that they are charged up with sentiments by participation in rituals." Efforts to memorialize Pearl Harbor during the 1990s had already contributed to this charging up; that process was intensified further still as the emotions evoked by 9/11 were plugged into the memory.[21]

Emotional responses to 9/11 intersected with pre-existing circulations of affect but also changed in content and intensity as the focus of media coverage shifted over time. The anthrax attacks made a special contribution to these shifts. Between October 4 and November 20, twenty-two cases of anthrax infection were reported at sixty sites. While only five resulted in fatalities, fear of infection was rampant. The Postal Service reported receiving almost 16,000 suspected anthrax envelopes by mid-December. Network and cable news programs offered steady coverage of the attacks, with little concrete information about their source. Analysts later separated the anthrax drama from 9/11, as investigators found links to a disgruntled researcher in Maryland.[22] At the time, however, there was no clear line between the two threats. The mystery surrounding the source of the biological attacks further complicated the fear circulating since early September. A physician and op-ed contributor to the *Washington Post* argued that the anthrax attacks had introduced an "entirely new fear" that undermined settled assumptions about the infallibility of science and the reliability of medical expertise. Cultural studies scholar Susan Willis explains: "The shock waves unleashed by the airplanes were displaced into vectors of biological attack, both real and imaginary."[23] Whereas the events of 9/11 had been horrific, the media frenzy surrounding anthrax prolonged those fears and affixed them to a mysterious new object.

Panic over anthrax was markedly disproportionate to the evidence of bioterrorism as a threat to Americans' safety.[24] Anthrax appears to have evoked strong fears because of its very unpredictability—its potential to affect anyone at any time. Surveys conducted in late October and early November indicate that 40 percent of Americans were exercising more caution in handling their mail; 35 percent reported that they had sought information on what to do in the event of a bioterrorist attack; and 34 percent were worried that they might become exposed to anthrax.[25] The fear of anthrax was uncertain and diffuse, permeating the daily lives of ordinary Americans. The circulation of suspicious mail caused school closings, airport delays, workplace evacuations, and other disruptions affecting day-to-day interactions. As Willis notes: "The trivial stuff of daily life—vanilla pudding mix, powdered sugar, flour, talcum powder—suddenly had the power to close schools, cancel the mail, shut factories, and otherwise halt business as usual." The anthrax threat also gave Americans concrete techniques for ensuring their safety in a post-9/11 world. A small but notable minority engaged in survivalist precautions, purchasing duct tape and plastic sheeting, assembling first-aid kits, and stockpiling emergency supplies.[26] The anthrax crisis intensified public anxiety partly by unsettling the routines of everyday life.

With a relatively low death toll, it is easy to recall the anthrax attacks as but a minor footnote between the attacks of 9/11 and the debate over Iraq that intensified during 2002. But the affair may have been a critical emotional ingredient in the prologue to war. Through popular prejudice, inaccurate reporting, and suggestive remarks from the White House, America's anthrax strain was imaginatively traced to an Iraqi weapons program.[27] Anthrax became a missing link between 9/11 and Saddam Hussein—and another moment in the slowly waning opposition to war in Iraq. As officials in the Bush administration later made arguments about Iraq and biological weapons, fear from the six-week media frenzy in late 2001 supplied a subconscious backdrop. The embodied interactions necessitated by the bioterrorist threat provided a process of emotional activation that helped to forge an association between 9/11 and anthrax, and between anthrax and Iraq. Collins notes that symbols are "charged up" through embodied participation in social interactions. The anthrax scare and its interaction rituals helped to consolidate a new constellation of counterterrorist symbols. Well before the official debate over Iraq and its controversial weapons of mass destruction program, "Iraq" was already becoming an affectively charged symbol of terrorism.

The anthrax scare demonstrates how, following 9/11, emotions circulated in and through the daily activities of ordinary Americans. Affective responses to 9/11 neither diminished gradually nor remained precisely intact but adapted incrementally to events on the ground. Elite manipulations contributed to these circulations but did not control them in a strictly instrumental manner. While the threat of bioterrorism ultimately became a useful antecedent for those advocating military intervention in Iraq, these efforts did not create the anthrax phenomenon. Indeed, the fear came before the public relations campaign, with the Bush administration marketing the war in Iraq well after the anthrax event had passed. The daily broadcasts and disruptions associated with anthrax changed the content and intensity of post-9/11 anxieties. Even as the phenomenon became subsumed by prevailing narratives concerning the war on terror, it also exhibited a creative capacity as an emotion-inducing public event in its own right.[28]

The Pearl Harbor and anthrax examples suggest that, in the upheaval following the 9/11 attacks, emotions migrated contagiously across actors and events that might not otherwise have found occasion to connect. In this environment, new symbols and ideas borrowed emotional viability from evocative precedents. As ordinary Americans memorialized the attacks and worried over new threats, their initial responses adapted. On the surface, Americans responded with fear and anger, and these feelings were consistently both trained upon terrorist perpetrators and sustained by elite rhetoric. But beneath this tidy appearance was a more complex array of fluid and intersecting circulations. Consistent with theories of "excitation transfer" and affective "carryover" discussed in the previous chapter, the cognitive content of emotions were not tightly bound to the excitations underlying them. Emotional associations attached to Pearl Harbor migrated contagiously into the national response to 9/11. The analogy did not in itself justify war in Afghanistan or Iraq, but it endowed public conversations with tones of moral clarity and confidence that made later justifications more palatable. And, as the emotional frenzy over anthrax amplified fears from 9/11, it reprocessed them in specific, politically consequential ways—by associating terrorism with the weapons programs of nefarious states. Such synergies are part of the distinctive manner in which emotions influence political action.

Creating the Terrorist Enemy

The above discussion suggests that the emotions triggered by the 9/11 attacks were more than generic expressions of fear, hatred, or anger. Such reactions—especially fear—were involved, but they were both connected to sentiments from the past and adaptive to social practices in the present. While we are therefore unlikely to find direct chains of cause and effect between a specific emotion and a correlated policy outcome, we might yet be able to trace some indirect and constitutive consequences. As noted in chapter 1, emotions underpin the normative commitments of a community. Perceptions of justice and fairness are often mediated by emotions, as sensitivities to suffering or injury imbue moral and legal standards with social legitimacy. Affective responses also play an important role in the ongoing process of normative change, provoking adjustments to which injuries a society deems most urgent and which beneficiaries it protects. In the aftermath of 9/11, emotions helped to shake up accepted norms and quietly extend legitimacy to new ones. This and the following section trace one thread of emotional change, which influenced popular tolerance for relaxing the legal protections available to terrorists.

Circulations of affect can help to explain how, following 9/11, Americans of Arab, Muslim, and/or Middle Eastern descent became socially recognized as the primary suspects of terrorism. This process took hold amid a relatively low level of public knowledge about the people behind the attacks of 9/11.[29] Americans were aware of corollary matters: the importance of the Middle East for oil resources, ongoing disputes with Saddam Hussein over weapons of mass destruction, and the ongoing conflict over Palestinian territories. And many had some recollection of signal events, such as the 1982 assassination of Israeli athletes in Munich, the Iranian hostage crisis beginning in 1979, and the Persian Gulf War of 1991.[30] But these fragments offered a weak foothold for comprehending the networked agents of terrorism. One result was that the Bush administration had latitude to shape public images of terrorism to suit strategic objectives. The vagueness of the enemy also created possibilities for other actors—from religious authorities to talk-show personalities and conservative bloggers. The result was a decentralized and creative construction of an enemy ambiguously defined as "Arab/Muslim/Middle Eastern."

These constructions were not, however, created through official discourse alone. President Bush and members of his administration did make use of the idea that 9/11 was part of a religious conflict. In a meeting with the press on September 16, Bush described the war on terror as a "crusade," sparking images of historical conflict against enemies of Christendom.[31] His September 20 speech described the attackers as representatives of a savage and cowardly enemy, opposed to the ideals of freedom and democracy. Their attack on America was an attack on Western civilization as such. Alongside these statements, however, Bush and other officials were forced to issue qualifications and clarifications aimed at forestalling the notion of religious conflict. The "crusade" remark provoked harsh and immediate criticism, for example, and prompted Bush to issue a series of caveats in subsequent speeches. The war was not, he later stressed, being waged against Muslims, and so Americans should respect Islam as a faith espousing peace.[32] The speech made to Congress on September 20 gave special attention to this point: "The enemy of America," he insisted, "is not our many Muslim friends." What is significant about this thread of official discourse, however, is that the later qualifications seemed unable to diminish the circulation of popular antipathy toward those perceived as Arabs, Muslims, and Middle Easterners. These discriminations were notably disconnected from the content of political speech.

One way to explain these developments is to suggest that the politics of terrorism merged with the already thriving discourse on the "clash of civilizations." As a result of influential writings by Bernard Lewis and Samuel Huntington, the idea of a post–Cold War clash between religious traditions had acquired significant interest among media figures, public intellectuals, and some scholars.[33] Lewis explained that anger over colonialism, modernization, and secularization surfaced within the Islamic world during the 1970s and '80s. America, he argued, was not the real cause of that anger but had nevertheless become its primary target. Huntington saw the tension between Islam and the West as the paradigmatic conflict in a world of clashing civilizations. For him, the end of the Cold War had given way to a greater salience of cultural and religious identities. Civilizations were the largest cultural group with which human beings identified, and the identification was most intense where civilizations converged: from Israel and Kashmir to Yugoslavia and Sudan. If most of these conflicts involved Islamic groups, it was because the Muslim world was beginning to assert itself after failed experiments with secular, pro-Western governments during the 1950s and '60s. As the news media and ordinary Americans sought to make sense of the terrorist attack on America, the idea of civilizational identity became a powerful lens.[34]

While the idea of a civilizational conflict undeniably played a role in defining America's enemies in the wake of 9/11, it alone cannot explain the social and cultural discriminations involved. To begin with, many public statements on the topic were in fact not direct allusions to a clash of multiple civilizations as imagined by Lewis and Huntington. Bush's November speech to the UN General Assembly, for example, explained that "civilization, itself, the civilization we share, is threatened."[35] Here he uses "civilization" not as a category of cultural difference but as a state of moral achievement. The speech presupposed that it was possible to distinguish between the enemies of civilization and its moral guardians. The ambiguity of the term "civilization" had arguably been part of the clash discourse from the start, as America's civilizational others were not presented neutrally but as culturally inferior adversaries. The post-9/11 rhetoric of civilization thus reflected the dual meaning accorded to the concept beginning in the nineteenth century—as both a normative hierarchy and racial/ethnic typology. The idea of civilization as a marker of moral authority was a significant element of post-9/11 discourse, but it did not in itself supply a substantive cultural profile of the terrorist enemy.

Another explanation suggests that the events of 9/11 simply augmented a constellation of cultural stereotypes with a longer history in American popular culture. Cultural studies of various kinds have noted that the image of Muslims and Arabs as potential terrorists originated with the Six Day War in 1967, the 1973 oil crisis, and the Iranian revolution in 1979. These stereotypes thrived on images circulated by the entertainment industry during the 1980s and '90s.[36] The 9/11 attacks only intensified a cultural process of classifying Arab Americans that had begun in the aftermath of these foreign policy crises.[37] Whereas Arab Americans have been historically and legally identified as "white," images circulated in popular culture and mass media effectively conflated Arabs, Muslims, and Middle Eastern Americans into a race-like constituency. That is to say, the person of Arab/Muslim/Middle Eastern descent became associated with specific phenotypic traits and other seemingly visible markers of identity, such as language and dress. This account seems indispensable if we are to make sense of the way in which these diverse social and cultural groups have become amalgamated into one and then essentialized with visible markers of identity.

What is less clear is how this process has succeeded in a liberal political environment where racial identity has become socially unacceptable. In such a postracial context, ideas and practices surrounding race also took subterranean forms. As scholars of race in America have suggested, an official politics of race can become taboo, and yet unofficial discriminations and prejudices continue to circulate.[38] The social phenomenon of racial profiling—experienced, albeit in different ways, by ordinary Americans—has played an important role.[39] Detentions, government eavesdropping, seizures of property, airline removals, FBI visits, mandatory special registration, and other security measures were experienced as technologies of social control by Arab Americans and others perceived to be Arabs, Muslims, or persons of Middle Eastern descent. By 2004, at least 100,000 Arabs and Muslims in the United States had been subjected to one or more of these measures.[40] The result has been a pervasive and well-documented feeling of fear on the part of Arab and Muslim Americans. Yet, even as secret detentions, wiretapping, and other measures were deliberately concealed from the public, many of these invasive practices also implicated a broader audience. When airport security personnel board an aircraft to remove a passenger, the operation becomes a public spectacle of counterterrorism. Or, when FBI agents arrive at a person's workplace to conduct a voluntary interview, employers and coworkers become implicated as coparticipants.[41] Such public interventions have not only instilled fear in targeted individuals but also socialized ordinary Americans into engaging members of their community on the basis of visible markers of racial identity.

These racialized interactions have both reproduced cultural stereotypes and "charged" them with new affective energy. As white Americans live through heightened security alerts, enhanced border controls, and the invasive practices associated with the Patriot Act, they participate in embodied interactions that fuse cultural meanings and symbols with racially coded affective stimulation. Where one author notes that "the American public was instructed that looking 'Middle Eastern, Arab, or Muslim' equals 'potential terrorist,'" he identifies a process of socialization that took place through the cumulative interactions associated with racial profiling.[42] These interaction rituals relied upon visible markers of an imputed racial identity: Arabic language and music; the Sikh turban, Islamic *hijab*, and other elements of religious dress; and brown skin and other phenotypic characteristics commonly associated with Middle Eastern populations in American culture.[43] Americans could plug the emotional lessons from such interactions into the stereotypes and symbols available in public discourse.

Such nonlinguistic interactions acquire special significance in an ostensibly postracial context where overt declarations of racial stereotyping are socially proscribed. One scholar even suggests that because multiculturalism and racial equality had acquired such authority, the overt public denigration of Arabs and Muslims was in fact more muted after 2001 than during the 1980s and '90s. Scholars have noted that retractions, caveats, and qualifications issued by Bush and other public figures seemed unable to quell the association of terrorists with Muslims. As one observer notes of Bush's September 17 clarification regarding "our many Muslim friends," "the association had been made and the damage done." A similar pattern occurred with evangelical pastor Jerry Falwell, who declared during an interview on *60 Minutes* in October 2002 that he considered the prophet Muhammad a "terrorist." He too offered a caveat: "Most Muslims," he later explained, "are people of peace [who] abhor terrorism."[44] Once again, the damage had already been done. These qualifications were ineffective in part because they were issued against an experiential backdrop of racial profiling systematically pursued by the US government and involving the coparticipation of ordinary Americans. A process of affective othering was taking place beneath official discourse and without overt linguistic endorsements. In a political context where racial discriminations are no longer socially acceptable, the process of exceptionalizing by race has tilted in favor of implicit and embodied channels of socialization.

The effects of official security measures were reflected in acts of harassment and hate taking place across the country during the immediate aftermath of the attacks. Popular anxiety was, it seems, fueling disaffection toward Arab Americans.[45] In the aftermath of 9/11, these racialized habits of recognition affected behavior toward a variety of individuals perceived to be Arabs, Muslims, or persons of Middle Eastern descent. The American Civil Liberties Union (ACLU), the American-Arab Anti-Discrimination Committee (ADC), Human Rights Watch, and other groups reported a massive increase in hate-based violent crimes in the three months after the terrorist attacks, and higher than usual levels in the months after that. The Council on American-Islamic Relations (CAIR) reported 42, 93, and 191 cases of anti-Muslim hate crimes during 2002, 2003, and 2004, respectively. Over 1,500 civil rights cases were referred to the organization during 2004 alone.[46] These acts took a variety of forms in a variety of locations—from mosque vandalism and private property damage to harassment and physical abuse. What united these actions was the use of the same visible markers associated with government profiling: skin color, facial hair, headscarves, and religious habits.

These acts of harassment were patterned, but also uncoordinated, as exhibited by the phenomenon of airline passenger removals. Incidents were often instigated by passengers rather than airport or airline officials, although the latter parties assisted readily. The pattern was consistent: A passenger "'felt uncomfortable'" in the presence of a person who raised suspicion because of her or his skin color, language, name, or religious accoutrements. Even conduct perceived as religious practice—such as reading the Qur'an—was sufficient to spark public concern. One report documents an episode in which the airline attendants moved quickly to ask the passenger to disembark. After he repeatedly refused, the flight attendant addressed the cabin: "Does anyone have a complaint with this man?" The appeal was met with a decisive response: "yes, kick him off the plane" and "I don't know why these people can't understand how we do things here in America." A lack of clear protocols allowed airlines to respond to popular concerns unquestioningly and without vetting the evidence. By March 2002, the US Department of Transportation had received ninety-eight complaints of discrimination, twenty-six of which involved passenger removals; in the year following 9/11, the ADC received over eighty reports of passenger removals.[47] Across the country, people were "feeling uncomfortable" about vaguely defined would-be terrorists. Passenger removals offer an indication that the racialization of the "Arab/Muslim/Middle Easterner" had begun to resonate among ordinary Americans. The patterns of conduct chronicled by the ADC, ACLU, CAIR, and other organizations suggest that racial discriminations were occurring even without the kind of overt rhetorical campaign proscribed by a multicultural and postracial society.

Emotional Habits and Legal Exceptions

Alongside identity-based discourses about al Qaeda, Iraq, and the enemies of "civilization," then, a constellation of unofficial and contagious affective habits was circulating. These emotions were helping to guide behavior in a social and cultural environment where recognizing others by visible characteristics of identity felt increasingly urgent to many Americans. The neuroscience of emotion can help to describe how such habits are constituted in the brain. Our brains are not hardwired to respond in fear to people who look differently than us. Rather, the brain is conditioned through experience to respond to certain stimuli with emotions considered appropriate to them. We internalize over time "emotionally competent stimuli" that often activate emotions synthetically, by simulating internal changes in the body; these "somatic markers" help to activate an emotion without the need for comparatively slower processes of intellectual recognition. Recent research has confirmed that visible markers of racial and cultural difference can affect the activation of these emotional responses. Exposure to "other-race" faces can generate implicit or unconscious fears even among subjects who explicitly declare their sympathies with racial others. Further, emotional simulation through mirroring is dampened in cases involving emotional displays by members of other cultural groups.[48] The visible markers of race change over time, as historical events endow new groups with social significance. Moreover, the way the brain uses these markers to stimulate emotional response also changes, as some groups become objects of empathy and others emblems of fear.

In the aftermath of 9/11, the social construction of the terrorist enemy occurred in and through a constellation of emotional changes affecting how Americans encountered perceived others in everyday situations. Even as racial differences are no longer accepted as the basis of political and social inclusion, racially inflected habits of affective recognition can shift patterns of social interaction on an implicit level. As William Connolly explains, the biology of race is a much more culturally and historically layered phenomenon than suggested by classical genetic theories. The cultural values associated with race are reproduced, sometimes without thinking, through a variety of visceral practices.[49] When airline passengers become alarmed at the sight of an Arab American–looking man switching seats, they perform an unconscious, affective habit of racial recognition. The affective nature of these habits means that a person can explicitly declare support for racial diversity while maintaining implicit habits of discrimination. It may also help to explain the existence of public opinion polling in the aftermath of 9/11 indicating a rise in public acceptance of Muslim-Americans just when one might expect its decline.[50] As more public attention is focused on the treatment of minorities, and as even the President calls for tolerance, conscious attitudes shift in favor of cultural pluralism. And yet, notwithstanding those conscious preferences, circulations of affect sustain distinctly negative associations.[51]

These implicit habits of emotional discrimination may help to explain public acceptance of Bush-era policies on terrorism. During the latter part of the twentieth century, prohibitions on torture and aggressive uses of force became widely shared norms both in international treaties and in customary international law. And, in the post–Cold War period especially, the legitimacy of military intervention has increasingly been tied to humanitarian objectives.[52] And yet, notwithstanding these normative and legal developments, the Bush administration mobilized substantial public support for both its use of torture and its preventive, military-strategic use of force. It is true that the details of the former policy were not circulated publicly until spring 2004, but even the support it received within the White House and Department of Justice is indicative of the policy's social acceptance. The doctrine of so-called pre-emptive war *was* circulated openly and received considerable public support when applied to the case of Iraq. In the wake of the attacks, elite and popular support for new legal exceptions on torture and the use of force seemed to rise.

The emergence of an affectively constituted terrorist enemy suggests that these normative shifts are more complex than a simple withering of international norms. A common worry in situations involving threats to national security is that the state will lift restrictions on the use of violence. Indeed, where international law is concerned, states are often legally permitted to derogate from legal commitments in times of war or emergency. The justification for preventive war in the 2002 *National Security Strategy* (NSS) seemed to follow this pattern, modifying standards concerning self-defense in light of new security threats. Similarly, American officials violated the ban on torture for the purposes of intelligence gathering. The emergence of an affectively constituted terrorist enemy suggests, however, that normative adjustment in the wake of the attacks was more subtle and qualified than standard worries suggest. Legal exceptions are not complete displacements of law but moments of selective suspension; as Giorgio Agamben explains, a moment of exception "releases a particular case from the literal application of the norm." The suspension of a norm in that particular case may result from a decision made by legal authorities, but such decisions are in turn the product of specific social environments and circulations of affect that diminish eligibility for legal protection.[53]

Political speeches, legal documents, and government reports could tap into prevailing circulations of affect without fully declaring the cultural discriminations guiding the application of new norms. The infamous torture memos, for example, proposed that the standards outlined in the Geneva Conventions could not be applied to Taliban and al Qaeda personnel. While these documents did incorporate a string of allusions to Afghanistan as a culturally backward society, they did not offer a racial or cultural doctrine of legal eligibility. And yet, even without an official statement of racial profiling, it seemed clear that new standards on torture were not being proposed as universal rules to be applied to just any American. As David Luban notes, the tradeoff between national security and human rights protection was always viewed through an implicit assumption that the recipients of state violence were not "regular Americans" but members of a different cultural group. By tracing these affective discriminations, we can account for the undeclared ways in which the application of domestic and international law continues to be filtered through cultural difference.[54]

Justifications for the Bush Doctrine came closer to an explicit declaration of America's cultural others, and yet they too stopped short of a racial or cultural doctrine of exceptionalism. The NSS, for example, included frequent references to "terror states" that "brutalize their own people" and "reject basic human values." And the document contended that deterrence could no longer work against "rogue states," "terrorists," and "tyrants" because such actors could not be counted on to act rationally. Presidential speeches from fall and winter 2002–3 spoke of Iraq as having a "deep hatred of America" and a "history of reckless aggression" and of Saddam Hussein as "merciless," "ruthless," and "deceptive."[55] Rather than a doctrine of cultural otherness, public statements incorporated only rhetorical fragments conveying a loose sense that America's enemies in the war on terror operated according to different standards of moral conduct. But such a doctrine was also not needed in a context where the terrorist enemy was already being defined through shifting habits of racial recognition. The feeling of a cultural exception lingered below the radar of public discourse but seeped into official arguments and policies nonetheless. The NSS spoke a more-tempered language and yet resonated with this implicit reservoir of prejudice. The legal exceptions devised after 9/11 were therefore not imagined to be applicable to all legal subjects; they were instead selective retractions applied to a specific class of affectively constituted others.

This process of affective exception reflects a distinctly nonlinear form of normative adjustment. As constructivists document the rising power of norms, realist critics often cite the frequency and impunity with which they are violated by self-interested states. The world, as Stephen Krasner contends, is replete with hypocrisy.[56] On one level, then, the wars in Afghanistan and Iraq, and the ascendancy of the Bush Doctrine, appear to support a skeptical rejoinder to the constructivist's world of norms. In this view, the Bush administration's response to 9/11 triggered a process of "norm regress" in the area of human rights and the use of force.[57] The evidence cited above suggests, however, that the normative aftermath of 9/11 was more complex than a simple "yay" or "nay" to international norms. The specter of terrorism induced a cultural exceptionalism that allowed those norms to be selectively suspended, for unspecified duration, in order to address an emerging threat. Constructivist accounts of norm diffusion have observed that empathy and other forms of affect can support the progressive extension of norms to new beneficiaries: new norms do not acquire force until we *feel* differently about their beneficiaries.[58] This case shows that affect generates alternative normative outcomes as well, as emotions inspire selective retractions of even an apparently settled norm. Whether affect supports, undermines, or selectively modifies a norm is ultimately an empirical question. In the aftermath of 9/11, the social modification of accepted norms occurred in a piecemeal and implicit fashion that neither constructivists nor realists are well equipped to conceptualize.

Normative and legal adjustments after 9/11 could be construed as standard products of a national security crisis: as a society experiences fear, it takes steps to eliminate possible threats, even if those efforts temporarily violate prevailing normative and legal standards. Since "radical Islamist" groups were responsible for the attacks, and since they were using a networked and truly global form of organization, it only made sense to apply counterterrorist security measures at home, in the Middle East, and around the world. While such a pattern did occur in the case of 9/11, it would be a mistake to interpret the emotional underpinnings of that response as somehow a natural byproduct of insecurity. The affective adjustments helping to construct the terrorist enemy were not automatic; they were products of a specific constellation of social practices and cultural meanings. In the aftermath of the attacks, the object of fear was mediated by pre-existing normative commitments, emergent cultural stereotypes, and ongoing rituals of security. To understand the affective impact of terrorism, we need to identify the mediating factors involved in a given case and then trace the peculiar emotional circulations they engender.

Terrorism and the Politics of Anger

A similar process can be applied to another emotional response to terrorism—namely, anger. It seems only natural that a large-scale terrorist attack would spark anger and a commensurate desire for revenge. People often feel anger in response to injury, and we generally expect that emotion to result in retributive acts toward those responsible. Moral philosophers contend that such a response is integral to self-respect: if we do not respond to injury with anger, we have failed to value the injured self.[59] After the 9/11 attacks, America had suffered not just violence but a challenge to its global authority and a wanton use of force against innocent civilians. In relation to Pearl Harbor and 9/11, John Mueller notes that "the shock, outrage, and fury they inspired impelled an intense desire to lash out militarily at the source of the assault."[60] Revenge is greatest when morality and honor are at stake, and many Americans saw the attacks as violations of both. As Jean Elshtain and others argued in the wake of 9/11, public anger was not a foolish or exceptional response but a valuable guide in assessing the injury from that event. Anger, in this view, serves as a beacon of moral transgression and injustice.[61]

While they may be intuitively compelling, images of anger and retribution as natural responses understate the complexity of emotional elicitation and attribution in social contexts. To begin with, we do not always know who exactly is responsible for an injury. Americans knew the attacks were perpetrated by nineteen hijackers associated with a group known as al Qaeda, but, as noted above, there was a high level of uncertainty surrounding the cultural, ideological, and geographical profile of these networked perpetrators. As experts debated how far to cast the tangled net of complicity, their efforts were invariably filtered through the historical analogies, extant rivalries, and cultural stereotypes discussed earlier in the chapter. In a clinical experiment, it might seem natural to assume that emotional responses are tethered to those persons or objects directly responsible for eliciting them. But in real-world situations, where social agency is diffuse and responsibility contested, the matter is often murky. The feeling of anger may be a natural response, but its direction and intensity are shaped by social conditions of elicitation.

For this reason, we can learn more about anger as an emotional response by tracing its social genesis across different cases. The affective aftermath of the 2004 bombings in Madrid illustrates this complex politics of emotional elicitation. The case is illustrative not because it departs per se from the politics of anger but because it tells us more about how anger is shaped and intensified by social circumstances. In the Spanish case, collective anger was amplified by a combination of lived protest activities and a peculiar pattern of official deception, censorship, and informal communications at the grassroots level. As a result of these factors, anger became targeted not externally toward terrorist perpetrators but internally, according to prevailing political narratives and collective memories. The case thus testifies to the range and malleability of anger in the wake of a violent political attack.

In the days following the March 11 bombings, the leaders of the governing Partido Popular (PP) tried to use the attacks to win support in the impending national election. Spanish president José María Aznar and other officials in the PP attributed responsibility for the bombings to the Basque separatist party ETA; by fixing public anger onto this familiar internal enemy, PP leaders hoped to win support for their party's aggressive stance on domestic terrorism. The strategy backfired, as disconfirming evidence emerged in the three days between the attacks and the national election. As the ETA thesis was progressively discounted and a link to al Qaeda confirmed, voters punished the PP for their attempt to curtail media coverage and manipulate public opinion. Despite an earlier lead in the polls, the PP leader lost to his Socialist Party challenger, José Luis Rodríguez Zapatero. Various observers have attributed the electoral swing to the PP's attempted deception, most agreeing that the PP's actions did not change the opinions of voters as much as it increased voter turnout among would-be abstainers.[62] There were important causal connections between the 3/11 attacks, the PP's response, popular outrage, and the electoral outcome.

Far from the "knee-jerk" reaction described by PP officials, anger over the March 11 attacks came into being through a peculiar sequence of social practices that shaped its intensity and focus.[63] As media and participant reports suggest, early reactions to the bombings were far from uniform. Media coverage pointed to conflicting emotional responses, including sorrow, fear, and anger, as well as more inchoate feelings of tension, anxiety, and panic. One study thus points to a "complex mixture of emotions"; another describes a "cocktail" of "anger and fury mixed with grief and mourning."[64] As foreign media and person-to-person networks began to uncover the PP's efforts at public deception, anger coalesced around the Spanish government.[65] There is evidence that some had from the beginning directed anger at the terrorists behind the attacks; as one Spaniard expressed to a *New York Times* correspondent, "we want an eye for an eye." But most reports describe instead a less coherent climate of confusion, shock, and sadness. Journalists variously noted that Spanish society was "winded," "in deep shock," facing "a terrible sense of unease," and experiencing a "mood . . . of shock and mourning." In the mass vigil of March 12, mourners displayed these ambiguous feelings of distress, and those who spoke to journalists seemed unable to identify the precise target of their anger.[66] Only over the next two days did this general reaction shift into a more defined anger toward the PP.

Because emotional responses are generated in and through such social interactions, it is significant that Spaniards were so widely engaged in political demonstrations and protests during those two days. These initial responses germinated in the flow of mass gatherings; as Castells writes of the March 12 vigil, "it was in this physical gathering that people first started to react." As the PP exerted its influence over the media, especially state-owned television networks and traditionally right-leaning print media, the public confronted a disquieting deficit of information about the possible link to al Qaeda. Foreign news reports suggest that the element of mystery intensified affective responses, as the process of waiting precipitated "a feeling of panic and desperation." Public emotion evolved as suspicions festered. The vigil of March 12 supplied an initial opportunity for shared grief and cautious anger. But, as the secretive behavior of public officials fueled speculation, facts initially concealed from public view began, as one Spanish sociologist remarks, to "spread like a contagious epidemic or a voracious moral fire."[67] As rumors of a cover-up intensified, a group of activists organized a demonstration for 6 pm on March 13, publicized primarily through SMS text messages. Official media channels were being bypassed by informal communications via SMS, listservs, and other person-to-person networking. The resulting "flash mobs" or "instant insurgent communities" helped to focus anger on the PP, as greater participation provided visual confirmation that public suspicions were well-founded.[68]

The profile of public anger shifted as new information about the bombings became available and as patterns of communication and protest adapted. SMS messaging and street demonstrations provided venues for expressive and contagious displays of discontent. Moreover, such communicative practices were not just neutral conveyor belts for a generic emotional response; they were changing the volume and focus of anger along the way. During the evening of March 13, for example, people in all Spanish cities banged pots and pans from their windows. Castells explains that "a form of protest adopted during the anti-war movement was spontaneously reenacted in thousands of homes." Widely used during the 2003 antiwar protests, the ritual injected currents of antiwar and pacifist sentiment into the 3/11 crisis.[69] The lived practice of protest thus helped to facilitate the growing association between the 3/11 bombings and the PP's controversial contribution to the Iraq War. The prevalence of this antiwar framing confirms that the political stakes were clear to most Spaniards: if al Qaeda were found responsible, the PP could be blamed for provoking the attacks through their involvement in the US-led invasion of Iraq. Emotional responses to terror were more than feeling-states created in the minds of individual citizens; they were contagious circulations of affect absorbed through adaptive and expressive social practices.

This case demonstrates that there is no automatic target for anger in the wake of a large-scale terrorist attack. Public anger can be amplified by efforts to manipulate information, and it can be redirected according to available memories, symbols, and narratives. The backlash against the Spanish government drew upon latent public frustrations over its commitment to the war in Iraq. Public opinion polls confirm that as many as 90 percent of Spaniards were opposed to Spain's involvement in the war between early 2003 and the March 2004 attacks.[70] The PP was out of step with Spanish voters, who were of like mind with other Europeans in opposing the use of military force to address terrorism. Since the Spanish military commitments were relatively small, the public opposition on this issue had not been expected to play a major role in the March 2004 election. But the events of 3/11 reopened the wound and reminded Spanish voters of the gap between government policy and popular opinion. Many Spaniards blamed the PP not only for its manipulation of information in the days following the bombings but also for its role in provoking those bombings in the first place. In one poll, 64 percent of respondents believed that the 3/11 attacks would not have happened if Spain had not supported the war in Iraq.[71] This political context made it possible for anger to focus not on the immediate authors of the attack but further back in the chain of responsibility, on the Spanish government.

The malleability of anger in this case tells us something about Spain's culture of national security. Whereas Americans treat terrorism as a threat to national security or a problem demanding military solutions, the phenomenon takes on different meanings among European publics accustomed to the use of terror as a vehicle, albeit a discredited one, for political advocacy. One study notes European skepticism toward the "new terrorism" declared by American officials after 9/11: "It has suited European attitudes to interpret this phenomenon more in terms of a reaction to specific policies and military deployments than as a general anathematizing of the West." Europeans tend to regard global terrorism as a symptom of a need for greater efforts to remedy inequalities through foreign aid and development policies.[72] Within this national security culture, it made little sense to treat the 3/11 bombings as unprovoked attacks on an innocent state; Spaniards saw them instead as responses to the policies of their own government. Indeed, six months prior to the Madrid attacks, Osama bin Laden vowed that Spain's involvement in Iraq and Afghanistan would be met with revenge. That statement was then offered by al Qaeda as a rationale for the 3/11 attacks in a video circulated the night before the Spanish election.[73] Public anger after the attacks of 3/11 was refracted through these pre-existing anxieties over Spain's commitment to war in Iraq.

Spain's national security culture helps to explain the absence of public hostility toward the country's Muslim minority. Unlike the racial profiling of Arab and Muslim minorities in the US context, Spanish officials and Spanish society abstained from targeting Moroccans and Spaniards of Moroccan descent.[74] Indeed, Zapatero's government deliberately pursued policies aimed at "mollifying" the Islamic world. It immediately withdrew Spanish troops from Iraq and pursued an ambitious experiment in multilateral dialogue known as the "Alliance of Civilizations."[75] The latter became Zapatero's signature foreign policy achievement, attracting the support of the UN and the prime minister of Turkey. Domestically, the Spanish government preserved immigration channels from North Africa, increased outreach to mosques and religious leaders, and insisted that terrorist suspects have access to standard legal protections and procedures. Such efforts were not universally in harmony with the needs and desires of Spain's Muslims; they sought, for example, to restrict the use of unregulated mosques and prayer rooms and promote "moderate" forms of Islamic practice. And yet, even as public anxieties about militant Islamist groups persisted, these policies never translated into widespread legal exceptions, security measures, or xenophobia.[76] This outcome is all the more significant given al Qaeda's repeated allusions to "the tragedy of Al-Andalus" and promises to reclaim the Iberian Peninsula.[77] Inhabiting a different security culture, Zapatero had the flexibility to respond to such provocations in a nonmilitarist fashion, channeling emotional memories of 3/11 into a political rhetoric of dialogue, bridge-building, and justice.

The Madrid bombings confirm that emotional reactions to violence, far from automatic or uniform, are shaped by expressive social practices and prevailing cultural norms. Anger may emerge in response to a perceived norm violation or breach of justice, but which norms are most likely to trigger response are a function of the sensitivities that are most acute within a community. Standard accounts of revenge suggest that human beings respond to injurious acts with anger directed at those deemed responsible. This case demonstrates that anger is not attached to a fixed schema of responsibility; depending on the normative expectations of a given society, responsibility for a violation may expand or contract to encompass different proximities of agency. The social chain of responsibility is a complex matter, mediated by cultural memories and moral commitments. Shaped by unfolding exposure to informal communications and street protests, public responses in Spain reached further back along that chain, targeting the authors of a pro-American foreign policy thought to have provoked the terrorist attack. Spaniards did not sustain a radical alternative to anger, and yet the species of anger they expressed was notably more complex than the "cycle of vengeance" image might suggest. We need to know something about the landscape of memories and sentiments before we can diagnose the varieties of anger an act of terror is likely to provoke.

Conclusion

The cases of Spain and the United States offer useful lessons on how modern societies respond to large-scale violence. Public discourse in the United States often assumed that Americans had reacted to the attacks of 9/11 with a few generic emotions, such as fear and anger—and that these in turn had automatically given rise to preferences for vigilance and retaliation. These emotion tropes spanned the political spectrum: Conservatives argued that 9/11 had provoked anger, that such feelings were justified, and that they could be harnessed to support a just war against terrorism. Even prominent Democratic leaders recognized the legitimacy of revenge.[78] These descriptions are not entirely mistaken, and yet they offer an oversimplified picture of how shared emotions are generated and how they achieve political impact. In social environments, emotions are not generic, and their political effects are not automatic. This chapter complicates that picture with three key contentions.

First, emotions are social circulations shaped and transmitted through media reports, public protests, and the quotidian rituals of a post-terror society. Although feelings can be deeply personal and often private, affective responses do not come into being in social isolation. Both cases discussed in this chapter illustrate the interactive process of emotion-generation. As Spaniards recalled latent frustrations over the Iraq War, text messages and street protests supplied the public venue where those emotions converged with anger over the 3/11 attacks. Anger was a common response, but not an automatic one: it came into being through a participative, public process of political expression. In the case of 9/11, public fear was forged through a relentless replay of the attacks in television news and digital media. The media spectacle allowed fears to shift from one object to the next: airline security to anthrax, al Qaeda to the Taliban and then Saddam Hussein. Emotions do not just pop into the heads of individual actors; they are transmitted through the social activities in which those actors are engaged.

Second, terms such as "anger" and "fear," while useful shorthand, stand in for an array of intersecting and reciprocally amplifying emotions. In complex social environments, emotions tend to resonate with one another. The intensity of public fear after 9/11 was partly predicated on, for example, a prior sense of trust and existential security. That fear then easily migrated from one object to another, with carryover from domestic terrorism to national security in the Middle East. Public reactions in the present also intersected with emotions past. Analogies to historical events such as Pearl Harbor brought with them currents of humiliation, fear, and anger. Anger tapped into latent feelings of frustration over Spain's involvement in Iraq and was amplified by revelations of political manipulation by the Spanish government. Emotions also adapted in the case of Spain, where anger was the cumulative product of mixed emotions that reverberated on the streets of Spanish cities. Anger was not automatic but developed through two days of public protest. Emotions such as fear and anger are common in the wake of large-scale violence, but they name something more than generic responses: these are dynamic social circulations capable of absorbing other sentiments, recombining them, and infusing them with new energy.

Finally, emotions can serve as engines of creativity, as the affective responses of a community are infused with its symbolic and normative commitments, old and new. Emotions are often tied to deeper social structures, such as national security norms, cultural identities, and moral and legal standards. When Spaniards reacted with anger, that emotion gave visibility to an underlying normative sensitivity over Spain's perceived provocation of the attacks. Emotions are partly expressive byproducts of more fundamental normative commitments. This chapter also, however, reveals a more complex process of normative change. The Madrid bombings show that collective emotional expressions of outrage can revive implicit norms. The process of person-to-person networking and expressive protest fueled normative contestation in the days after the attacks. Giving public expression to those implicit commitments is itself an act of invention, recombining otherwise latent sensitivities with contemporary policy challenges. In such situations, emotions serve as beacons of injustice, giving new urgency to some gap between the principles a community considers legitimate and the actions committed in its name.

The American case highlights the importance of fear and shows how that emotion supplies a political environment with ambiguity and normative malleability. Post-9/11 fears appear to have intensified what Jane Cramer calls the culture of "militarized patriotism"—the idea that patriotism in late twentieth-century America required an obligatory vigilance within foreign policy.[79] Such fears also served as vehicles for legitimizing new norms of vigilance and legal exception. A tradition of legal exceptionalism was creatively adapted to the new circumstances associated with terrorism. The Bush administration devised a more flexible approach to the ban on torture and advanced a new doctrine of anticipatory self-defense. These new norms were publicly discussed, but their scope of applicability remained implicit; these standards secured social legitimacy in part because they relied on implicit cultural associations regarding the legal subjects whose rights would be compromised. Under the radar of a liberal culture otherwise committed to ethnic, religious, and racial equality, new legal exceptions rested on images of a terrorist enemy forged at the level of affect. Circulations of affect did not cause US military policy, but they did lay a social groundwork for its requisite legal adjustments.

FOUR

Emotions and Ethnic Conflict

During the 1990s and early 2000s, as journalists, foreign-policy advisers, and scholars traced the politics of ethnic identity back to resentment and hatred, the connection between ethnic conflict and emotion seemed obvious. Some assumed that, since reasonable people are not usually willing to risk their lives for cultural identity or national honor, conflicts in places like Yugoslavia, Chechnya, Rwanda, Kenya, and the DR Congo must surely be rooted in atavistic passions. This diagnosis reflects the notion that ethnic and religious conflicts are rooted in long-standing historical resentments. Samuel Huntington, for example, argued that these destructive patterns occurred wherever two or more civilizations converged. Others concurred that the collapse of communism in Eastern Europe had released pre-existing hatreds; communism was, in this view, a momentary hiatus in a protracted and perverse ethnic competition. For Robert Kaplan, the Balkan conflicts revealed a perversion of historical memory; and violence in Africa was, in his account, an equally irrational product of "tribalism."[1] The common denominator in these diagnoses was an alarming propensity for hatred.

Subsequent scholars have generally agreed that the idea of ancient hatreds simplifies the complexity of ethnic conflict, and yet hatred still sits comfortably at the top of the list of emotions commonly associated with the phenomenon. Indeed, many studies of transitional justice accept the ubiquity of hatred as a useful starting point. Yet few who cite the importance of this emotion linger on its limited applicability to real-world social environments. Even constructivists seeking to discredit primordialist accounts of hatred often accept some form of ethnically directed animosity as the net result of the social processes under study.[2] Meanwhile, empirical research has recently found that witnesses to and participants in ethnic conflict rarely cite "hatred" as a motivation for violence. In interviews with over 200 Rwandan *génocidaires*, for example, Scott Straus finds that hatred was rarely expressed. Lee Ann Fujii makes a similar discovery in her study of two local communities in Northern and Central Rwanda. Ethnographic research on Serb nationalists in Bosnia shows that, while people often spoke of hatred, they did so in a clichéd manner indicating a highly scripted response.[3] My approach capitalizes on this empirical evidence—not to discredit the role of emotions but to demonstrate its complexity in cases of nationalism, ethnic conflict, and genocidal violence. By investigating the circulation of affect at the microlevel, I breathe fresh air into a literature polarized between those who emphasize emotions but treat them as fixed, deterministic causes and those who replace emotions altogether with strategic logics of behavior. Studies of hatred are correct about the emotionality of these phenomena but are held back from theorizing it by abstract conceptualizations of "hatred."[4]

This chapter revisits two cases, the former Yugoslavia and Rwanda, focusing on the early stages of conflict in each. These cases represent a special opportunity, since both are familiar to scholars in the Anglo-American social sciences, both have been widely discussed as cases involving identity and emotion, and yet both involve forms of emotional exchange whose creative dimension has not yet been appreciated. In both conflicts, key events and social interactions induced circulations of affect and thereby engendered powerful new forms of collective agency. In the former Yugoslavia, I look especially at political protests, workers' strikes, and political rallies taking place in 1987–89. I also discuss a less overtly political form of interaction—reburials of World War II victims—from the period immediately prior to war, between 1990 and 1991. In Rwanda I discuss political speeches and radio broadcasts during the two years prior to the genocide, and use the opportunity to extend the book's theorization of emotional discourse.[5] While the emotional significance of such group gatherings would have been clear to nineteenth-century sociologists of the crowd, recent studies of ethnic conflict tend to treat them simply as byproducts of ideology, identity, or interests. My analysis appeals to fine-grained descriptions—journalistic, historical, and ethnographic—in order to capture the affective circulations generated by these social events. For reasons discussed in earlier chapters, I steer away from an exclusive reliance on self-reports, even where these are used by secondary research. My case studies supplement secondary research based on interview and survey data with broader ethnographies of social practices and interactions that can reasonably be expected to induce surges of affect.

My investigation highlights the role of fear in both cases but also finds it is often associated with multiplying threats and existential unease rather than the explicit content of elite discourse. This creative productivity of fear thus raises new questions about the role of elites in ethnic conflict. It seems clear that Slobodan Milošević and other Serb leaders deliberately manipulated popular emotions in pursuit of political ambitions. Even in Rwanda, where decisions to kill generally took place at lower levels, people in positions of authority also bore direct responsibility for eliciting popular participation. Nevertheless, in both cases leaders made decisions and took actions against the background of powerful affective changes in their respective social environments. Even the cleverest of elites could not control the many affects circulating through popular gatherings, mass media, and word of mouth. Political speech matters in setting the stage for violent conflict, but often because of paralinguistic elements not fully controlled by its authors. Where I examine the interventions of Milošević and other "emotional entrepreneurs," I therefore supplement existing research on symbolic mobilization by examining elements—such as tone of voice, rumor, and ambiguity—operating on less-intentional registers. In both cases, political speeches capitalized on ambiguous forms of expression that resonated with popular emotion, often without explicitly appealing to ethnic identity.

The idea that nationalism is a "creative" force may seem counterintuitive: are nationalists not unimaginative people who filter all problems through the singular lens of national identity? Without denying that such a tendency exists, my concern is to account for the success of nationalism as social phenomenon, not to assess its validity as a political program. The affective dimensions of nationalism are, I argue, central to its appeal. As discussed in earlier chapters, affect tolerates high levels of ambiguity and flexibility. New symbols, historical analogies, and suggestive rumors thrive in situations of affective density. By tracing the emotions generated by social events, I show how the politics of ethnic nationalism absorbed anxieties, grievances, rivalries, and hopes from different areas of political, economic, and cultural life. When football hooligans channeled sports enthusiasm into nationalist activism, they sustained creative transfers of excitation from one social domain into another. Where ordinary Rwandans were exposed to ambiguous radio propaganda, they filtered these provocations through local fears and insecurities. Through circulations of affect, political and economic struggles are absorbed into cultural politics; ethically troubling as they are, genocide and nationalism are creative forces that capitalize on this fugitivity.[6]

By appreciating the creativity affect brings to nationalism, I demonstrate the political significance of social and cultural processes often missed in constructivist research. Studies of identity often focus on continuities such as the repetitive appeal to well-worn myths of a nation. I adopt a more dynamic view of ethnic nationalism and violence. My account regards "national identity" as a variable and open-ended phenomenon, whose myths and symbols are continuously invented and reinvented, combined and recombined. Emotional contagion creates new patterns of political conduct without the intervening influence of national identity. Where emotions do come to underpin a given identity, they do not always sustain a long-standing association with it. The habits, rituals, and prejudices that inspire nationalist movements are often more contingent than constructivist studies of identity suppose. I therefore cast a wider net than most: rather than focusing on familiar symbols of a nation, I trace the emergence of new symbols through a diverse array of emotionally charged social interactions. Football games, reburial rituals, political demonstrations, radio listening—all are microlevel interactions that "charge" the politics of ethnic identity with new sources of emotional energy.

Fear as a Circulation of Affect

An unfortunate legacy of the ancient hatreds hypothesis is the assumption that the emotions involved in ethnic conflict are bound to the politics of identity. The escalation of conflict in both Rwanda and Yugoslavia indicates a more fluid and creative process of emotional circulation. Collective emotions were not natural or pregiven but forged through a patchwork of lived events. In Yugoslavia the period from spring 1987 to summer 1991 hosted a flurry of political rallies, demonstrations, workers' strikes, and reburial rituals, the emotional impact of which was often extended by television broadcasts to the Federation's furthest corners. In the three and a half years prior to genocide in Rwanda, political speeches, radio broadcasts, and, ultimately, participative forms of violence altered the landscape of collective emotion in significant ways. Through social interactions such as these, people became exposed to contagious displays of various emotions, from fear and anxiety to frustration and anger, jealousy and resentment. In some cases, these emotional responses migrated from one event and context to another in ways that energized emergent symbols and laid the emotional groundwork for new constellations of collective agency. To begin to understand these processes, I examine circulations of fear, trace their emergence over time, and assess the connections they had to ancillary emotions.

The years leading up to genocide in Rwanda reveal that fear is more than a generic condition. Many observers have recognized that fear played an important role in preparing ordinary Rwandans for genocide. And yet its precise characteristics during this period are often obscured by standard conceptualizations of emotions as mere repetitive impulses. It is true that intense periods of fear had occurred at earlier points in Rwanda's postcolonial history—in the aftermath of the 1959 revolution, during the early 1970s, and other moments where political events triggered violence. But to suggest, as Franche does, that the emotional environment of 1990–94 simply continued a "vicious cycle of fear and revenge" misses the special qualities fear had at this particular moment.[7] To begin with, the proliferation of fear during the early 1990s had the distinctive mark of the Hutu Power movement, which sought to not only incite fear of impending attacks by the Rwandan Patriotic Front (RPF) but also cement visceral associations between the RPF and the broader Tutsi population within Rwanda. Through radio broadcasts, print media, and word of mouth, extremists translated latent anxieties into explicit fears of violence. The fear that made genocide possible was in fact a social construction, erected upon the beliefs, memories, and social habits of a distinctive period. As Mamdani argues, the fear induced by the RPF attacks and subsequent massacres was not a "timeless cultural reflex" but a "timebound response to a rapidly shifting political and social context."[8]

Transformations taking place in Rwanda during the late 1980s and early 1990s help to account for the specificity of fear during this period. After the Habyarimana government accepted assistance from the International Monetary Fund and other international donors, everyday life in rural Rwanda was affected by pressure to democratize economic opportunity and political competition. As Belgian anthropologist Danielle de Lame documents, daily interactions had historically sustained a sophisticated and delicate balance between formal public events and the many secrets reserved for private life. The result, she argues, was a "crisis of transparency."[9] Seemingly minor adjustments to everyday rituals—the public sharing of beer during once-private celebrations, for example, or the enlarged and newly public events surrounding the giving of a cow—disrupted the social fabric of Rwandan society. More people had access to wage-earning jobs, and more young adults migrated to the capital, Kigali, in search of greater opportunity. By placing greater value on outward demonstrations of material wealth, these changes altered older institutions of authority and heightened the uncertainties of daily life. These proliferating anxieties became available for politicization. De Lame's account chronicles the pervasive but ill-defined fears that existed even before the threat of war in 1990 or the advent of genocide in 1994.[10]

Throughout this period, the exact source of popular fears and anxieties remained elusive, and the result was an especially plastic definition of threats to Rwandan society. In the context of fear, the parameters of response to the RPF invasion were stretched. Fear in the present stimulated recall of fears associated with previous attacks. Hutu peasants felt the RPF attacks as a threat to security because they associated them with the massacres following the Inyenzi invasions of 1963 and the experience of violence among Hutu refugees in Burundi in 1965, 1972, and 1988. But pregenocide fears were not automatic reflexes recapitulating fear experienced at earlier moments; more recent fear combined the lived experiences of the present with highly memorialized and mythologized images of these earlier events. Mamdani argues that the category "Tutsi" had at various points since 1959 referred to both an ethnic and racial group. When the term denoted the former, Tutsis were a national minority that could in principle be accommodated by quota systems and other government remedies. When Tutsis were understood as a race, however, they became outsiders with no legitimate claim to a life within Rwanda.[11] The result was a specifically racialized version of fear, in which those perceived to be Tutsis were regarded as dangerous foreigners. The climate of fear following October 1990—magnified by the anxieties associated with recent social changes—allowed the Tutsis-as-ethnic-minority view to slide into its racialized variant. That slippage reveals the creative potential of fear.

Circulations of fear allowed the social category "Tutsi" to become gendered as well. During the 1980s, Rwandan society saw a transformation in norms and practices surrounding gender and sexuality. As a class of educated or "Europeanized" women (mostly in cities) introduced new fashions and sexual practices, guardians of moral conduct reacted with vigilance. Fear of changing sexual practices was heightened by the spread of HIV/AIDS. Many women were intimidated and assaulted by soldiers and police, and hundreds were sent to rural detention facilities for moral "straightening-out." Popular stereotypes cast the guilty women as prostitutes using their bodies to obtain power and wealth, degrading the purity of those men who succumbed to them.[12] Since these alleged sex workers were also widely perceived to be Tutsis, the Tutsi woman became a complex mixture of sexual desire and moral corruption. As extremist propaganda intensified in the years prior to genocide, it resonated with these fears. In addition to her possible association with the ethnic group of Tutsis, a woman could also be targeted for her perceived sexual deviance. These gendered norms and behaviors may explain in part why women, generally not included in Rwanda's earlier episodes of violence, were more often seen as legitimate targets in the 1994 genocide.[13]

These developments were more than a mobilization of anti-Tutsi sentiment, since they involved a fusion of ethnic/racial identity with cultural habits and perceptions of sexuality. Much of the discussion of women's experiences of the genocide, in both scholarly literature and civil society reports, has addressed the tragic phenomenon of war rape. As the International Criminal Tribunal for Rwanda (ICTR) succeeded in showing in showing in *Prosecutor v. Akayesu* (hereinafter *Akayesu*), the raping of women was part of a deliberate and systematic campaign to exterminate the Tutsi people. Various scholars and activists argued early on that rape was being used in Yugoslavia and Rwanda as a tool of genocide, and these studies triggered considerable scholarship and jurisprudence concerning the intentions (material and symbolic) of those who encouraged and/or sanctioned rape. But the presence of genocidal intent does not tell us about the prior social habits and prejudices fueling popular antipathy toward Tutsi women. The association of a particular population of women with promiscuity made it possible for social habits pertaining to sexuality to inspire violence aimed at ethnic extermination. One study speculates that Hutu extremists were unable to resolve the contradiction between their sexual desire for Tutsi women and their moral castigation of them; sexual violence was the tragic result of that ambivalence.[14] The "Tutsi woman" was a collection of fears and convictions that had become contingently attached to an identity.

Viewed after the fact, the record of violence in Rwanda's postcolonial history suggests that myths about Tutsis as a foreign race were longstanding justifications for violence—vicious political doctrines driving acts of violence against Tutsis. Such a view overestimates, however, the planned, coherent quality of racial hatred as an ideology and underestimates its dependence upon contingent circulations of affect. Straus's account confronts the difficult problem of how much autonomy to grant emotional responses. He acknowledges their importance when he emphasizes that ethnic categorizations are dependent upon certain psychosocial environments. The ideology that targeted Tutsis as a group "depended on an awareness of ethnic/racial categories," he argues, "but the mechanisms driving the categorization and violence appear to have been insecurity and uncertainty." This "insecurity and uncertainty," or fear and anxiety, were crucial for translating the vague idea of a "Tutsi" into assessments of actual people and their circumstances: "Tutsis stop being neighbors, friends, and a disparate population: they become a single entity with identical—and permanent—intentions."[15] The ideology of genocide existed in abstract form, but to resonate with real people and concrete situations, it had to draw inspiration from more ambiguous and multifaceted escalations of fear.

In the former Yugoslavia also, fear contributed to conflict through an economy of interconnected emotional circulations. The death of Tito in

1980 created a political vacuum within the Yugoslav Communist Party, but it also provoked an existential crisis across the federation. As one anthropologist notes, the institutional changes following Tito's death were not just abstract ideas; they were lived realities: "As state structures crumble, institutions lose their legitimation, and there is no money left, people feel lost (a way of life is disappearing)."[16] During the 1980s, as overt fears were still to congeal, Yugoslavs reported a variety of subtle and indeterminate anxieties and frustrations. They had lost confidence in the policy of Brotherhood and Unity and the system of self-management that had defined Yugoslav society since the 1970s. Discontent among Albanians in the semiautonomous province of Kosovo became a key node in the escalation of popular emotions throughout the federation. With street protests in March 1981, the Albanians provoked military response from the Yugoslav People's Army and drew the ire of the Serb minority within the province. In the following years, Serbs in Kosovo and Montenegro formed a protest group to solicit support for the plight of Serbs outside Serbia proper. The movement received official legitimacy in a memorandum written by a committee of the Serbian Academy of Sciences and Arts and leaked to the press in late 1986.[17] The document offered a catalogue of injustices experienced by Serbs and, as such, condoned a discourse of ethnic identity that had long been suppressed under Tito's federalism. It put into words the discontent of Serb activists, giving intellectual justification to their public acts of dissent. The document changed the climate in the former Yugoslavia; as one account suggests, "the country was convulsed."[18]

These affective changes did not cause war directly but raised thresholds of tolerance for violence within Yugoslav society. Mounting fears were heightened by public displays of violence. A series of paramilitary attacks changed the atmosphere in Croatia, and almost immediately after in Bosnia. Serb and Croatian forces became highly skilled at using "ethnic cleansing" as a technique of fear. The practice brought violence incrementally to one village after another, rather than containing it at a distant battle line. The ethnic cleansing pursued in the Bosnian and Croatian countryside was itself a form of social interaction that induced patterns of collective emotion. Moreover, the practice had an expressive dimension that elicited fear among participants and observers alike. Even among those who did not experience it directly, the very prospect of attack had devastating effects. Rumors of violence served as warnings of impending war. Each captured village and each execution served as a visible and visceral precedent for further violence. The result was an escalating, contagious, and unpredictable circulation of fear. Fear was not just a belief about a tangible threat; it was also a dispersed affective response to the spectacle of violence and drew inspiration and direction from lived social events.

As IR scholars turned during the 1990s to the phenomenon of ethnic conflict and civil war, many emphasized the importance of fear. In showing how fear and insecurity precipitate group competition, they uncovered an important aspect of ethnic conflict.[19] My analysis supplements these insights with an account of the specific properties of fear, its production through social interaction, and its connection to ancillary circulations of affect. Empirical research reveals contagious social exchanges of fear rather than abstract security dilemmas. In both cases discussed here, fears were neither monolithic nor tethered to a specific political object; on the contrary, as Fujii notes in her study of the Rwandan genocide, "the object of fear shifted to different groups at different moments."[20] Whereas rationalist theories conceptualize fear negatively, as an absence or blockage of information, ethnographic and historical studies often find that fear coincides with a *proliferation* of beliefs, memories, and sentiments. Fear, insecurity, and anxiety are more than proxies for the absence of objective facts; by supplying viability to new symbols and identities, they play a positive role of their own. People react to a complex social world by activating comparisons, memories, and sentiments; as fear spreads through emotional contagion, it can both intensify and dampen these activations.

Reburial in Yugoslavia

As Yugoslavia's communist leaders lost power to nationalists during the late 1980s, many anticipated the demise of Tito's federalism. After nationalist leaders in Croatia, Serbia, and Bosnia won the elections of 1990, they escalated the rhetoric and propaganda of ethnic politics. One topic that surfaced over and over was the unresolved matter of atrocities committed during World War II. Tito's regime had not allowed public discussion, let alone mourning, of the many victims of the war. The nameless dead were referred to only abstractly as "victims of fascism." As nationalist mobilization intensified, a heated debate ensued over which ethnic groups were responsible for atrocities, and over precisely how many victims of each group had perished. Tudjman and other Croatian nationalists argued that atrocities committed by Partisan forces (mostly Serbs) had been unfairly ignored under Tito, and those committed by Ustaše forces exaggerated. Serb nationalists for their part rekindled interest in the precise numbers killed at the Ustaše camp of Jasenovac. During summer 1990, newspapers in Croatia and Slovenia published stories about previously concealed massacres by communist

forces. Meanwhile, the media in Serbia was talking about Jasenovac and
Ustaše atrocities.[21] By mid-1991, popular interest in the topic had reached
a new intensity, and both groups turned attention to actual burial sites.
Some mass graves had been officially memorialized; others were previously
unknown to all but those who lived nearby. Local communities began the
emotional process of exhuming and reburying the dead. Their ritual practices spawned new circulations of affect, experienced locally and transmitted nationally through newspaper and television.

Most accounts of the controversy over World War II atrocities treat them
as familiar symbols of nationalist sentiment.[22] As leaders mobilized support
for nationalism, they looked to the collective memory of World War II as
reliable triggers of popular emotion. The more people thought about the
atrocities previously committed against their ethnic kin, the more loyalty
they would feel toward their nation. Thus, in accounts such as Kaufman's,
Jasenovac and other World War II images are symbols of the nation, used
by nationalist leaders cognizant of their emotional appeal.[23] While this view
captures an important dimension of the mobilization process, it misses the
ambiguity of the emotion involved and overlooks the participative dimension of reburials as emotion-generating social interactions. As Katherine
Verdery's brilliant study of reburial suggests, the dead bodies were not naturally tools of nationalist mobilization but had to acquire symbolic importance. Dead bodies, she argues, were especially amenable to a new symbolic
charging:

> A body's symbolic effectiveness does not depend on its standing for one par-
> ticular thing, however, for among the most important properties of bodies,
> especially dead ones, is their ambiguity, multivocality, or polysemy. Remains
> are concrete, yet protean; they do not have a single meaning but are open to
> many different readings. Because corpses suggest the lived lives of complex
> human beings, they can be evaluated from many angles and assigned perhaps
> contradictory virtues, vices, and intentions.[24]

While the dead bodies may appear as natural markers of national identity, we need to recognize that they *became* symbols through the embodied
process of reburial. Reburial rituals did not simply recapitulate pre-existing
myths and symbols; they created new symbols by investing them with emotional energy.

Accounts that regard World War II as a repository of ready-made symbols miss the affective force of reburial. When Kaufman, for example,
notes that World War II "added a new set of symbols to the Serbian myth-

symbol complex," he removes from the picture the positive contribution made during more recent episodes.[25] By assuming that the dead bodies already have symbolic meaning before the summer 1991 reburials, he overlooks the ongoing investment of dead bodies with symbolic force. The dead bodies had not been recognized under Tito as victims of ethnically targeted killings; they were considered through the abstract categories of "victims of fascism" or "domestic traitors," or else knowledge of them was suppressed entirely. Before reburial, the graves did not contain the bodies of "Serbs" or "Croats" as those categories were being used in the late 1980s and early 1990s. Thus, for Verdery, they remained malleable receptacles of potential power. Prior to reburial, the bodies had significance not as symbols of national identity but as concentrations of emotional energy. The suppression of public discourse on World War II atrocities had created a silence, and the silence enhanced the bodies' affective power. As one account suggests, the atrocities became "secret histories"; officially their memory was suppressed, but unofficially it continued to circulate.[26] The dead bodies and burial sites contained a reserve of affect; the interactive process of reburial creatively plugged that virtual energy into the politics of ethnic identity.

While it may seem strange to talk about a silence as having its own emotional force, the ethnographic context surrounding burial rituals helps to explain why. Verdery notes an especially strong sense of proper conduct surrounding burial of the dead in the former Yugoslavia, especially among Serbs. People felt a responsibility not only to bury the dead properly but also to visit them regularly. By interrupting these social obligations, Tito's ban on memorializing created a climate of spiritual tension and anxiety. The corpses acquired, Verdery suggests, an "aura of sanctity."[27] Recognizing this potential is different from saying the bodies had symbolic importance for nationalist politics. Symbolic significance was involved, but it was generated by the process of reburial. These rituals were, moreover, both discursive and visceral practices. Because the identities of the dead were not known, large groups of people—entire communities—participated in the reburials. As the bones were unearthed and placed in plastic bags, participants had the opportunity to handle them personally. In this tactile process, participants could imagine and hope that each bag might contain the bones of a relative.[28] In a context where the atrocities of World War II had been remembered only in private, the 1991 reburials were, as public expressions of private emotion, a novelty.[29] Because the bodies had a "polysemous" quality, these private emotions—memories of family members, deferred feelings of grief, and anxieties over improper burial—were folded into the interaction. Verdery thus observes that reburial "*blends* the personal grief of kin with rage against the enemy, nationally conceived."[30] The mass graves were useful for nationalist politics, but their usefulness was as a creative social practice rather than just a symbol awaiting deployment. Through reburial, diverse and hitherto implicit emotions were fused with the project of ethnic politics.

For many observers, the politics surrounding World War II atrocities signaled a pathology within Yugoslav society. In the collective consciousness of the former Yugoslavia, historical memory seemed to be bubbling dangerously close to the surface. The Balkans were, as Kaplan puts it, "a region of pure memory."[31] The implication of this view was that, in healthy modern societies, the rule of law allows us to lay aside old grievances rather than use them to justify continual acts of vengeance. Kaplan and other primordialists were not the only ones articulating such a view, which, after all, resonated with the common assumption that memories fade over time. The idea of linear memory is integral to the very idea of endemic hatreds, supplying the benchmark against which so-called cycles of hatred are assessed. Ignatieff, for example, writes: "These places are not living in a serial order of time but in a simultaneous one, in which the past and the present are a continuous, agglutinated mass of fantasies, distortions, myths, and lies." For Ignatieff, the wars in Yugoslavia during the 1990s involved simple recapitulations of unresolved animosities from earlier times: "yesterday and today were the same."[32] He illustrates the conceptual affinities between the idea of cycles of hatred and the image of memory as a repetition of the past. This conception of memory inherits much from the Freudian conception of repression. Painful emotions from earlier periods become repressed in an unconscious storage bin; when circumstances permit, those affects—preserved since the original moment of trauma—are released intact. The cyclical view of memory is especially enticing for those attuned to the tragic dimension of politics.

Such mnemonic exchanges seem less pathological, however, when we recall the creativity of emotional contagion. While folk psychology often presumes the linearity of memory—wherein each memory diminishes progressively until the experience is forgotten entirely—research in the psychology and neuroscience of memory tells a more complex story. Memories are in fact deeply intertwined with emotion, as they are recalled against a rich background of emotional conditions. Sadness, joy, and other moods may affect the way memories are recalled. For example, a condition of sadness in the present can elicit memories of unhappy life events.[33] Prior to these moments of creative recall, memories exist in nonconscious form: they comprise what psychologist Daniel Schacter describes as a repository of "implicit" memories and what cultural theorist Gilles Deleuze calls a "virtual" reservoir of emotional habits. Both scholars extend the influential account of memory in the works of Henri Bergson, who explained that latent memories are continually plugged into the experiences of the present.[34] Emotionally intense memories—from personal fears to the emotions connected to collectively memorialized events—can find their way into later experiences; such memories are more likely to be recalled, and recalled in greater detail, than those without overt emotional resonance.[35] Seen from this perspective, the layering of emotional memories in the former Yugoslavia during the late 1980s and early 1990s was more a showcase of the human brain's sophistication than a display of cultural backwardness.

Emotional reburials, by recharging memories with vitality, were thus opportunities to forge collective agency. Collective memories do not exist as perfectly preserved psychic "things," hardwired within members of a group. As Maurice Halbwachs—a student of Bergson—argues, collective memories crystallize only "because the same group is . . . able to call them to mind at the same time."[36] Where he assumes, however, that in any given situation the contours of the group are self-evident, the reburials suggest that the groups involved were constituted through ritual practice. As Verdery writes, "A (re)burial creates an audience of 'mourners,' all of whom think they have some relation to the dead person. The question is, *which* aggregate of people is brought together (directly or indirectly) for this event?"[37] Since the reburials of 1991 were organized according to ethnic community, the emotional memories called to mind became those of the "Croat" or "Serb" nations. Previously, they had been publicly suppressed memories with no necessary significance for ethnic identity. The reburials helped to fabricate ethnic groups as sites of collective memory.

This example reveals important aspects of memory as a product of social interaction. First, it shows how the recall of collective memories is less an automatic repetition than an active endeavor, shaped by the social context of the present. What we are doing when we recall memories, and whom we are doing it with, shapes which memories come into focus. Second, the memories that are recalled have a loose, rather than tightly determined, relationship to present practices. Because the mass graves were not symbols of national identity until reburials made them so, studies of identity need to recognize that diverse memories can resonate with the identities and projects of the present. Third, historical memory is not a linear process, in which the intensity of a memory corresponds inversely to its proximity in time. While we often assume that memories progressively fade until they are erased from consciousness, the Bergsonian view tells a different story: even distant memories are often available for activation in the present. Finally, this case illustrates that, outside the artificial constraints of clinical experimentation, emotional memories cannot be neatly parceled out in tidy packages. As noted in chapter 1, the emotions activated by a social interaction do not exist in isolation. Rather than look for the repetition of memories concerned with endemic hatred, we should look for diverse, overlapping circulations that mix past and present emotions.

The Neuropolitics of Incitement

As international tribunals and third-party states are holding leaders criminally responsible for "incitement to genocide," the emotional nature of this crime warrants close scrutiny. Incorporating language from the Genocide Convention, the statutes of the ad hoc UN tribunals authorize the courts to charge leaders with real and attempted acts of genocide, conspiracy to commit genocide, complicity in genocide, and "direct and public incitement to commit genocide."[38] National courts, seeking to fulfill responsibilities under the Convention, have recently heard similar cases on an extraterritorial basis. These juridical efforts reveal some enduring mysteries surrounding what exactly it means to "incite" a person or group to commit the crime of genocide. The international legal documents and jurisprudence reveal a tight association between incitement to violence and the emotion of hatred. The International Covenant on Civil and Political Rights accordingly includes a prohibition on "any advocacy of national, racial or religious hatred that constitutes incitement to discrimination, hostility or violence." In the ICTR's media trial, the terms "hatred" and "incitement" are often used in tandem: where they reveal an intent to destroy members of the targeted group, eliciting expressions of hatred is tantamount to inciting genocide.[39] Genocide is, by definition, a crime directed at members of a group; inciting populations to participate in that crime seems naturally to involve beliefs and emotions that help to demarcate its specific object of violence.

Notwithstanding the close connection between hatred and incitement in the emerging jurisprudence, there are many indications that the emotions associated with violence are complex and multifaceted. There is no rule requiring that acts of violence against members of a group must be predicated on hatred or resentment toward that group, intuitive as such an association might be. Ethnographic research in conflicted societies suggests that leaders can motivate popular involvement also through ancillary emotions, such as fear and jealousy, that may or may not have an out-group as clear objects of elicitation. The specific emotions capable of moving people to participate in violence are thus products of context rather than a standard recipe. In addition, given the varied degrees of conscious awareness and cognitive complexity involved in emotional response, not all forms of incitement to hatred are likely to involve clear and distinct definitions of an enemy. In environments of fear especially, vague allusions, rumors, and urgent tones of voice can serve as powerful provocations. These linguistic and paralinguistic vehicles of incitement may influence social actions without causing them. Indeed, the ad hoc tribunals have recognized that the causal connection between emotional speech and political acts is often less "direct" than the Convention's definition allows. To explore the affective complexity of incitement, I begin with a case that worked its way through Canadian courts between 1998 and 2003.

One week after Rwanda's President Habyarimana spoke in neighboring Ruhengeri to denounce the Arusha Accords, and seven months after the largest pregenocide massacre at Bugesera—Léon Mugesera delivered an impassioned speech in a western Rwandan village calling for vigilance. Mugesera, an official within Rwanda's then-governing party, the Mouvement Révolutionnaire National pour le Développement et la Démocratie (MRND), assembled a litany of observations, anecdotes, and arguments concerning recent political events. He spoke of the need to bring to justice all RPF collaborators, including the prime minister and those who had sent their children to fight for the invading RPF forces; unjust actions taken in Kigali by an opposition party official to discipline school inspectors working for the MRND; the illegitimacy of the Arusha Accords and international diplomatic efforts undertaken in Brussels by opposition parties; the resistance among opposition parties to immediate elections; and attacks on MRND members at a nightclub in Kigali.[40] In the following weeks, the speech was rebroadcast on radio, published in one newspaper, and discussed by leaders and intellectuals in Kigali.[41] Just two months later in nearby Gisenyi, a large massacre killed approximately 300 Tutsis. Human rights groups and other observers quickly highlighted his speech as a key moment in the prelude to violence in 1994.

Mugesera fled to Canada in 1992, where he then faced deportation as an accused inciter of genocide. He was ultimately found guilty of inciting genocide by the Supreme Court of Canada, which ordered that he be deported in accordance with both Canadian and international law. He was deported on January 23, 2012, and is now the first high-profile figure to stand trial for genocide within Rwanda's domestic courts. Before the Canadian Supreme Court's ruling, however, lower courts and the Ministry of Immigration's own bodies for adjudicating deportation cases deliberated over the nature of incitement to genocide. In 2003 a federal appeals court in Quebec offered a remarkable and telling judgment in Mugesera's favor. The case is worth closer scrutiny for what it reveals about the complexity of incitement through political speech.

Mugesera was acquitted at the appellate stage because the appeals court misunderstood the speech's affective potency. The court maintained that the only way to determine his responsibility was "by establishing the meaning of the speech itself."[42] Lawyers and experts thus attempted to reconstruct the definitive meaning behind each of its statements. Based on this analysis, the court reached some surprising conclusions: that Mugesera had used the word "Tutsi" only once and not in a way that represented Tutsis as a group; that the "we" on whose behalf he spoke were the citizens of Rwanda; and that the enemies to which he referred (the "Inyenzis") were "aggressors from abroad" and did not include Rwandan Tutsis. The court deemed the speech a provocation to self-defense but not an incitement to genocide. The exoneration stemmed in part from the court's unwillingness to consider the speech's emotional context as a legally relevant matter. While it is true that Mugesera does not explicitly target Tutsis, his calls to action would have been applied according to sentiments and prejudices circulating at the time. Although the Canadian judge laments that his expert witness missed Mugesera's "extreme language," his judgment is unable to account for the speech's peculiar force.[43]

Despite its efforts to parse the exact meaning of the speech, the appeals court was unable to capture the extent to which its factual content worked in tandem with emotional currents. The speech's emotional dimension is twofold. First, it incorporates vague and suggestive allusions whose ambiguity appeared to augment rather than temper its audience's fears. Alongside his references to the military force invading Rwanda, Mugesera makes a casual reference to those "people living among us" who also represent a threat, or who act as "accomplices" to the invading forces. If Mugesera meant to identify only outsiders as a threat, he would not state that "these people should begin leaving while there is still time and go and live with their people, or even go to the 'Inyenzis.'" By underspecifying the enemy in this suggestive manner, he creates space for listeners to apply the general argument to whatever fears, sentiments, and memories circulated locally. To speak explicitly of "Tutsis" would introduce an abstract category rather than resonate with local fears; like other extremists, Mugesera well understood that the latter had greater mobilizing potential. The speech contained enough literal material to crystallize fear, but not so much that it impaired the imaginative application of that fear to the most broadly conceived enemy. Because the power of the speech lay partly in what it left unsaid, focusing on its explicit content misses the emotional potential involved.

After considering more closely the "social and historical context" of Mugesera's speech, Canada's Supreme Court overturned the judgment of the federal appeals court.[44] Mugesera did not offer a detailed plan for killing Tutsis, but direct instruction was not necessary at that time and place. Speaking of a political opponent, for example, he offered a thinly veiled threat to expel him to Ethiopia "by the Nyabarongo [River]." Alluding to the Hutu Revolution of 1959, which had failed to eliminate "political" adversaries, Mugesera spoke of "the mistake we made in 1959." Here, the reference to 1959 was a sufficient substitute for overt identification of Tutsis. The Supreme Court concluded that no listener would have failed to see that the invading "Inyenzis" repeatedly cited by the speech were Tutsis: that is precisely how these forces had been popularly perceived since 1959. The idea of an unfinished conflict was vaguely expressed but nevertheless widely understood. Alongside the speech's explicit statements, parsed so clinically by the lower court, there was an implicit thread of emotional allusions that resonated with fears, memories, and prejudices. Mugesera's responsibility for incitement rested on his statements but also on inferential evidence that he had diagnosed and appealed to these affective circulations. By abstracting the meaning of the speech from the "psychology of [its] hearers," the lower court had missed these connections.[45]

In addition to this affective power of ambiguity, the speech also adopted a tone of urgency capable of provoking powerful emotions. Mugesera repeatedly urges his listeners to "rise up!," "wake up!," and "unite!" Over and over, he posits a central imperative: "Do not let yourselves be invaded!" "This," he declares, "is forbidden!"[46] The Supreme Court recognized from the start that a speech must be interpreted both in relation to its audience and "the manner and tone used." Even the federal appeals judge conceded that he "would have preferred that the brutality of certain passages be made clearer" than the court's linguistics expert had done.[47] Mugesera had, he noted, chosen "extreme language that appeals to the imagination." And yet the "gentler reading" prevailed, and Mugesera's intent was determined to be advocacy on behalf of immediate elections, but not incitement to genocide. The case raises a significant problem for jurisprudence concerning the crime of "direct and public incitement to commit genocide," since it faces a higher threshold for establishing responsibility than the sociology of political speech recommends. Indeed, the ICTR has recognized this very problem, noting in its so-called media trial that "the tone of the statement is as relevant to this determination as is its content."[48] As practitioners of international criminal justice move toward more flexible legal treatments of incitement, the emotional tones of political speech are becoming a timely area of study.

The neuroscience of emotion demonstrates how tones of voice help to facilitate the process of emotional stimulation discussed in earlier chapters. Research in sociolinguistics has noted the importance of gesture and other "nonverbal" dimensions of language; hand and facial gestures, far from optional enhancements, are integral to human communication.[49] Recent studies in neuroscience suggest that tone of speech and other elements of prosody are also important vehicles of emotional expression. "Prosody" as it is used in this literature encompasses various paralinguistic elements of speech, such as loudness, pitch, rate, stress, and tone of speech.[50] As we listen to others speak, the brain's capacity for emotional simulation is triggered by these paralinguistic factors.[51] Because human brains and bodies are equipped with these diverse sensory capabilities, the social transmission of emotion needs to be understood as multimodal. The emotions in a given environment circulate through combinations of facial expression, hand gesture, tone of voice, and other paralinguistic channels accompanying the linguistic content of speech. Prosody cannot be separated from explicit, verbal dimensions of language or be disqualified as inherently less significant. In the complex world of political speech, tone is integral to emotional potential.

This neuropolitics of incitement can help to explain the much-discussed role of radio and other forms of mass media in the Rwandan genocide. The contribution of the media was confirmed in 2003 when the ICTR found owners and broadcasters criminally responsible for incitement to genocide. The earliest efforts at incitement were made late in 1990 in Rwanda's most widely read newspaper, *Kangura*. The paper published the much-discussed "Hutu Ten Commandments," a catalogue of reasons to fear Tutsis, both outside and within Rwanda. The document tapped into existing prejudice, forging a moral, political, and cultural equivalence among different groups of Tutsis: militants in the RPF, civilians in present-day Rwanda, and all those who held positions of privilege and power in prerevolutionary Rwanda. The document's aim was to spur complacent Hutus into fear and, through fear, vigilance: "The enemy is still there, among us, and is biding his time to try again, at a more propitious moment, to decimate us."[52] Versions of the same message appeared in issues of *Kangura* over the following four years. Radio, too, contributed to the process of incitement. Beginning July 1993, the radio station Radio et Télévision Libres des Milles Collines (RTLM) broadcast racist propaganda similar to that of *Kangura*. These and other media communications circulated a vicious and suggestive discourse; they not only encouraged ethnic and racial hatreds but also, and perhaps principally, instilled fear among Hutus.[53]

While the evidence of propaganda from this period is profuse, it remains unclear how widely known it was among ordinary Rwandans. Straus has recently argued that the importance of mass media has in fact been exaggerated. Based on survey and interview research, he shows that fewer than 3 percent of genocide perpetrators were even aware of the "Hutu Ten Commandments." Only 15 percent attributed their participation to radio broadcasts. As Straus emphasizes, Rwanda is a predominantly rural society, and most perpetrators lived in rural areas. The propaganda circulated by *Kangura* would have been well known to the educated elite in Kigali, but its influence beyond that was likely limited. And while Rwanda's radio audience was much broader, many accounts of the genocide have been too quick to presume a causal connection between exposure to radio propaganda and participation in the killing.[54] Straus makes a powerful case for a more systematic, interview-based account of what motivated individual perpetrators.

Research on emotion and prosody suggests, however, that not all affective dimensions of speech are consciously understood by its audience.[55] We can thus reassess the effects of radio broadcasting by situating the content of broadcasts in relation to their tonal qualities. Some observers have tended to assume that RTLM listeners were passive recipients paralyzed by a "stupefied fascination" or "blind obedience."[56] As with the Mugesera speech, however, the process of reception is more complex than such statements suggest. Starting in late October 1993, broadcasts shifted from mostly music to political commentary. News reports and call-in shows sought to relax and ingratiate listeners at the same time as elicit anxiety and seriousness of purpose: "Although punctuated with good humor, the shows were usually serious in content and intense in tone, and often engendered heated debate."[57] Radio personalities grafted their broadcasts onto familiar, everyday forms of public exchange. As a former director of Radio Rwanda explains: "The broadcasts were like a conversation among Rwandans who knew each other well and were relaxing over some banana beer or a bottle of Primus in a bar."[58] Warnings of violence were conveyed upon a tone-induced foundation of trust and conviviality. Radio communications thus became integral to a casualness about violence—what de Lame has termed the "extreme banalization of cruelty."[59]

The jurisprudence of the ICTR has recognized the importance of these tonal qualities. In a 2003 judgment in *Prosecutor v. Nahimana*, the Tribunal concluded:

The power of the human voice . . . adds a quality and dimension beyond words to the message conveyed. In this setting, radio heightened the sense of fear, the sense of danger and the sense of urgency giving rise to the need for action by listeners. The denigration of Tutsi ethnicity was augmented by the visceral scorn coming out of the airwaves—the ridiculing laugh and the nasty sneer. These elements greatly amplified the impact of RTLM broadcasts.[60]

The tribunal's assessment confirms the importance of tone but also treats it as a supplementary "amplification" of broadcasts. This formulation warrants two caveats. First, the research on emotional expression suggests that prosodic elements of a speech are parallel rather than subservient to its intended verbal content. Given the content of RTLM broadcasts, and given the tribunal's forensic objectives, it may make sense to privilege verbal components of speech in this manner. But a neurosociology of this phenomenon recognizes that emotional speech combines verbal and nonverbal elements into a compound, multimodal expression. Second, the power of the words used in radio broadcasts was not only enhanced by tone but fundamentally constituted by it. The informal tone of broadcasts lowered expectations about the veracity of their content. This familiar and relaxed ambiance released broadcasters from any obligation to verify the content of their reports.[61] News stories were often entirely fabricated, and few listeners would have had access to alternative sources that might disconfirm false reports. Radio broadcasts circulated suggestive rumors whose veracity was possible but yet to be confirmed; the ambiguity of these speculations helped to motivate listeners to seek out their own reasons to contribute to the task of killing.

Emotions and the Crowd

Nationalist and genocidal discourse is thus a multifaceted emotional phenomenon. Emotions travel through verbal and nonverbal elements, and speech combines familiar myths with emergent symbols and ambiguous forms of expression. Together, these features maximize the potential for a presentation to resonate with a wide audience. Moreover, and as the example of reburials suggest, all of these discursive interventions are not passively consumed by audiences but actively received by participants. Standard accounts of manipulative leaders inciting nationalist hatreds tend not to attribute causal significance to popular modes of receptivity to official discourse. Political actors do not generally consume political speeches through a calm, philosophical reading of printed texts. Instead they participate in political demonstrations, attend sporting and other cultural events, and watch television news with friends and coworkers. In the case of Rwanda, radio broadcasts were integral to new forms of social interaction—"listening groups"—that may have shaped the way political speech was internalized by audience-participants.[62] Members of the Interahamwe militias were exposed to radio invective not in the privacy of their homes but at checkpoints and on group patrols. Investigating the participative dimension of political discourse offers a more nuanced understanding of how and why elite interventions acquire power.

The four years prior to war in Yugoslavia showcase the importance of lived participation to nationalist mobilization. Many assessments of this period focus on the content of political speeches, or on documents such as the provocative memorandum of Serbian Academy of Sciences and Arts. But the period beginning April 1987 also involved an intensification of public events attended by ordinary people. From football matches and spontaneous street protests to highly organized political rallies, cities across the former Yugoslavia hosted new forms of social interaction with great emotional potential. These events created opportunities for the kind of face-to-face participation that microsociologists consider ripe for emotional entrainment and that research in neurobiology suggests might facilitate emotional contagion. Members of an audience are exposed, together, to the emotions expressed in a political speech. Moreover, those who attend such events display their own emotional expressions to coparticipants. In prewar Yugoslavia, the impact of these face-to-face interactions was further extended by television coverage that distributed emotional arousal to a broad audience of mediated, non-copresent participants. Together, direct and mediated forms of interaction supplied venues for the sort of affective simulation discussed in chapter 1.

During 1988 and 1989 Milošević used a series of rallies to ignite the fiery politics of ethnic nationalism. These began in Kosovo but spread to Vojvodina and Serbia, then Montenegro, and Slovenia. Dubbed "meetings of truth" and "happenings of the people," the rallies were a key dimension in Milošević's campaign to undermine pro-Albanian (and pro-Yugoslav) leadership in Kosovo. The first demonstrations, held during the summer and early fall 1988, were set for Novi Sad and several Serbian towns, viewed as hospitable environments in which to cultivate anti-Albanian nationalism. Only after a series of rallies of increasing intensity did the communist leadership in Vojvodina finally resign. Just a day later, the first of numerous rallies was held in Titograd in an attempt to generate a similar concession from the Montenegrin leadership. In this case, too, an escalation of pro-Serbian public protest led to the resignation of pro-Yugoslav leaders in January 1989. The rallies formed part of a systematic political campaign to gain control of a majority of the seats in the eight-member Yugoslav Federation.[63]

As these rallies contributed to the complex emotional climate of pre-war Yugoslavia, they also, however, involved an unplanned escalation of emotional expression. On one level, the meetings celebrated well-known symbols of the Serb nation. Even as the demonstrations migrated beyond Kosovan soil, the "Kosovo problem" remained their focal point and nominal source of inspiration. Speakers claimed that Albanians, unfairly rewarded under policies of decentralization in effect since the mid-1970s, were discriminating against the Serb minority. They routinely alluded to the historic significance of Kosovo in Serb folklore, pledging that Serbs would not stand to lose Kosovo.[64] Yet, the result of the rallies was not limited to the expression of nationalist symbols and ideologies: public meetings siphoned a wide range of popular emotions into the absorptive politics of nationalism. Participative events activated memories and symbols in ways that invested ethnic identities with popular energy.

These creative processes became especially apparent as nationalist mobilization converged with the politics of economic disillusionment. During 1988 and 1989, economic deprivation had sparked a wave of strikes and demonstrations in several parts of Yugoslavia.[65] Factory workers in Montenegro and Vojvodina instigated a number of demonstrations. Disputes arose between relatively well-off bauxite miners in Eastern Bosnia and the poor and unemployed of neighboring towns who wanted a stake in the wealth.[66] In Kosovo Albanian miners were pushing Belgrade for greater autonomy and economic security. On November 17, 1988, as Serb leaders were preparing to recognize the negotiated resignation of two Albanian leaders who were continuing to support Titoist federalism, a group of disgruntled Albanian miners from Trepča marched thirty miles to Pristina to ignite mass protests. But, as several secondary accounts confirm, they were not motivated by anti-Serb nationalist ideology; indeed, protestors in Pristina reportedly chanted "long live the brave Serbian people."[67] Reports reveal instead the centrality of honor and despair: the miners felt passionately that their actions were in defense of truth, but had little optimism that reform would be achieved. The depth of the Trepča miners' moral commitment became clear as they initiated a hunger strike on February 20, 1989; some threatened mass suicide if the strike was ended by force.[68] The strikes were dramatic and public displays of various emotions—honor, despair, and anger—seemingly disconnected from ethnic hatred.

The confluence of economic deprivation and ethnic nationalism seems perplexing until we consider the emotional exchanges involved. Although nationalism alone did not promise a direct remedy for economic troubles, the former gained popular enthusiasm from the economic protests coursing through the Federation during this period. Emotional events became sites of the "excitation transfer" described in theories of social psychology. Circulations of affect were decoupled from the economic struggles that inspired them and instead plugged into the absorptive politics of ethnic nationalism. Historical narratives of economic discrimination arguably helped to legitimize the transfer of affect into ethnic politics, but the emotions involved did not originally take the form of ethnic hatred. The conflict thus exhibits some of the tendencies cited by Deleuzian and other cultural theorists. In affectively dense environments, emotions tend to migrate across social fields, objects, and actors; as Ahmed describes it, affect moves "sideways" from its initial object of elicitation to some acquired target.[69] Emotional events permit fugitive connections across fields that appear separate by cognitive standards.

Beyond Kosovo, the miners' protests sparked a cascade of emotional ripple effects. As the massive pro-Milošević demonstration of November 19 (one day after the first strike and march to Pristina) suggested, these actions energized Serb fears. The November 19 rally was the first at which Milošević himself spoke and was allegedly intended to be the end of the 1988 "meetings of truth."[70] While Milošević was by now comfortable with the emotional energy of Serb nationalism, the next few months would make it clear that he and his organizers exercised no monopoly on popular emotion. As the miners' strike in February prompted Belgrade to send troops into Kosovo, Slovenes responded by expressing support for the Albanians at a gathering in Ljubljana. Following televised coverage of the rally, a group of Serbs responded in kind. The broadcast "sent electric jolts through Serbia," provoking a spontaneous rally of as many as one million anti-Albanian Serbs in Belgrade the following day. The Belgrade demonstrators called for the arrest of Azem Vllasi, one of the Albanian leaders who had been forced to resign and whose reinstallment was being demanded by the miners. At this stage, however, the protestors had no clear connection to nationalism; as the head of Belgrade TV explained, they "were upset for no clear political reason apart from one transmission from Slovenia where they had heard so much abuse against themselves."[71] These unplanned ripple effects show that circulations of affect were not confined to the time and space of single events. Crowd activities were connected by a chain of affective reverberations.

Efforts at nationalist mobilization are thus qualitatively and quantitatively altered by the lived events and practices present in a given sociocultural environment. Through events such as the Trepča strikes, the November 19 rally, the Ljubljana meeting, and the February 28 protest in Belgrade, the politics of ethnic nationalism absorbed an array of popular humiliations, frustrations, and tensions. Each event refueled circulations of affect with more energy but also inflected them with an array of different memories and emotions. Ordinary people did not evaluate new political movements as logical propositions but absorbed them in and through everyday interactions. Not all these social interactions were new; indeed, some were embedded in long-standing rituals. Čolović has argued, for example, that popular enthusiasm for nationalism and tolerance for violence emerged in and through attendance at sporting events. Football hooligans in Serbia, like their counterparts in Italy and Britain, had developed what Čolović calls a "sub-culture" of "alcoholism, barbarity, vandalism, madness, free sex and a pornographic vocabulary."[72] As football matches became imbued with interethnic rivalry during 1990 and 1991, these dispositions seeped into the politics of nationalism. The affective transfer between football hooliganism and nationalist violence does not detract from the responsibility of those such as Željko Ražnatović ("Arkan"), who organized the use of football clubs as paramilitary organizations. But tracing these circulations of affect does help to explain how and why their efforts succeeded.

The cascade of public events prior to war in Yugoslavia demands a reassessment of elite mobilization. Milošević, Tudjman, and various other leaders played a vital role in orchestrating rallies and protests, which escalated tension and sometimes incited hatred. But, as with the conflict in Rwanda, we need to reconsider the kind of force these mobilizing efforts had in Yugoslav society. Elite interventions are only effective where they resonate with social emotions and memories. The latter are the product not only of the nationalist ideology expressed at public gatherings but also of the expressive and performative practices that accompany the rhetoric of nationalism. Because some crowd activities reveal instead a more experimental process, the question of whether support for ethnic nationalism was "planned" or "spontaneous" needs to be reconceptualized. Commentators with various political agendas have sought to discredit mobilization seen to be orchestrated from above: if the event is planned, it is elite-driven, merely political, and not an authentic expression of popular sentiment.[73] Milošević's "meetings of truth" have attracted the most attention in this regard, appearing to many observers as the product of internal party disputes, constitutional revisions, and other "elite" issues.[74] But even these orchestrated events flowed from a more experimental process, and we cannot therefore assume that Milošević and other elites were consistently aware of which symbols and myths held emotional potential.

The early stages of nationalist advocacy in fact suggest that Milošević was not the passionate nationalist he was later taken to be. Milošević first articulated his defense of Serb minorities in Kosovo at a meeting with local Serbs in Kosovo Polje in 1987. The televised event galvanized him as the de facto leader of Serb minorities in Kosovo but also Bosnia-Herzegovina and Croatia.[75] Milošević was later embraced for having taken "resolute action" on behalf of Serbs. More fine-grained accounts reveal, however, that the trip to Kosovo was not motivated by a desire to support Serb nationalism. At an initial meeting with Serb leaders, Milošević only agreed to return in several days for a town-hall event. At the later meeting, he unexpectedly confronted an organized demonstration of 15,000 protestors. As the crowd's energy escalated, protestors began throwing stones at Albanian police. When informed of the situation, Milošević delivered a seemingly impromptu address outside the meeting hall. It was then that he uttered a sound-bite widely televised by the Belgrade media: "No one should dare to beat you!" The response was electric: The crowd began shouting, "Slobo, Slobo." His "partially prepared and partially intuitive" address became the focus of intense media hype, and it made Milošević the new, accidental leader of Serbian nationalism.[76]

While Milošević clearly recognized the political value of his relationship to the Kosovo question, his commitment to Serb nationalism was remarkably lacking in enthusiasm. His response to the crowd at Kosovo Polje contained no specific promises and only restated to the crowd what he took to be its own demands: "I don't suggest that you stay, endure, and tolerate a situation you're not satisfied with."[77] Not only were his statements vague, his demeanor was far from what one would expect from a speaker offering "resolute action." Observers present at the event noted that Milošević had been "pale and shaking," "visibly upset, physically shaken, and trembling." Television clips show him paused before the crowd of protestors, listening passively and without visual response to their complaints, interjecting with only vague pledges of support. Milošević was not offering a coherent and forceful platform for Serb nationalists but channeling the expression of popular energy. The speech was not, as an instrumentalist account might suggest, "aimed at the people's emotions"; on the contrary, those emotions were aimed at it.[78] While, Milošević later became a key spokesperson for Serb nationalism, his efforts rarely displayed charisma and conviction. With his vague promises and reluctant energy, Milošević represented instead something more like a conduit for collective anxieties, fears, and frustrations.

Even later speeches betrayed elements of emotional experimentation. The climax of nationalist demonstrations was a stage-managed celebration of the 600th anniversary of the Battle of Kosovo on June 28, 1989. Although one source suggests that Milošević had by then "become routinized into a systematic formula of mass political mobilization that left very little to chance," the affective potential of this event is notably disconnected from the content of his speech.[79] Milošević alluded repeatedly to the events of 1389, when the Serb nation allegedly entered a long period of suffering and humiliation at the hands of its enemies. Like Mugesera, however, he remained intentionally vague in describing purported enemies. After the events of 1987–89, the 1–2 million Serbs in attendance—and those who viewed the speech on TV—would very likely have regarded Kosovo Albanians as among the enemies of Serbia.[80] But Milošević's formulation placed no limit on the potential list of Serbia's enemies; they could be Albanians but also Croatian nationalists, Islamic fundamentalists, or the family next door. He described present-day enemies only in vague and confused terms, alluding to an unstoppable "wave of suspicions, accusations and intolerance" that had recently heightened ethnic tensions. Milošević concluded that, while "armed battles" had not been used, "such things cannot be excluded yet." Since the speech never declared a target for this possible violence, its audience would have to define the threat in whatever terms were locally most meaningful.[81]

There is some evidence also that the tone of Milošević's speeches resonated with popular emotion. The nervousness and emotional dryness that characterized his performance at Kosovo Polje was not simply a political immaturity to be overcome but a lasting feature of Milošević's populism. Even at the June 1989 event, Milošević's performance was remarkable for its ordinariness. He read the speech word for word and his delivery lacked the fiery enthusiasm often associated with nationalist mobilization. Moreover, the speech contained no explicit call to arms. Asked by prosecutors at the ICTY about his statement concerning the coming of "armed battles," Milošević argued that he was merely reporting on the continued existence of political contestation in the "modern world." It was, he argued, "an ordinary type of sentence that everybody uses today."[82] There is some truth to this claim, and it reveals something important about the tone of Milošević's populism. His popularity appears to have stemmed less from boldness or confidence than from banality. Milošević's performance succeeded by mirroring the sentiments circulating among Serbs—including humiliation, confusion, and powerlessness. One Serbian journalist and commentator offers a telling assessment:

Milošević easily and naturally fitted into the majority "ambience," into the dumb mind-set of the Majority, by slyly insisting, in the stages of consolidation of his power, on sending, through every gesture and word, conduct and appearance, a coded message to the "people": I am one of you, you like me for in my contrived greyness—both physical and spiritual—you recognize a somewhat more "sophisticated" version of yourselves.[83]

These speculations suggest that Milošević succeeded in part by emulating the habits and moods already circulating in Serbian society. His brand of populism rested not on fiery provocations but on reflecting—in his halting gestures, vague statements, and flat tones—the sentiments prevailing within his audience. Even as that audience "appeared wildly eager to follow their determined new leader," they related on a nonconscious level to his own hesitations.[84]

Conclusion

Ethnic conflict is the product of powerful emotions, but the latter are neither hardwired cultural sentiments nor individual feeling-states. Circulations of affect occur when individuals coparticipate in social interactions of various kinds: demonstrations, rallies, radio and television broadcasts, football matches, and reburials. These events are more than products of identity-based mobilization; they are participative endeavors that generate new patterns of collective emotion. These surges of affect can in turn lend energy to the symbols and identities of the nation. By investigating the emotional interactions and rituals that become associated with ethnic conflict, we learn something new about the politics of identity. In the Yugoslavia of the 1980s, ethnic identities were reinvented and infused with popular aspirations to political and economic stability. In the period leading up to genocide in Rwanda, "Hutu" and "Tutsi" existed as virtual communities of fear more than cognitively recognized identities. The names used to talk about identity too often obscure the affective processes comprising collective agency. These processes turn out to be broader and more varied than we might glean from explicit discourses concerning resentment or hatred toward out-groups. The emotions associated with violent conflict extend beyond these initial suspects and include economic grievances, historical memories, local jealousies, and the abundant anxieties and insecurities associated with "fear." Tracing these circulations of affect helps to illuminate the multidimensional genesis of violent conflict in multiethnic environments.

Doing so also suggests the need to reassess the phenomenon of political mobilization. By looking first at circulations of affect and secondarily to the contributions of individual actors, my approach generates a new picture of who is involved in the politics of nationalism, what kind of influence they have, and how their efforts are affected by socially circulating emotions. Treating emotions as transsubjective, social phenomena enables an alternative to rationalist accounts focused on the willful manipulation of intentional agents. Through coercion, persuasion, and symbolic politics, elites play an important role in precipitating conflict. As the UN tribunals for Rwanda and Yugoslavia have aptly demonstrated, many individuals bear criminal responsibility. At the same time, however, we underestimate the potency of elite mobilization if we subtract the emotional contexts in which it becomes effective. Circulations of affect exist wherever groups of people interact, and elites multiply opportunities for interaction and plug the resulting emotions into new political projects. But the degree of control leaders exert on the objectives and outcomes of popular affect should be assessed empirically and not presumed in advance.

One place to view the payoff of an affective approach to ethnic conflict is the politics of speech. Cultural studies have rightly examined the content of official speeches, government documents, and other discursive vehicles of ethnic identity. But we still lack a full understanding of the many levels on which these discourses affect political action. Verbal content is undeniably part of their power, since it involves narratives, myths, and other social constructions of ethnic identity. The speeches of Milošević, Mugesera, and others suggest, however, that verbal content is often more ambiguous than it seems at first, and this ambiguity appears to be integral to their emotional potential. Further, there is a strong theoretical basis for tracing this emotional potential back to various paralinguistic elements of political speech. In contexts where impending conflict is widely known and tensions are mounting through other social events, the tone of speech may work alongside its content to endow violence with urgency, moral acceptability, or banality. While neuroscience has yet to address large-scale social violence, its broader findings on topics such as the role of prosody in emotional expression can help to define new directions for future research. While this chapter is not itself a neuropolitical study of ethnic conflict, it does confirm the need for one.

Contrary to standard images, ethnic conflicts are products of intense creativity more than either emotional campaigns or instinctive animosities. While constructivist accounts of nationalism often acknowledge the power of narrative, myth, and symbol, they tend to miss the creative syntheses through which these become fused to new objects of mobilization. In environments of emotional upheaval, affective energies can become attached to unexpected objects. By permitting political projects to resonate with a wide variety of local sentiments, ambiguous political speech can have emotional effects that exceed the intentions of its author. Social interactions give rise to shared emotions that become available for a variety of possible projects. Circulations of affect, because of their flexibility and ambiguity, forge connective tissues between locally generated sentiments and the larger political movements advocating violence. The process is less a repetitive cycle of hatred than a creative synergy of affective dispositions circulating in a given social context. "Hatred" may be useful at times as a manner of speaking, but the category cannot underpin an effective sociology of emotions. By uncovering a broader range of mixed emotions involved in violent conflict, we are in a better position to locate responsibility and to assess possibilities for social recovery. I turn to these tasks in the following chapter.

FIVE

Justice beyond Hatred

While the previous chapter shows that emotions can play a creative role in violent conflict, this chapter assesses their contribution to justice after conflict. At the core of my analysis is a challenge to an assumption shared by many theories of transitional justice—namely, that legal and political responses must be contemplated against the possible resurgence of hatred. The idea stems from a laudable appreciation for the trauma of violence: where conflicts involve not only competing interests but also clashing identities and intense emotions, institutions concerned with justice and reconciliation must be attuned to that psychological depth.[1] Juridical processes are indeed fragile constructions in situations of powerful emotion. Too often, however, political and legal studies pair this recognition of emotional intensity with the assumption that, in conflicted societies, emotions are tightly bound to cultural identity. In this view, identities guide decisions about whom to trust and whom to fear, they permit injured groups to seek revenge upon those responsible for violence, and they dictate the terms on which social groups pursue reconciliation. By tying emotion to identity in a vicious cycle of hatred, efforts at transitional justice perpetually recreate the very emotions they seek to overcome.

The ubiquity of hatred reflects an idealized conception of identity-driven politics: clearly defined ethnic groups ostensibly locked in insidious and repetitive battles. The ethnographic research cited in the previous chapter suggests, however, that the emotions associated with violent conflict are rarely so simple. These emotions are not natural impulses but shared responses generated through coparticipation in social interactions of various kinds—from protests, demonstrations, and political speeches to television broadcasts, commemorative rituals, and cultural events. The emotions these events generate are, moreover, creative social exchanges connecting social fields that might otherwise remain distinct. Economic grievances can fuel nationalist resentments, for example, and popular fears can migrate from one source of emotional elicitation to another. Circulations of affect contribute to violent conflict, but not in predictable or direct ways. Instead of causing actors to unite with ethnic kin in pursuit of security or cultural recognition, affective circulations engender more subtle political effects, such as fueling new symbols, synthesizing emotional energy across disparate social fields, and sustaining the ambiguities on which political mobilization can capitalize. While standard accounts of conflict may find evidence of clashing, identity-bound emotions, social and cultural analysis reveals a complex phenomenology of conflict at the microlevel.

This alternative conceptualization of affect suggests that the popular emotions encountered in the pursuit of transitional justice are both diverse and mediated by social context. In Rwanda, for example, victims of rape felt genocide not abstractly—as the "intent to destroy an ethnic group"—but concretely, as a violent social practice mediated through local relationships, memories, and norms of sexuality. Returning refugees report experiences that are more complex than simple resentments: memories of violence in exile, feelings of betrayal by international humanitarian agencies, or social alienation and exclusion upon return.[2] While some emotions are organic products of everyday social interaction, others are products of government-sponsored campaigns for public awareness and commemoration. Moreover, juridical institutions can alter the intensity, significance, and profile of popular emotions: a criminal trial could, for example, augment fear by exacerbating tensions among local audiences, but so too could it transform fear into trust through public participation. This chapter is an attempt to explore how transitional justice institutions might engage productively with this complex terrain of emotional politics.

My aim is not to identify winners and losers among institutional alternatives but to reconceptualize the emotional contexts in which the full range of transitional justice institutions do their work. International tribunals, community-based courts, truth commissions, and informal/grassroots initiatives respond to the emotional contexts of violent conflict in different ways.[3] Tapping research in legal anthropology, journalistic sources, and widely available primary documents makes it possible to replace generalizations about vengeance with a varied and dynamic topography of popular emotion. And, while the statements and experiences of local populations are relevant starting points, research derived from interviews and other forms of self-reporting needs to be supplemented with historical and microsociological analysis of everyday social rituals. By assembling a broad range of theoretical resources, this chapter offers not a last word but an exploratory account of what an emotionally engaged form of transitional justice might look like.

Tribunal proceedings, truth commission hearings, and community-based trials are social events capable of engendering circulations of affect among both participants and observers. This chapter therefore treats the International Criminal Tribunals for Yugoslavia (ICTY) and Rwanda (ICTR) as social rituals with the potential to shape popular emotion in the aftermath of war crimes and atrocities. International tribunals, ambivalent about the political status of emotions, have become embroiled in some unexpected circulations of affect: strains of liberal hope and guilt in the West, as well as forms of resentment, fear, and frustration in their target societies. Quasi-juridical institutions, such as the South African Truth and Reconciliation Commission (TRC) and state-sponsored programs associated with commemorating the Rwandan genocide, have recognized the need for emotional transformation and yet have tended to bind emotions to ethnic or racial identity in a limiting way. Focusing on reconciliation between ethnic or racial groups narrows the emotions considered admissible in these venues and underestimates the affective resources available in everyday social interactions. Such limitations are also visible in the much-discussed gacaca courts in Rwanda. Although largely subsumed within Rwanda's policies of national unity, these courts had the potential to become more genuinely participatory rituals capable of transforming powerful and negative emotional energy into a public process of trust-building. Conflicted societies are emotionally complex environments; the challenge for transitional justice institutions is to develop venues and processes that give public expression to this complexity. My analysis thus calls for a piecemeal practice of social repair that builds upon local relationships and personal experiences rather than nationally orchestrated commemorations or pledges of forgiveness. Institutions concerned with reducing violence cannot afford to assume that emotions are obstacles rather than resources for justice and social repair.

Beyond "Cycles of Hatred"

Efforts at promoting transitional justice are animated by the goal of arresting cycles of emotionally induced violence. The image of emotional cycles is so integral to how we talk about resolving ethnic conflicts that it mostly goes unnoticed. When news media cite the emotional cycles fueling conflict in far-off places, the underlying image of cyclicality thus seems unremarkable. In April 1998, for example, a front-page article in the *New York Times* described a public execution of leaders convicted of playing key roles in the Rwandan genocide, attended by a large crowd said to be "gripped with blood-lust."[4] The executions were presented as symptoms of a pathological pursuit of justice that failed to translate vengeance into retribution. Those in attendance were quoted making statements such as: "They killed and they have to be killed." The account implicitly assumes that a reciprocal desire for violence is widely shared but also treats the "they" to whom vengeance is directed as self-evident. Such framings appear in scholarly discourses as well: Martha Minow, a respected and thoughtful scholar of transitional justice, quotes the *Times* article in a way that accepts and reproduces its cyclical view of emotion. "Rather than ending cycles of violence," she explains, "the [Rwandan] trials themselves seemed to observers another phase of revenge."[5] These discourses effectively install at the heart of transitional justice the task of arresting repetitive, violent behaviors among clearly demarcated cultural groups.

The idea of cyclicality not only ties violence to identity but also posits emotion as the engine of repetition. Although anger is sometimes cited, the presumed ubiquity of identity gives hatred special salience within this discourse. The result is a powerful and widespread assumption that "cycles of hatred" are the primary problem to be remedied by the institutions and organizations involved in transitional justice. Indeed, their primary goal is, as the title of one of Minow's works suggests, "breaking the cycles of hatred."[6] The idea owes some of its appeal to the literature on collective trauma, which anticipates the return of allegedly repressed aspects of emotion. Insofar as a person is unable to express or confront a traumatic experience, the unresolved emotions it generates become prone to resurfacing in the future. When a group experiences trauma, the repressed emotion is shared; as long as the community is unable to mourn or otherwise confront its trauma, the outstanding emotional baggage goes unresolved.[7] The notion of impotence in the face of emotion implies that political agency guided by some purer form of rationality might recognize the need to express and thereby transcend destructive emotions. As with the discourses on emotion discussed earlier in the book, "cycles of hatred" limits the way emotions are imagined. We cannot understand the relationship between justice and affect with these preconceptions intact.

The image of a cycle of hatred above all influences the kind of political effects we can attribute to emotions. Optimistic that cycles of hatred can be overcome by some process of retributive or restorative justice, advocates of transitional justice do not generally subscribe to the notion of "ancient hatreds." And yet the assumptions that violent conflicts conform to a pattern of repetition—and that the emotions involved in violence are the reason for that pattern—affect the way theorists and practitioners imagine the relationship between justice and emotion. Diagnosing a cycle of hatred entails, for example, a disparaging evaluation of the political agency of conflicted populations by undermining their capacity to achieve justice and social repair without external intervention. The discourse of emotional cycles is not only a theory about how human beings experience conflict but also, as Vanessa Pupavac shows, a technique of international governance. By stressing the "cycles of emotional dysfunctionalism" in a postconflict society, international agencies can justify interventionist forms of humanitarian aid and peacebuilding. Pupavac does not dismiss the reality of emotional suffering but contests the move to "[pathologize] people's unhappiness, anger and frustrations."[8] Violent conflict becomes akin to a "crime of passion" in which the perpetrators of violence experience a loss of rational competence in the face of debilitating emotions. Politically, the preoccupation with cycles of hatred implies an impoverished form of political agency necessitating external assistance.

This discourse on hatred forms the centerpiece of a specifically liberal practice of justice. A strain within the liberal tradition assumes that the only thing we need to know about emotions is that, to build a well-ordered political system, we in fact need not know much about them at all. This liberal prejudice views emotions as symptoms of impaired reasoning: as private afflictions, they should not be allowed to infect the neutral deliberations of the public sphere.[9] The flip side of the liberal view of normal political conduct is a diagnosis of abnormal conduct that points the finger at emotion. These ideas resonate with Orientalist prejudice concerning cultural and historical backwardness. The assumption is that, while modern, liberal societies mediate conflict through the rule of law, weak states and traditional cultures are mired in emotional battles over identity.[10] As long as we view emotions in these ways—as undesirable aspects of human behavior or as pathologies of a primitive society—we are content with superficial descriptions of them. Focusing on developing rational frameworks for peace and stability entails approaching emotion on a need-to-know basis. Only against the backdrop of this intellectualist strain of liberalism does the "cycle of hatred" seem like an adequate conceptualization.

The literature on transitional justice retains a subtle investment in these liberal myths. Most institutions concerned with justice or reconciliation still adhere to rarified conceptions of which emotions should be addressed and what kind of role they should play in postconflict situations. Tribunals aim to "stay the hand of vengeance" in situations where tyrants have abused power and the rule of law has failed.[11] War-crimes trials uncover acts of political violence and thereby allow conflicted societies to confront collective traumas publicly. Doing so prevents future episodes in an otherwise cyclical resort to violence. A tribunal thus promises to replace resentment with a balanced, public process of retribution: "The transfer cools vengeance into retribution, slows judgment with procedure, and interrupts, with documents, cross-examination, and the presumption of innocence, the vicious cycle of blame and feud."[12] This process remains indebted to the liberal image of emotion, as trials seek to displace emotions as legitimate forms of political agency. On the work of truth commissions and other quasi-juridical institutions, some similar assessments result. By exchanging truth for justice, truth commissions solicit the forgiveness of victims who might otherwise succumb to the desire for vengeance.[13] And they assemble a broader corpus of testimony in order to memorialize the event based on a new, more truthful, public record. Nevertheless, such institutions embark on these endeavors in order to achieve the underlying goal of arresting cycles of hatred. Viewed in terms of how they understand the emotional context of conflict, juridical and quasi-juridical models have much in common, both addressing only a limited spectrum of emotions and emotional processes.

The goal of arresting vengeance thus continues to affect the way these institutions are evaluated, and indeed the literature on transitional justice is well attuned to the risks of displacing emotion through legal practice. If not planned well, the legal process itself may begin to fuel the cycle of vengeance. Recall Minow's assessment of the Rwandan executions. She is above all concerned that institutional practices not become additional phases in Rwanda's recurrent conflict. With international tribunals, she argues, supporters of an accused leader may experience further humiliation and antagonism. These trials may induce "new waves of frustration, cynicism, disappointment, and anger." Truth commissions, by granting amnesty to perpetrators, may risk further provocation of victims' families.[14] In each case, Minow's concern is that the emotions elicited will compound the emotional loyalties and prejudices of pre-existing groups and thereby fuel the cycle of vengeance. And so abstraction draws us into an evaluative framework abstracted from the many other emotional dynamics of a conflicted society.

By placing a simple repetition at the heart of violent conflict, the discourse surrounding "cycles of hatred" risks hindering the practice of transitional justice. Violent political conflicts admittedly involve important continuities and recurrences: Conflicts in Eastern and Central Europe, for example, connect with historical antecedents in the communist era and earlier. Those in

Africa bear the marks of both colonial rule and decolonization. Treating a society as locked in an emotional cycle denies its members agency by presuming their affective capabilities are unchanging. A society may experience successive violent events, and each may involve reactivation of emotions. But, as the discussion of reburials, protests, and political speeches in the previous chapter suggests, antecedent emotions are also revitalized, reappropriated, and transformed by successive episodes. We gain analytical leverage by regarding violent conflict as original mixtures of emotion, memory, and creative rituals rather than a protracted conflict divided into repetitive phases. Understanding these contributory factors may improve the capacity of institutions to adapt to, and engage with, the emotional currents in a conflicted society.

Tribunals and the Emotional Politics of Audience

Notwithstanding liberal images of law as a realm of calm deliberation, institutions of transitional justice in fact have powerful emotional effects. A war-crimes trial, for example, is a political spectacle involving human participants, evocative crimes, and sensitive audiences. While the official goal of a criminal tribunal may be to displace emotions—by shunting personal revenge into institutional retribution—as a participative event it cannot avoid leaving an affective footprint of its own. Modifying the classic Durkheimian account of legal rituals, Mark Osiel argues that Nuremburg, Eichmann, and other war crimes trials function as secular rituals capable of promoting social solidarity. In his view, institutions of transitional justice are inherently dramaturgical, staging "cultural performances involving the wholesale disruption, self-examination, and reconciliation of a society by means of legal or other ritual procedures."[15] A war-crimes trial in this view is not just a computation of forensic evidence but a collection of social interactions among participants who advance arguments, exchange stories, and express emotions. Because the actions under consideration are intrinsically violent, contested, and traumatic, the emotions expressed can be intense and contagious. The face-to-face interactions of the courtroom are, moreover, relayed to broader audiences through television news, Internet, and word of mouth. War-crimes trials, truth commission hearings, and other practices of transitional justice are among the many social interactions that generate circulations of affect.

This emotionally engaged conception of law finds support in legal philosophies. As various scholars have suggested, legal argument and practice frequently reflect the emotional commitments of participants and evoke, in turn, strong responses among observers.[16] Deleuze traces the re-engagement of law and emotion back to Hume, whose eighteenth-century account treated justice as a mechanism for recreating a society's emotional dispositions. Reason, according to him, was not at all antithetical to emotion but in fact erected upon its calmer forms. Social institutions succeeded in establishing order in part by substituting "violent" for "calm" passions.[17] The legal process for Hume was concerned not with removing emotions but with recreating them in a manner consistent with the broader needs of society: "Passions are not limited by justice," Deleuze explains, "they are enlarged and extended."[18] In this framing, certain emotions are socially preferable to others, but purging emotion as such is no longer the guiding objective of legal practice. These ideas suggest that we regard the legal process as a series of opportunities for public expression of emotion. In American criminal courts, for example, victim impact statements have both forensic and emotional significance; as Austin Sarat explains, "Private pain and grief is heard, but it is also subject to public judgment." Because emotions are present in such legal practices, we cannot afford to assume that law operates against a "neutral, emotionless baseline."[19]

Recent war-crimes tribunals demonstrate the complexity of emotional production involved in international legal events. On the one hand, these trials generate new circulations of affect by revealing facts, airing secrets, and personalizing responsibility. An early case at the ICTY, for example, offered the dramatic confession of Dragan Erdemović, a young Bosnian Serb soldier who participated in the massacre at Srebrenica. "He recounted in chilling detail," one source reports, "how, at the age of 23, he personally killed dozens of unarmed helpless Muslim civilians."[20] In the ICTR, similar testimony revealed the extent of the killings, the breadth of complicity, and the daily horror endured by victims and survivors. Through dozens of cases, the UN tribunals have offered venues for the public exchange of emotionally charged testimony. On the other hand, these emotional expressions have circulated among broad and diverse audiences, with different effects on each. The proceedings in Arusha, for example, were received by survivors in Rwanda, by perceived *génocidaires* living in exile, and by a globally dispersed audience of human rights supporters. Similarly, the ICTY was observed by human rights advocates in the West but also closely scrutinized by Serbs within the former Yugoslavia. In each location, the courts' performances were received against a different context of pre-existing emotion. To begin evaluating the emotional product of these legal events, we need to move beyond establishing their emotionality and into an assessment of how their emotional productivity intersects with expectations and memories in different locales.

Assessing the UN tribunals across these multiple registers reveals some mixed results. While their war-crimes trials have in theory offered an opportunity for evocative, emotional performances, in practice their affective work has encountered some significant blockages. These tribunals, popular among human rights advocates abroad, have been less successful in stirring the interest of local populations in Bosnia, Serbia, and Rwanda. The result has been international institutions lacking popular support at the local level.[21] The Hague Tribunal's opening case (against Dušan Tadić), for example, is now a widely cited lesson in mismanaged media relations.[22] Western viewers became bored, and many Serbs, in the absence of accessible media coverage, could only assume that the tribunal represented Western, anti-Serb interests. The volume of forensic detail, along with the use of simultaneous translations "stripped of all emotion," led to what one observer describes as "a complete emotional disconnect."[23] Furthermore, in their earlier stages, the ICTY and ICTR both neglected to recognize public relations as part of their mandate. Under the pretense of neutrality, the ICTY made no direct effort to develop the countervailing convictions that would modify passion among Serbs—especially surrounding the issue of Kosovo. By avoiding a direct engagement with emotional context, the institution allowed Serb feelings of victimization to continue unabated. Serb nationalists, still in power until after the war in Kosovo, had successfully portrayed the ICTY in public discourse as "a political anti-Serb Tribunal, one more instrument that other nations would use to victimise the Serbs." In place of Muslim and Croat aggressors, the tribunal inadvertently affirmed the West as the alleged new source of anti-Serb sentiment. Only more recently have the tribunals worked to overcome these problems through public outreach initiatives.[24]

The tribunals' "emotional disconnect" is further illustrated by the ICTR's treatment of witnesses. Concerned with securing the necessary evidence to convict war criminals, prosecutors have appealed to survivors to provide testimony in Arusha. The tribunal has gone to great lengths to maintain the anonymity of witnesses, many of whom fear retaliatory violence for their participation. Nevertheless, the legal process has in fact compounded the suffering of victims through its public acknowledgment of stigmatized crimes. The *Akayesu* case ultimately became the first successful prosecution of rape as an act of genocide. Western feminists and human rights activists hailed the conviction as a landmark moment in the campaign to end violence against women.[25] But these jurisprudential advances had the unintended effect of intensifying the social stigma surrounding the crime of rape. Many victims of rape were either abandoned by their own family members or else demonized by their communities for involvement in a crime traditionally seen to involve responsibility on the part of the woman. Women have been ostracized for what is seen by some as a willful exchange of sex for survival.[26] In this climate, most of Rwanda's estimated 250,000 rape victims have been reluctant to speak of these crimes. The Arusha proceedings solicited testimony without altering popular sentiments about the forms of crime they adjudicate. This case highlights the tension between the hopes and expectations associated with international jurisprudence and the emotional needs and struggles of victims and local communities. The tension may not be severe enough to justify abstaining from efforts to prosecute rape cases, but it does suggest an important challenge facing criminal tribunals.

Empirical research confirms the depth of public ambivalence toward the UN tribunals. In interviews conducted in Rwanda in 2002 and 2003, one study found that most interviewees see the ICTR as having "little relevance to processes of reconciliation in Rwanda." Of the three levels of justice in Rwanda—community gacaca courts, national genocide trials, and the international trials in Arusha—the latter are routinely identified as the least likely to contribute to reconciliation.[27] Moreover, many Rwandans who are aware of ICTR proceedings have expressed resentment that the leaders of the genocide have received better treatment in Arusha than the lower-level perpetrators have within Rwanda. One author writes: "There is a deep, widespread, and understandable feeling of a dramatic imbalance between the extreme evil of the genocide and the refined judicial treatment afforded the detained leaders." In the minds of many, the international community was effectively protecting and thereby rewarding the architects of the genocide. Perhaps more significant in the Rwandan case is the fact that most Rwandans possess little or no knowledge of the ICTR.[28] In a society where illiteracy levels are high and access to mass media limited, the proceedings taking place in centralized courts are unlikely to attract widespread public attention.

Although the Arusha trials appear not to have resonated with popular expectations concerning justice, it would be premature to conclude that the tribunal's problem amounts to a failure to cultivate certain emotions, such as forgiveness, uniquely disposed to reconciliation. The lack of popular resonance is more likely a product of a tendency to underestimate the complexity of achieving justice at microlevels. While it has made important jurisprudential innovations in recognizing the crime of rape, and in broadening legal conceptions of complicity and criminal intent, the ICTR has done little to address problems facing Rwandan society in a concrete way. The genocide was, after all, a conflict involving mass participation and thus wide, ambiguous networks of responsibility. It left national courts and prisons utterly overwhelmed. Eight years after the genocide, the country's prison population remained near 120,000. Women were burdened with new obligations to visit husbands and sons in prison. The conflict left local communities deeply damaged and desperate for a public process to redress not only the high-level planning of genocide but also the local aftermath of mass violence. Popular expectations concerning justice emerged from this context, and the proceedings in Arusha offered scant remedy.

Even as the UN tribunals encountered emotional blockages among some audiences, so too did they give rise to powerful emotions for others. Enthusiasm for these institutions in the West, for example, poses a stark contrast to the tepid response within the nations they ostensibly serve. As far as human rights advocates, international lawyers, and liberal internationalists were concerned, these institutions represented an important step toward a permanent international court for trying war crimes and, especially, genocide. Although Cold War tensions put legalist aspirations on ice, the UN had by the early 1990s revisited the idea of prosecuting war crimes in international courts. In 1998 a group of 120 states voted to adopt the Rome Statute of the International Criminal Court (ICC), a permanent body for trying war crimes, crimes against humanity, and genocide. In the interim, however, events in Yugoslavia and in Rwanda prompted Western states— the United States in particular—to support the creation of ad hoc tribunals for prosecuting crimes against humanity and, they hoped, genocide. As social events, the war crimes trials in Arusha and the Hague received some of their emotional gravity from not only the nature of the crimes adjudicated but also the norms that inspired them. As Kamari Maxine Clarke writes, "the spectacularity of international justice performances are seen in their ability to go beyond the limits of national courts and responsibilities that were formerly considered the domain of sovereign states and in reassigning responsibility on the basis of growing international conventions."[29] These courts were thus inseparable from what legalists saw as an inspiring and progressive march away from unquestioned deference to state sovereignty.

The tribunals may also have had specific significance as gestures of moral redemption on the part of Western states. After pulling UN peacekeepers from Rwanda and failing to authorize a stronger intervention, and after neglecting foreign policy commitments in Bosnia, many observers in well-endowed Western states regarded the ensuing conflicts with a guilty conscience. Then–US president Bill Clinton famously offered an apology of sorts during a hasty visit to the Rwandan capital in 1998.[30] Kofi Annan, the former UN Secretary-General, made a similar pilgrimage in May 1998; after acknowledging the failings of the international community, Annan proclaimed: "the world must deeply repent this failure."[31] Set against this backdrop of grief and guilt, the emotional work of the tribunals sometimes focused less on the emotions of conflicted societies involved and more on those of the international community. In these instances, foreign journalists were quick to seize on controversial testimony. When, for example, former UN commander Major General Roméo Dallaire testified at one of the ICTR's first cases, his emotional statement was widely reported.[32] In tearful and shaken testimony, Dallaire expressed the utter incomprehensibility of the predicament he faced as head of the incapacitated UN mission in Rwanda. The attention paid to these moments confirms the speculations of those who regarded the ICTR, ICTY, or both as a "reaffirmation of the international community's own morality."[33] The ascendancy of international criminal justice cannot be separated from these shifts in global concern.

The effectiveness of international tribunals cannot therefore be understood in the abstract, and particular attention is due to the emotional contexts in which they function. War-crimes trials are emotional events that offer unique opportunities for public expression of grief, anger, and hope from witnesses and defendants. By holding individuals criminally accountable, and by displaying their guilt publicly, a trial can safeguard against perceptions of collective guilt. Ideally, such a process can amass a public record of facts and facilitate collective memorialization in ways that restore civility in the aftermath of atrocity. However, that a tribunal has the opportunity to engage in this emotional work does not mean the institution succeeds in capitalizing on it. In the case of the UN tribunals for Rwanda and Yugoslavia, legal rituals have had very different kinds of emotional impact depending on the audiences and interests involved. Serbs at home either lost interest in the proceedings at the Hague or, perceiving the institution as biased against Serbs, intensified their support for nationalism. Many Rwandans similarly remained either disconnected or fearful of the ICTR process. Meanwhile, throughout their lifespan, these institutions have served as unanticipated catalysts for global waves of enthusiasm over human rights and international criminal justice. The contribution of these tribunals to transitional justice is mixed partly because their impact has been splintered across such varied and interconnected emotional contexts.

Reconciliation and Social Repair

While criminal tribunals have had an ambivalent and hesitant relationship to the emotions they evoke, quasi-juridical institutions have been more explicitly receptive. Recognizing the shortcomings of a formal and technical legal inquiry focused on criminal responsibility, many advocates of transitional justice have looked to nationally and/or internationally sponsored commissions of inquiry, or truth commissions.[34] These institutions were first created in Latin America during the 1970s and have since been used by states in Africa and Southeast Asia. Reconciliation, as conceived by these institutions, is a social and psychological process achieved by encouraging public expression of truth. Less concerned with amassing forensic evidence and displaying strict adherence to the protections of criminal law, some commissions have exchanged judicial amnesty for truth-telling.[35] Foregoing criminal prosecution is justifiable, supporters argue, in contexts where broader goals of social healing outweigh the more narrow need for establishing individual responsibility. Criminal courts allow some victims to testify, but only where minimally necessary to secure conviction; these institutions are not specifically concerned with the participation of victims and victims' families. A truth commission aims, above all, to provide institutional space for a public exercise in healing.

The South African TRC placed special emphasis on public forgiveness and mutual understanding. It consistently recognized the emotional dimension of this reconciliation process. This aspect of its work centered on its Human Rights Violations Committee (HRVC), especially the public hearings into "gross violations of human rights." These events became dramatic rituals soliciting a public commitment to forgiveness from a broad cross-section of victims.[36] After sharing personal violations, each witness was asked if she or he was willing to forgive the perpetrator.[37] The HRVC aimed to provide what criminal justice could not: a disavowal of revenge and commitment to reconciliation. As witnesses and perpetrators told their stories, new elements of terror under apartheid were made public through widespread media coverage. Its proceedings contributed to an "on-going national drama" rather than a technical and legalistic process.[38] Rather than allow injured groups and individuals to control definitions of the past, the commission worked to express memories of apartheid in public settings devoted to the goal of national reconciliation. Some critics saw this as a dangerous process of reliving past injuries.[39] But the commission presupposed that memories would not, in the absence of public attention, automatically fade over time.

Nor would public attention to them automatically engender a return to divisive emotions; with the right atmosphere, and a consistent narrative frame, memories of pain and suffering could be redirected toward national unity and reconciliation.

While the commission made an important contribution to South Africa's historic exit from apartheid, it has faced considerable criticism over its pursuit of national unity and forgiveness. Mahmood Mamdani, Richard Wilson, and others note that it often turned away South Africans whose injuries did not meet the requirements of "gross violations" of human rights. Those who had suffered years of discrimination were not given the space to express their frustration and anger. The contentious issue of land reform was deliberately excluded from the process. Mamdani argues that a broader discourse of social justice would have held greater appeal for those whose primary concern was overcoming dispossession and securing livelihoods.[40] The language of universal sin was for many a captivating framework helping them to embrace the politics of forgiveness. For others, however, Archbishop Tutu's religious narrative of redemption suppressed the individuality of pain. The idea of a universal experience of pain—expressed by Tutu in the statement "your pain is our pain"—allowed little room for individuals to present their own framework for public expression of private suffering.[41] The result was a perception of the TRC as lacking moral authority and/or political legitimacy. The commission's discourse of benevolence and goodwill increasingly had to contend with this challenge.[42]

Institutions aimed at promoting reconciliation thus face a central paradox. They aim to facilitate recognition of and respect for diversity in pluralistic societies. But, to achieve these goals, they must construct narrative frames that restrict and essentialize the emotions, memories, and identities that can be expressed. To accomplish "reconciliation," there must be parties to reconcile. The goal of "unity" generalizes certain social cleavages awaiting unification. And so an institution must offer public descriptions of the tensions it seeks to remedy and the identities it tries to reconcile. In the South African case, the TRC unavoidably restricted the kinds of experiences and emotional memories that could be given public expression. It adopted a singular discourse of national unity that required a uniform expression of forgiveness from all victims. As critics have argued, the insistence on this discursive frame of national unity effectively marginalized those whose experiences were not as tightly governed by the violence of "gross violations" and police repression. These failures engendered an emotional consequence of their own. The institution's discourse of unity stifled popular support and weakened emotional commitment to reconciliation and forgiveness.

This paradox reflects a tension between the practice of *reconciliation*, on the one hand, and the broader process of *social repair*, on the other. Social repair involves an attempt to create anew the diverse rituals, interactions, and memories damaged during violent conflict—to "rebuild broken ties, broken communities, and broken lives." The anthropologist Veena Das approaches social repair—or, as she describes it, "the delicate task of repairing the torn spider's web"—as a process of reinhabiting the complex interactions and subtle negotiations of everyday life.[43] The politics of ethnic nationalism succeeds by concentrating diverse beliefs and emotions into exclusive, oppositional loyalties. A practice of social repair involves a countervailing effort to restore the mix of emotions that comprise everyday life; it decouples popular beliefs and emotions from the identity-based groups to which they were temporarily attached. A strategy of reconciliation, on the other hand, accepts opposing loyalties but seeks to reduce the tension and resentment that calcify around them during conflict. Reconciliation is shaped by macrolevel understandings of identity and assumes that, left to their own devices, conflicted communities will cling to bitterness, resentment, and hatred. Social repair is guided by lived experience at the microlevel, and presupposes that, while relationships, memories, and emotional circulations have been temporarily assimilated into the politics of ethnic identity, they do not belong to it naturally.

A strategy of social repair recognizes and builds upon work individuals and communities perform in routine interactions.[44] As legal scholar Roberto Unger notes, institutional experiments can gain "seductive force from their resonance in personal experience."[45] In Rwanda, for example, formal and informal networks of women have forged relationships through cooperative economic ventures and efforts to recover from sexual violence. A report published under the auspices of the Rwandan government cites examples of grassroots organizations that have successfully facilitated dialogue between women survivors and the wives of those accused of genocide. The authors explain that women's "long experiences" with resolving disputes within family and community make them "natural teachers for peace."[46] But we need not appeal to essentialist images to appreciate the specificity of women's social position following the genocide. Because more men than women were victims of the genocide, and because more men were imprisoned as suspected perpetrators (between 2 and 3 percent of genocide suspects were women), women comprised a majority of adults in Rwanda after 1994 (from approximately 70 percent immediately following the genocide to 54 percent in 2003). As such, women were propelled into new social relationships and responsibilities. In larger numbers, women (mostly widows) headed households and engaged in joint enterprises and micro-credit networks.[47] The demographics of conflict reconfigured the social dynamics of Rwandan society.

Within this modified social context, women struggled to restore daily routines and repair social connections within their communities. This work includes but is not limited to reconciliation with neighbors of opposing ethnic groups. The injuries connected to genocide were never shaped exclusively by the ethnic categories routinely cited by foreign journalists. Ethnically targeted killing was mediated by corollary disruptions to the social fabric. Many women, for example, faced not only rape and sexual violence but also the social stigma associated with a crime that was frequently attributed to the alleged promiscuity of the victim. Retreating from public venues for giving testimony on sexual violence, women have created survivors' groups, some of which cut across ethnic and social categories. In other cases, women whose husbands were killed and/or imprisoned confronted new challenges relating to property rights, home-building, and the provision of food for their imprisoned family members.[48] Grassroots organizations have capitalized upon this shared experience of widowhood to forge new arrangements for mutual assistance and economic cooperation.[49] Where these efforts have explicitly promoted reconciliation, it is through the shared realities and struggles of everyday life. Women have occupied a special position in relation to social repair in Rwanda by virtue of these concrete circumstances rather than an inherent disposition to forgiveness.

These examples suggest that the discourse of reconciliation is too tightly bound by the ethnic categories it seeks to overcome. Rarefied ethnic categories create the expectation that members of each group are united by shared cultural characteristics. And yet victims of sexual violence were stigmatized by the community as a whole, according to popular perceptions that mixed sexual norms with ethnic stereotypes. Similarly, the mostly Hutu refugees who returned to Rwanda in 1996 were greeted with hostility not just by Tutsi survivors but also by Hutus who had remained within the country following the genocide. The refugees, perceived en masse as *génocidaires*, for their part returned with memories and hopes deeply shaped by the experience of exile.[50] In some cases, these memories pertained to lost property or living conditions in internationally administered refugee camps rather than, or in addition to, the violence of genocide. Institutional practices need to penetrate beneath abstract identities to examine the various social circumstances and interactions that erode and sustain trust.

Focusing on social repair reverses the priority, implied in some approaches to reconciliation, of reflective deliberation over participative interaction. Rather than relying on an early intellectual recognition of an overarching identity or guiding ethical principle, the work of repair builds upon lived experience. More important than strengthening the rule of law is "the development of grassroots programs that facilitate interpersonal interaction." As one scholar describes in the Rwandan case, "daily actions and interactions had become a way of dealing with the past." Interactions associated with agricultural work, communal sharing of beer, co-participation in community celebrations, or assistance with illness—all of these, Ingelaere argues, "may have been catalysts in restructuring emotions and relationships." Through coparticipation in everyday tasks and social events, members of a conflicted society can build a stock of shared experiences. Appadurai sheds light on this possibility in a study of local coalitions to provide housing for India's urban poor. He emphasizes the importance of "precedent-setting" in building people's capacity to engage emotionally in a common future. As members of a community engage in acts of cooperation, they forge what he calls a "common terrain of aspiration."[51] Institutional programs and grassroots initiatives need not engage in explicit declarations of national unity or new meta-identities. The process of interacting together as a community builds trust through reciprocal display of commitment. Efforts at reconciliation may build upon these exchanges, but they are unlikely to either initiate or exhaust the work of social repair.

The theoretical resources assembled in earlier chapters can help to explain why everyday interactions are important to achieving repair. Collins, Giddens, and other sociologists have demonstrated the importance of continual interaction to the establishment of trust and solidarity.[52] Trust, in this view, consists of emotions forged through lived social interactions. It is also more than simply an intellectual belief that others will honor their obligations.[53] Trust consists of affective dispositions that cannot always be reduced to articulable beliefs. In a study of diplomatic relations, Pouliot treats trust in this manner: an "inarticulate feeling derived from practical sense." Investigating the neural processes involved in generating trust, research in neuroscience has confirmed that trust is often associated with emotional processing below the threshold of consciousness.[54] Trust involves a process of recognition that takes place through both explicit judgments of the intentions of others and implicit, gut-level assessments. These findings complement Collins's sociological account of the unconscious "rhythmic entrainment" generated through on-going interaction: "there is a very fine-grained, micro-anticipation that happens within the interaction itself . . . as well as a more long-term expectation of being able to enter into such micro-coordination with particular kinds of people."[55] The beliefs associated with a trusting relationship are thus forged through emotion-generating interactions at the microlevel.

The neurosociology of trust highlights the importance of interaction to social repair. The everyday encounters and exchanges that build trust are organic elements of social life and need not involve an explicit ideology of unity or program of re-education. The Rwandan case suggests, moreover, that such didactic efforts may in fact impede the process of repair. Reconciliation requires a paradoxical engagement with the politics of identity it seeks to overcome. And, as suggested by those who see in the South African TRC a kind of forced reconciliation in the name of national unity, the discourse on identity can interfere with the goals of social repair. Similar concerns emerge from the Rwandan case. Since the end of the genocide in 1994, the RPF-led government has pursued an active campaign of unification with the explicit intent of dismantling social attachments to ethnic identity. Each year in April, the government has exhumed mass graves and conducted public reburials; these ritual commemorations are an attempt to use the horrific memory of genocide to promote national unity. They also launched a series of mandatory training sessions or "solidarity camps" for government officials, university students, returnees, and released prisoners—combining basic military training with unity-minded civic education. But these official efforts at promoting unity have been widely perceived as politicized strategies to justify and sustain the power of the Rwandan government.[56]

Rwanda's initiatives have sought to achieve unity by overcoming ethnic identities. Nowhere is this more evident than in a government document published in 1999 under the title "The Unity of Rwandans." The document states the government's official position on the history of ethnic identity in Rwanda, which it regards above all as an invention of colonial rule. While the report acknowledges disagreement over the history of ethnic identity in Rwanda, in the end its aim is to establish a singular and authoritative account of the ostensibly unified origins of the Rwandan people.[57] Divisive tensions between Hutu and Tutsi are, it argues, artifacts of colonial intervention rather than permanent features of Rwandan culture. The argument finds some support in the scholarly literature on the colonial history of Rwanda and Burundi. Politically, however, the document has legitimized a policy of enforced unity, and this has come at a cost. As one interview-based study has shown, most Rwandans are familiar with the government's discourse on unity, and many express support for it in public. But privately its reception has been more complex. As the authors report, disagreement with official policy can be gleaned subtly, between the lines of what is explicitly said.[58]

While there is agreement over the need for unity and reconciliation, the beliefs, memories, and sentiments of ethnic division remain unaddressed.

The enforcement of unity fails in part because it focuses on ethnic identities without addressing the interactively generated emotions underpinning them. Under South Africa's apartheid, for example, racial identities were more than intellectual categories; they became embodied habits of social privilege and power. Living as a black South African meant internalizing a truncated sense of aspiration and, often, a fear of state repression. The Rwandan government's policies of unity replaced ethnically defined identities with an overarching identity based on citizenship. While these measures modified prevailing discursive categories, they left social habits of identification intact. In Rwanda, "Tutsi" was not only the subject of a rich symbolic discourse; it also stood for a range of social habits concerning recognition and privilege. As one woman from Kibuye (in Western Rwanda) states, "the ethnic label remains in people's hearts."[59] The situation is captured in a different idiom by Mamdani, who distinguishes between "cultural" identities, which are artificial and subject to modification, and "political" cleavages, which have largely remained untouched in South Africa and Rwanda.[60] Understanding the emotional depth of identity suggests another way of viewing the persistence of social distinctions in these cases. The privileges that remain are social habits that have not yet been altered by a shift in official discourse. As Mamdani explains, residual cleavages reflect expectations for "social justice" that go deeper than what has been achieved by abstract concepts of reconciliation or national unity.

These intellectual efforts at achieving national unity may not only miss but also intensify the emotions associated with identity. The pursuit of unity reflects an assumption that divisive identities should be forgotten in order to facilitate reconciliation. In previous chapters, however, I have noted unorthodox theories of memory that challenge this image of forgetting. Drawing from Bergson, the Deleuzian view replaces the tradeoff between memory and forgetting with a distinction between memory's virtual and actual modes. A virtual memory is implicit but continues to have emotional potential. Das appeals to Deleuze to show, for example, how unspoken memories of violence acquired a virtual power in the aftermath of India's anti-Sikh riots in 1984. This virtual power is made visible, she argues, through indirect forms of expression such as rumor.[61] Rather than see a simple act of forgetting, we might consider Rwanda's unification strategy as giving rise to both actual and virtual memories. While the government allows and encourages the official memory of unity, memories of ethnicity and social discord persist on an implicit level. Implicit memories are not forgotten; they are remembered in a distinctive fashion—as ambiguous, virtual circulations below the surface of public discourse. The official policy of unity did not erase memories of violent conflict and social suffering but confined them to private life. As a participant in one study explains: "We can't speak freely, only in whispers."[62]

Official policies involving suppression of identity may, moreover, create auras of power around divisive identities and memories. As Judith Butler shows, the attempt to limit public expression can inadvertently give emotional weight to that which is curtailed.[63] The force of ethnic identities as implicit memories was only strengthened by public skepticism concerning the policy of national unity. Rwanda's official efforts at promoting unity and reconciliation have failed to acknowledge the RPF's own involvement in massacres, and government-sponsored commemorations have refused to include Hutu victims in memorial projects and burial sites.[64] These and other policies have contributed to an unarticulated but pervasive perception that the government has unfairly politicized the genocide in an effort to secure international sympathies and to legitimize a Tutsi-dominated government. The sense of unresolved injustice has fueled rumors, speculations, and implicit memories of as-yet unacknowledged killings. Official efforts at suppressing a collective memory may contribute to its power as an implicit, virtual circulation. Success in social repair may therefore be impeded by certain efforts to reshape public consciousness.[65]

Conflicted societies are home to contested memories and layered allegiances, and these inflect the lived experience of violence. Social repair requires tolerating emotional plurality in the wake of violence: repairing severed loyalties; cultivating free expression of painful memories; and acknowledging the many emotional processes (resentment but also frustration, anxiety, and fear) that contributed to conflict. Efforts to force certain forms of commemoration and emotional expression can become counterproductive in this context. Both cases discussed above involved tensions between official programs of unity and reconciliation and the more organic work of social repair. The tension arises where these programs obstruct public expression of certain emotions and memories. It also happens where practices of unification or reconciliation lend emotional support to the divisive identities whose influence they seek to diminish. Because divisive identities have shaped popular understandings of conflict, efforts to erase painful emotions may breathe new life into them as virtual memories. Everyday social interactions and grassroots projects can contribute to social repair more effectively in the absence of enforced unification.

Popular Justice and the Politics of Vengeance

In 1998 the Rwandan government began exploring options for a community-based justice system to accommodate burgeoning prison populations in the aftermath of genocide. The result was a system of 11,000 "gacaca" courts hearing genocide-related cases in every local jurisdiction throughout the country between June 2002 and April 2010. Ostensibly modeled on traditional community hearings for property-related crimes, the local courts were presented as a "middle path" between a conventional criminal trial and a truth commission.[66] The courts were originally empowered with the ability to hand out all but capital sentences and try all suspected *génocidaires* except those charged with planning the killings. Beyond the practical need of alleviating overcrowded prisons, the Rwandan government saw that the gacaca system could make a valuable contribution to the work of national unification. The government had looked especially to the South African case and seen the importance of public participation to national reconciliation. Gacaca courts were designed, according to a government report, to "not only reprimand the culpable but also, and above all, to re-establish social dialogue and restore society to a firm foundation."[67] Each court consisted of a general assembly composed of the entire adult population of a local jurisdiction. Local gatherings were a form of participative justice rather than a technical process insulated from public view.

Focused on evaluating its work in practice, studies of the gacaca experiment have not generally explored the significance of its participatory objectives. A common trend among critics of Rwanda's gacaca courts has been to note the middling levels of popular participation, which many argue are the product of key flaws in the institution's design and implementation. Human rights organizations and critical scholars have variously argued that judges lack experience with criminal justice (indeed, individuals with legal qualifications were barred from participation); that few safeguards exist to protect against corruption and false testimony; that the sessions are consequently being used as platforms for pursuing grievances; that insufficient protections were available for witnesses producing testimony on sensitive topics such as rape; that cases involving land disputes, and those associated with crimes committed by the RPF, were excluded; and, finally, that the institution generally was steeped in the Rwandan government's rigid ideology of unity.[68] These are serious and widely documented problems, and there is evidence—albeit contested—that they have led to a reluctance to participate among some Rwandans.[69] However, the institution's imperfect record of public involvement only point to further questions about why and how a participatory model of transitional justice is so potentially significant for promoting social repair.

The literature on transitional justice is largely ambivalent on the merits of popular participation. Some regard direct observation of criminal trials or personal exposure to hearings of a truth commission as necessary for reconciliation. Others consider public involvement as a potential obstacle to procedural fairness.[70] Assessments of gacaca courts have often noted the additional risk of retraumatizing participants by exposing them to painful memories of violence. Local courts can, in this view, reopen old wounds, activate resentment, and undermine trust. The psychological risks of participatory justice seem undeniable in this case, and even those sympathetic with the gacaca experiment overall have documented such problems.[71] And yet the ambiguity and fluidity of emotions gives reason to pause before concluding that the negative expressions of emotion are necessarily or automatically impediments to justice or contrary to the goals of social repair. The Rwandan courts provide an opportunity to examine more closely how shifting patterns of affect might circulate in and through a participatory juridical process.

At the empirical level, there is evidence that the process began with relatively high levels of public enthusiasm. Studies conducted prior to the process and during its pilot phase indicated high levels of support for the new idea of gacaca justice, and public enthusiasm did not appear to be the product of a desire for revenge. One study suggests that 84 percent of respondents regarded the gacaca courts as likely to contribute to reconciliation.[72] Sometimes with little knowledge of the procedural details reflected in the proposals, they indicated a high willingness to participate. Another report adds that, of the almost 1,700 respondents surveyed, 96 percent declared their intention to participate in the election of judges and 87 percent were willing to give testimony before the trials.[73] Most saw the participative dimension of these courts as a benefit over criminal trials; 87 percent stated they were either "highly confident" or "fairly confident" in the success of the gacaca process. The study notes that the community-based courts "seem to kindle a lot of hope in Rwandans." Another report notes: "people were looking forward to gacaca."[74] The enthusiastic anticipation of the gacaca initiative during the late 1990s and early 2000s indicates a basis for participatory justice, even if actual attendance ultimately waned over time.

There is also reason to doubt the assumption that resentment, anger, and other negative emotions were the natural baseline for these popular justice initiatives. During early stages of the gacaca process, victims expressed a greater desire to hear truthful testimony and statements of remorse than to see punishment.[75] Perpetrators too indicated a strong desire for justice, whether out of genuine remorse or a more pragmatic desire to return to normal life.[76] Many regarded the process as having the potential to produce not just reconciliation but also forgiveness—despite the fact that this more ambitious goal was never part of the Rwandan government's official justifications for gacaca. Moreover, the emergence of unofficial forms of gacaca courts, initiated in prisons and church communities, underscores the urgency of justice in Rwandan society.[77] Many Rwandans converged on the importance of a participatory process that would solicit truth and address criminal acts in a fair and public process. Available reports suggest that, by the early 2000s, Rwandan society was less concerned with punishment per se and more with unearthing evidence to corroborate suspected crimes, exonerating those unfairly accused, and facilitating acknowledgment of individuals' suffering. Although participants arrived with different interests and experiences, many shared in this overarching desire for justice.

The empirical record aside, there is also reason to question the notion that local justice automatically retraumatizes participants by reactivating painful memories and negative emotions. While these concerns highlight some of the failings associated with the implementation of community courts in Rwanda—for example, the need to integrate counseling into the judicial process—they may also underestimate the extent to which emotions are affected by their contexts of elicitation. As Sarat notes in the context of witness impact statements in US courts, private grievances are expressed, but in a context where they become "subject to public judgment." Rwanda's community-based courts offered a similar synthesis of private memory and public judgment. Because emotions have loose, flexible connections with their contexts of elicitation, even seemingly negative emotions such as anger and resentment can be altered by the public process of giving testimony. The social climate established by juridical institutions makes it possible for participants to express many emotions that, in a different environment, might become fuel for continued conflict. Against a background of trust, another person's failure to act may be felt as a great betrayal. But where institutions create a climate of hope or a sense of fairness, a feeling of anger may contribute to solidarity rather than vengeance. Part of the value-added of juridical and quasi-juridical institutions is to couple emotions with new social platforms.

Participatory justice processes are dramaturgical opportunities to circulate and modify expressive displays of emotion, akin to the Durkheimian events theorized by Osiel. That a participant recalls an experience of suffering and publicly expresses anger as a result does not mean that she or he automatically desires revenge against a perpetrator. Moreover, the participatory dimension of local trials may give them more potential to generate shared emotions than conventional statutory courts. As participants congregate to listen to testimony from members of their community, the interaction has the potential to generate trust and social solidarity. The participative dimension of the event supplies another opportunity for the kind of organic, microlevel transformation already taking place—in the Rwandan case, through daily work, beer consumption, and other communal activities.[78] Approaching local justice in this manner does not presuppose that the content of a legal hearing is entirely amicable or magically replete with empathy for survivors and perpetrators alike. But local institutions can offer participative venues for building trust through shared emotional expression. By participating in a public ritual, people can, Osiel argues, "achieve a sense of lived experience that is mutual."[79] In this view, the lived act of co-participation yields its own social and emotional benefits, alongside whatever substantive arguments are exchanged in the process.

Understanding the affective potential of participatory courts helps to locate more precisely the "short circuits" in the Rwandan case. A juridical or quasi-juridical event can contribute to social repair by creating a climate of hope and fairness in which would-be divisive emotions can be shared publicly. Several of the shortcomings most often attributed to the gacaca courts involve limitations placed on the scope of this public participation. In this reading, gacaca courts have failed in promoting social repair not by reactivating emotions per se but by restricting their scope. Critics have noted, for example, that crimes committed by the RPF have not been addressed, that witness protections have not been secured, and that public attendance at gacaca sessions has been constrained by economic need. Each of these problems entails some restriction placed on public participation: whether witnesses or defendants, some constituency is effectively excluded from the opportunity. As Ingelaere argues, the gacaca courts never became the participative rituals of restorative justice suggested by their traditional namesake. Instead, they became a forensic pursuit of truth associated with certain atrocities and not others—and guided by the state's political agenda for promoting national unity.[80] The opportunity for restoring trust through shared participation was thus impeded by the political circumstances surrounding its implementation.

There is a crucial difference between forging trust through participation in local courts and using those courts as part of a political campaign to promote national unity. From the beginning, the Rwandan government saw gacaca sessions as public events aimed at "the rediscovery of a lost sense of

Rwandan unity."[81] The official discourse of unity treated this goal as a pre-existing cultural fact that had been obscured and undermined by political forces during colonial and postcolonial times. Participation was thus not about developing something new but returning to an older, golden age of social harmony. While many Rwandans espoused these ideas themselves before inquiring researchers, others registered deep skepticism and resentment off the record. The goal of achieving lost unity entails not only a fixed end point but also official standards by which to evaluate participation. For example, the government deemed counterproductive and illegal any resort to the use of ethnic labels in discussing the 1994 conflict. Building trust through participation, however, places fewer restrictions on popular testimony. Stories appealing to ethnic categories to describe injustices of the past, for example, become admissible contributions to a public exchange. Expressions of anger, likewise, are publicly relevant expressions of suffering rather than obstacles to procedural integrity.

While the gacaca experiment offers no model for other cases, it does highlight the importance of treating popular emotions as resources rather than obstacles in the pursuit of justice. And the specific emotions involved need not be limited to "forgiveness," "empathy," and other select responses celebrated in the literature on transitional justice. Courts can meaningfully incorporate into a public process of justice even those emotions normally viewed as disruptive. As victims and victims' family members display anger, disappointment, and resentment, these expressions inspire public support for social repair in a way that an abstract and technical pursuit of retribution cannot. These emotions are not the raw, psychological responses often associated with vengeance but ingredients in a new circulation of affect. They combine with the hope and trust established by the institutional process soliciting them. The challenge facing transitional justice institutions is to admit a diverse range of emotions and memories as eligible contributors to popular justice. Sometimes these responses map neatly onto official conceptions of identity-based injuries, as with the goal of forgiving members of an out-group. But the emotions involved in complex conflicts often tap into more layered forms of suffering, shaped not only by oppositional identities but by different experiences of violence, local narratives, and personal memories. Each victim holds a distinct "sense of injustice," and the challenge of law is to develop institutional responses flexible enough to adjust to that specificity.[82]

Critics and human rights advocates are right to have raised red flags about Rwanda's gacaca courts. And yet the broader project of restorative justice deserves some precision concerning the role that emotions do and do not play in these juridical processes. It is true that nothing guarantees that a victim's testimony is motivated by public objectives rather than "merely private" grievances and jealousies. A participative process cannot be sure, moreover, that the anger and other emotions expressed in it do not fuel reprisal attacks and further violence. But these worries become less paralyzing once we reconceptualize the way emotions function in social contexts. Critics often assume that emotions take the familiar form of hatred or anger and are by nature private and potentially disruptive, whereas the lived experience of participatory justice extends beyond the narrow confines posited within such abstractions. Anger expressed in a context of public alienation from official institutions differs from forms of anger surfacing amid a climate of hope surrounding participative justice. Transitional justice institutions should not seek to eliminate emotional expression but, on the contrary, to ensure it is not impeded by narrowly conceived political interests and discourses.

Conclusion

Too often the discourse of transitional justice assumes the need to suppress simple, recurrent, and undesirable emotions. This assumption is not confined to legalist proposals for war-crimes tribunals, as even quasi-juridical institutions are often trained on the ever-present specter of resurgent hatred. Images of emotional repetition presuppose that victims and perpetrators comprise clearly demarcated social groups: I fear revenge when I categorize others as potential aggressors whom I suspect of having a clear perception of me as responsible for their injuries. And yet violent conflicts often implicate more fluid and ambiguous emotional connections. As long as we remain fixed on repetitions, cycles, and resurgent emotions, we are poorly positioned to see the emergent, context-specific forms of popular emotion affecting recovery from conflict.[83] My concern in this chapter has been to show that promoting social repair after violent conflict can benefit from a better understanding of the social interactions and practices giving rise to circulations of affect. Juridical and quasi-juridical institutions are more than conduits for the public expression of pre-existing hatreds; they are participative events giving rise to new constellations of shared emotion. Anger and other emotions may be expressed publicly, but such responses have no necessary social profile—and no automatic affinity with a politics of revenge. Even seemingly negative emotions can be transformed through the ritual enactment of justice.

By assuming that emotions are tightly bound to ethnic and other identities, the practice of transitional justice risks obscuring the diversity of emotional experience associated with multidimensional conflicts. Theories of ethnic conflict generally aggregate individual beliefs and emotions as either products or ingredients of group identity. But emotional connections in a real-world social environment are more layered and composite than such images suggest. While macro-level theories fix on the emotions of abstractly conceived groups, institutions concerned with justice need once again to disaggregate the lived experience of violence through a public process aimed at social repair. The emotions displayed during the legal process can and should take many forms; as Minow argues, individuals are "entitled to their own reactions, whether these take the form of anger, thirst for revenge, resignation, forgiveness, hope, stoicism, pride in survival."[84] Some identify with ideologies of the nation, but many others resist official discourses aimed at mandatory unification. Some harbor memories of past injury, but these are both varied and contingent upon the context of retrieval. Some may favor a politics of reprisal, but many others, feeling either moral imperatives or just the pressure to restore social order, support formal and informal efforts at social repair. Participants in a process of transitional justice possess a multiplicity of possible responses to violent conflict, and one challenge of juridical and quasi-juridical institutions is to allow public expression of these.

To suggest that public exchanges of emotion might contribute to social repair does not require a utopian faith in the benevolence of human nature. Nor does that process require tapping into some special class of "good" emotions, such as forgiveness, empathy, or compassion, that might be uniquely disposed to reconciliation. It is only historical prejudice that creates the expectation of a neatly polarized field of hatred and compassion. In concrete social situations, popular emotions take more complex forms. A neo-Jamesian view of emotion suggests that responses to conflict are more diverse than even Minow's vocabulary suggests. For James, "revenge," "resignation," "forgiveness," "hope," and so on are only linguistic representations of a broader field of affective experience. Such categories stand in for clusters of interconnected emotional response. Approaching emotions as social circulations of affect thus replaces the hatred/compassion schema with a more diverse field of affective states and responses.

The South African and Rwandan cases underscore the emotional fragility of social repair and the importance of a pluralistic and participative approach to justice. In both cases, governments concerned with promoting national unity have pursued a mandatory discourse of unity and an emphasis on direct forms of emotional cultivation. The hearings of the South African commission often insisted on receiving explicit statements of forgiveness from those who offered testimony. The Rwandan government has appealed to a singular discourse of ethnic unity in which "Tutsi" must be understood as an artificial construct of colonialism with no political relevance in the present. Moreover, the official practice of commemoration has relied on dramatic rituals designed to promote the shock and horror seen as necessary antidotes to resurgent violence. As various critics have contended, these efforts pose serious risks for the success of social repair. Rather than promote unification, they legitimize the rumors, tacit memories, and unstated grievances not receiving official public expression. And yet there is reason to believe that social repair is possible without magnanimous gestures of forgiveness or direct, literal commitments to unity. Examining the social and psychological context of reconciliation suggests that forgiveness may require more piecemeal strategies. And these strategies are more potent where they focus less on reconstructing official identities and loyalties and more on giving expression to the diverse senses of injustices in a conflicted society.

Conclusion

Events of the last two decades confirm that we inhabit a world of emotion. Hijacking and suicide bombing, prisoner abuse, financial crises, earthquakes, and pro-democracy movements—each of these phenomena brings emotions to the fore and often distributes them globally. Such high-profile political events have roots at the microlevel, in emotion-generating social interactions such as commemoration rituals, legal processes, or political protests. Local emotion-generating events are increasingly being disseminated through communications technologies to broad, diverse audiences. The original location of emotional elicitation no longer serves as a reliable predictor of its cultural and political impact. The more we study emotional politics, the more it seems woven into the fabric of everyday life in a globalized and interconnected world. And, while emotional interactions and processes are not contained by familiar units of analysis in international relations, they have proven to be of great consequence for the actions of states. In an era where sub- and trans-national movements thrive on circulations of affect, the architects of foreign policy cannot afford to sweep emotions under the rug.

A central aim of this book has been to equip scholars interested in international conflict, and global affairs more generally, with a new conceptualization of emotion. My argument is not that emotions are ignored or neglected in the study of international politics. Indeed, certain traditions within IR theory have devoted considerable attention to emotions: the role of fear in security dilemmas, for example, or the perils of overconfidence in group decisionmaking. My concern lies instead with how emotions are conceptualized within theories that purport to study them. Too often, emotions are treated as periodic aberrations from some baseline of "rational" competency. The result is an assumption that affective motivations can be set aside by standard models of rational action. Studies of violent conflict often take emotions more seriously, but nevertheless theorize them as repetitive, psychological impulses. Such abstract models offer a weak foothold in a complex and dynamic world of emotional interaction. A wide variety of affects regularly influence the conduct of politics—by promoting the viability of norms, legitimizing power relations, alerting us to sources of insecurity, or announcing moments of injustice. As a result, taking emotions seriously demands not just adding a few new variables to the science of politics but revising its cherished foundations more deeply.

One of the key challenges in the study of emotion and politics is their accessibility to empirical investigation. Sometimes emotions are readily available at the surface of political conversation; other times they function as implicit moods running in the background. Research in neuroscience is revealing the many ways in which implicit emotions—from latent personal memories to racialized norms of social recognition—affect judgment and decisionmaking. This book maps one possible strategy for studying both explicit and implicit manifestations of emotion. Treating emotions as products of social interaction offers an opportunity to infer the presence and movement of affect by combining observation of what people say and what they do. Not all socially and politically relevant emotions are consciously felt by actors, and not all are products of strategic or intentional manipulation. Without denying that emotions are strategically appropriated in many situations, I show how intentional acts take place through and alongside nonintentional forms of emotional agency. Some effects of emotion can be detected by surveys, discourse analysis, and other conventional methods, but others cannot. This book retools IR theory with concepts and methods calibrated to the elusive nature of emotion. It offers a revised social constructivism that is equipped to study not only discourses about cultural norms and identities but also diffuse, informal, and embodied forms of affective socialization.

To support this endeavor, the book embraces a variety of theoretical resources from across several disciplines. Emotions are a multidimensional phenomenon—psychological, physiological, social, cultural, and political—and therefore demand a multidisciplinary approach. From microsociology, I extract the central insight that people exchange emotions through social interaction. By attending protests, rallies, and other political events—but also by bearing witness to a media event, political speech, or other communications event—coparticipants become exposed to shared patterns of emotional elicitation. From neuroscience, I find crucial insights into the neural basis of emotional transmission. Human beings produce emotional responses not in isolation but in social settings where the expressions of others are available for replication. Brain-scanning technologies have unveiled the sophisticated neural machinery behind this sort of emotional simulation and thereby confirmed the claim that sociologists of emotion have long noted: that emotions are expressive, public capabilities that bring individuals into contact with others. The result of these theoretical resources is a neurosocial model that complements, and also challenges, the cognitive psychology of emotion.

The book thus offers a fresh account of what emotions are, attuned to research in these adjacent fields and tailored to the study of complex social environments characteristic of global politics. I treat emotions as both psychological and social responses. Emotions are in our hearts and minds, but they also connect us to other people: emotions exist inside individuals and fill the space between them. The book thus investigates the social interactions that generate, intensify, or otherwise modify socially transmitted blocks of emotion that I call "circulations of affect." The term is less important than the idea behind it: in social contexts, emotions have a life outside the hearts and minds of individual actors; they are part of what connects us as human beings and social actors. A circulation of affect is a conscious or nonconscious transmission of emotion within a social environment. Social actors involved in these circulations may be participating face to face in a common activity, or they may be connected in a mediated fashion through communications technologies. The emotions they share are products of affective simulation across participants, as the expressive displays of one are emulated by another. Those responses are also products of parallel exposure to emotion-eliciting objects or communications, as participants listen to an evocative speech, observe a televised event, or celebrate some emotionally resonant symbol. By releasing emotion from the confines of the psyche, this book opens up a vast domain of research into the social exchange of affect and its impact on political relations.

One consequence of treating emotions as products of neurosocial exchange is that fixed emotion categories become analytically less reliable. As emotions are transferred across social settings and actors, their content and form can change in the process. Throughout the book, I have traced contagious circulations of affect in which excitation can migrate from one eliciting object to some other, seemingly unrelated one. Emotional contagion possesses specific properties that affect the form emotions take in social situations. Not all emotional exchanges can be neatly packaged into individual emotion categories, such as "fear," "hatred," or "empathy." Emotions readily change form as the individuals and groups experiencing them live through successive emotion-generating events and interactions. Fear can change objects—from terrorism, say, to rogue states—but it can also enter into synergistic relations with adjacent emotions, such as resentment or anger. There is no fail-safe way to trace these fluid exchanges of affect. My illustrative case studies, drawing on several cases of ethnic conflict and several of terrorism, combine journalistic and ethnographic materials in an attempt to reconstruct these emotional dynamics in a plausible way.

The resulting investigation persistently questions the adequacy of familiar emotion tropes. Several cases in the book require critical interrogation of images such as "ancient hatreds" or "cycles of hatred," which continue to guide conceptualizations of emotion in international relations and adjacent disciplines. I argue that these stereotypes become limiting in two ways. First, they restrict our attention to a narrow band of emotions—familiar to folk psychology but not adequate to complex, real-world environments. Hatred, anger, fear, and compassion are loud emotions that often attract public attention. One of my goals in the book is to attend also to quieter moods and background emotions—for example, enthusiasm, anxiety, or frustration—that affect political behavior without claiming the spotlight. Some emotions are easy to identify, while others are vague, fleeting, or nested within ancillary moods and sentiments. Second, these discursive representations understate the complexity of emotion by treating them as repetitive impulses rather than dynamic social responses. As long as our sights are trained on recurrent cycles of hatred, we are unlikely to see that "hatred" is in fact a shifting composite of many constituent responses. Because the affective ingredients of hatred change according to social context, the notion of repetition does us analytical disservice.

One of the book's key conclusions concerns the actors whose emotions matter in international conflicts. One approach to studying emotion in global contexts is to begin with familiar actors and then look for evidence of emotional motivations behind their conduct. Official representatives of a state, for example, are affected by powerful emotions, as post-9/11 biographies of American leaders amply attest. An institution, too, can become defined by a prevailing mood, as when the UN tribunal for Rwanda became a magnet for global humanitarian sentiment in the West. Even substate actors are sites of collective emotion: the literature on ethnic conflict suggests, for example, that ethnic groups adopt and express certain emotional profiles, such as fear of historical rivals, or hatred of out-groups. In these cases, emotions become part of the normative and cultural profile of a group; social groups conduct themselves in accordance with distinct forms of emotional agency. Moreover, standards of socially acceptable emotional display can become part of the normative context shaping official behavior. The more visible these constitutive emotions are, the more they are susceptible to appropriation by elites and other political entrepreneurs within a community. These are important locations of collective emotion and will likely continue to attract attention, quite rightly, by IR scholars.

My contribution focuses, however, on emotions less tightly connected to willful and recognizable actors. The communities united by emotion are not always coincident with states, organizations, and other formally constituted groups. We are used to thinking of "communities" as social formations rooted in geographic proximity. But, as Benedict Anderson famously demonstrated, communities are imagined through the social interactions and communications technologies of the day.[1] In the nineteenth century, those technologies were largely located within the nation; now they are digital and transnational. The result is that emotional exchanges need to be followed across conventional levels of analysis. Business networks, financial communities, diasporas, and religious movements—these are emotional assemblages with national investments but also global extension. Emotional assemblages are informal, dispersed, and emergent actors created by circulations of affect. As seemingly local interactions—from religious rituals to political protests—fuel sub- and trans-national movements, they give rise to emergent, geographically dispersed forms of collective agency.

The case studies in the book find that political problems populated by ethnic groups, nation-states, and other recognizable actors often involve such emotional assemblages. Because contagion facilitates emotional exchange across social settings and actors, it can forge new locations of collective agency. We cannot afford to assume a one-to-one relationship between familiar social groups and prevailing circulations of affect. A distinguishing feature of several circulations discussed in this book is that they bring into concert people with only a minimal conception of themselves as a group. Contrary to the accounts of Western journalists, "Tutsi" was a category employed relatively rarely within Rwandan society; what made genocide possible was not the pre-existence of strong identities but the intensification of emotions that could later be mapped onto vaguely defined ethnic and racial categories. And the war on terror activated pre-existing cultural stereotypes concerning Arab, Muslim, and Middle Eastern peoples, but it also cobbled all these together into a new, racially defined enemy. Emotional assemblages are constantly emerging around us, coming into being whenever an evocative event triggers the hope, fear, or anger of a population.

Viewing emotional associations as assemblages rather than groups helps to make sense of the social networks and movements that populate global politics in an age of digital communications. Circulations of affect are increasingly giving rise to temporary, ad hoc formations such as the Save Darfur movement, al Qaeda network, or pro-democracy movements in the Middle East. Such assemblages have unique properties—spatially dispersed, temporally localized, and organizationally informal—not well accounted for in conventional models of hierarchical, formal organizations and political units. Treating emergent groups as assemblages also helps us reduce the risk of essentializing culture. The perpetrators and victims of genocide in Rwanda, for example, are more usefully conceived as contending assemblages than as long-standing ethnic groups; they were united by temporary circulations of fear rather than durable, group-based hatreds. Scholars interested in the phenomenon of nonstate security threats but wary of the dubious association between terrorism and Islam can capitalize on this conceptual decoupling of agency from culture. Because formal actors are increasingly answering to these communications-driven and emotional assemblages, political analysis can benefit from adding them to more familiar units of analysis.

By reconceptualizing these forms of agency, the book secures a better hold on the political impact of emotion. One of my key conclusions is that emotions can have political effects beyond those associated with the willful intervention of elites. Even as leaders and activists tap into popular emotions, they rarely control them fully. The cases discussed in the preceding chapters suggest that emotional events can jump-start, accelerate, or redirect the efforts of elites and norm entrepreneurs. Neoconservatives wanted to remove Saddam Hussein from Iraq well before September 11, 2001, but the events of that day supplied the necessary affective conditions for their goals. Without the attacks, some rival policy would likely have succeeded in the marketplace of ideas and emotions. Emotions also played an important role in the ascendancy of ethnic nationalism as a normative framework in the former Yugoslavia. In a political culture previously dominated by the federalist commitment to "Brotherhood and Unity," the rise of ethnicity as a site of political loyalty was a complex product of popular unrest, impending violence, and evocative ritual. Slobodan Milošević succeeded in promoting Serb nationalism, but his movement used often experimental and tactical footholds. From the disaffections of zinc miners to the grieving families of World War II victims, a confluence of affects aided the rise of nationalism. Emotions can affect political outcomes in unexpected ways.

I trace these surprising dynamics back to the creativity of affect. Exchanges of emotion in and through social interaction allow high levels of ambiguity and flexibility. Theories of emotional contagion and excitation transfer suggest that emotions change as they travel across actors and social settings. Objects of emotion are thus unstable, as when fear migrates from one eliciting object to another, and emotions themselves often resonate with one another, as when fear amplifies sentiments of hatred. Successive emotional responses are contingently tied back to antecedent emotions and memories, creating a web of overlapping circulations rather than a clean series of stable emotions. These findings are supported in different ways by research in social psychology, microsociology, and neuroscience. The underlying idea that emotions endow human agency with creativity is, moreover, supported by a longer tradition of philosophical investigation. My theorization of creativity thus draws important lessons also from turn-of-the-century work by figures such as William James, Henri Bergson, and Théodule Ribot. Because the creativity of affect pushes at the limits of existing science, tapping into work presented in a more speculative key helps to focus theoretical inquiry on emerging challenges.

Future Research

This book advances a new conceptualization of affect and illustrates its analytical leverage through several case studies of sub- and trans-national conflict. While I offer new insights on ethnic nationalism, transitional justice, terrorism, and foreign policy, the book leaves many stones unturned. Future research is needed to extend my agenda to additional cases, both old and new. Understanding the creativity of emotional politics could illuminate some enduring puzzles. The end of the Cold War, for example, involved emotional changes that remain unaccounted for in even the most multidimensional explanations. While constructivists have argued persuasively that the winding down of the Cold War needs to be understood as the product of a new normative environment, we still have an incomplete picture of the emotional interactions engendering affective shifts within Eastern European and North American societies. A theory attuned to affect could also uncover the microlevel genesis of terrorist movements. We still know relatively little about the emotional processes that contributed to the organizational success of the 9/11 attacks. Terrorism experts have elucidated the strategic interests of al Qaeda leaders prior to 2001, but these insights tell us little about the disaffections sustaining Islamic radicalism across spatially dispersed participants.[2] The location of power and authority in global politics is not a direct function of material resources, symbolic capital, or persuasive efforts; it is instead a synthetic product of the emotional circulations with which these factors interact. My framework shows how seemingly small-scale emotional interactions can become amplified into globally visible assemblages.

One particular avenue for further investigation is in the relationship between emotions and norms. Several cases I discuss in the book reveal the importance of emotions for international and domestic norms. I find, for example, that the Bush Doctrine was more than a strategic plan for US foreign policy; it is a norm that resonated with emerging sentiments in American society about enemies in the war on terror. Conflict in Yugoslavia revealed the depth of contention between proponents of ethnic separation and those espousing pluralism through federation. In Rwanda, violence was a product in part of perceived threats to prevailing social norms, from agents of sexual misconduct to those who, it was said, would restore a form of colonial rule. The norm of reconciliation in postconflict societies also engenders emotional responses—over and above its intellectual status as a legal and political proposition. Changing social norms after violent conflict involves a public process of affective expression, which juridical and quasi-juridical institutions can both facilitate and impede. In each case, emotions do not obstruct moral and political agency but serve as its vehicles. If political conflicts involve intense emotions, it is because they stem from contention over deeply held moral and/or legal frameworks. Emotions signal not the weakness of norms but the depth of conviction behind them.

More research is needed to explore how emotions give norms this urgency and appeal. For example, there is now a burgeoning literature on why strategically minded organizations adopt some issues and not others.[3] And yet relatively little is known about why certain norms are more successful in garnering popular enthusiasm than others. We know about how norm entrepreneurs "graft" campaigns onto pre-existing framings and established norms, but less about the contingent and implicit associations and resonances that also fuel norm diffusion.[4] The Save Darfur campaign offers one example, since that humanitarian effort intersected synergistically with available sentiments within the American public—doubts about US military involvement in the Middle East and, conceivably, cultural stereotypes about the malevolence of Arab perpetrators.[5] In each issue area, an economy of emotional events and symbols modulates and mediates popular support. Some of these are predictable: the Holocaust, for example, still serves as a powerful caution against genocide, and post-apartheid South Africa now serves as an evocative reminder of the promise of transitional justice. Other points of emotional resonance are less intuitive, as in the synergies between conservative evangelical values in America and the diffusion of human rights norms abroad.[6] We still lack a full account of how and when circulations of affect supply normative regimes with viability.

Another open question concerns the affective weight of lived participation in political and legal processes. We often treat norms and institutions as political things rather than emergent products of social interaction. IR scholars, trained to look at the interests and capabilities behind global governance, sometimes overlook the procedures through which they are engendered. The recent attention to argument and deliberative process is pushing beyond these conventions in important ways.[7] And yet the affective significance of coparticipation in governance processes remains poorly understood. Consider the politics of climate regulation, which has been cited as a "hard case" for international regime development due to a lack of public appeal. Cass Sunstein argues that the absence of strong emotions about global warming leads the general public to underestimate its risks.[8] And yet the global outrage that followed the Bush administration's unsigning of the Kyoto Protocol suggests that emotional investments were present after all. Perhaps feelings of hope and trust were generated by the process surrounding the Framework Convention rather than the content of the norm. By expanding its focus to include these varieties of affect, IR theory can uncover factors heretofore concealed within global controversies.

One almost entirely unexplored question concerns the way normative deliberations are affected by *how* participants are talking. Several cases in the book suggest that the tone of a speech can contribute to its emotional impact. While there is extensive research in social linguistics and neuroscience into tone and other paralinguistic elements of discourse, IR scholars have yet to address these factors. Doing so could accentuate the now well-established interest in political discourse and its cultural significance. Behind a diplomatic dispute, for example, we might find that parties are affected by a combative mood that stems from both content and tone of public discussion. Although research on nuclear proliferation, to take another example, has made great strides in understanding the psychological politics of nuclear weapons acquisition, we still lack a full account of how such policies function within domestic political discourses.[9] Behind each move in the chess game of nuclearization, there are emotional gains and losses felt by sensitive leaders and publics; a savvy foreign policy needs to anticipate these emotional dynamics. Taking emotions seriously means that we cannot afford to diminish the importance of seemingly minor utterances in the sensitive world of diplomatic communication.

Understanding emotions thus requires extending interpretivist research in IR deeper into processes of socialization and cultural reproduction. Constructivists have generated rich accounts of norms and identities in world politics, but these need to be enlivened with attention to how people actually inhabit those social structures. We can do this by supplementing concerns for the content of discourse with the everyday social interactions that give it emotional energy. Studies of emotion need to adjust the kinds of activities accepted as sociologically relevant in global politics. International relations theory has come a great distance to admit the importance of symbols, narratives, and other sources of meaning. Investigating affect now demands attending to the paralinguistic elements of communication and other expressive interactions that circulate emotion among social actors. Understanding emotions requires accounting for the sustained patterns of communication that contribute to the steady consolidation of norms and identities. But it also calls for tracing the way fluid and volatile circulations of affect can disrupt those routine forms of socialization. For example, we might investigate whether an official state apology changes the tone of diplomatic interaction with a former rival, or how multilateral conferences create or erode confidence among communities of experts. Such events are not simply window dressing but critical factors shaping the affective environments we inhabit.

There is much room for empirically oriented scholars to pursue, refine, and test the exploratory ideas presented in this book. The methodological challenge for future research is to devise and combine methods that are sensitive and appropriate to the peculiar characteristics of emotion. Some forms of emotion are quite amenable to conventional methods: feelings might, for example, be detected through an open-ended interview or even a carefully constructed survey. Other emotions, if they are familiar and durable within a community, may be observable in official speeches, documents, and texts. My case studies find, however, a dimension of nonconscious affect that requires alternative methods attuned to implicit processes and exchanges of emotion. Sometimes political actors are driven by emotions they do not know they have; others may be aware of their emotions but unable to describe them accurately. We cannot afford to allow methodological conventions to cut us off from emotion's less easily detected effects.

More generally, the study of emotions points to the need for greater cross-fertilization across areas of specialization within IR and the social sciences more generally. Consider, for example, future research on the topic of war. We cannot understand large-scale violent conflict without some consideration for the norms over which it is waged. Constructivist theory has gone a long way to establishing that anarchy, conflict, and war are social and normative phenomena. This book finds in turn that emotions are integral to these guiding normative frameworks: the norms and beliefs at the center of violent conflict are generally ones that matter to people. Moreover, the norms and rules that govern the use of force are, following a long history of violent wars, themselves invested with powerful hopes and revulsions. The result is that the emotions involved in war are products of contention over normative orders with great emotional weight. We cannot understand the convergence of norms and violence in war—a class of topics typically of great interest to IR—without plugging into security studies knowledge from global governance but also fields such as legal studies, sociology, cultural anthropology, and neuroscience.

As IR scholars turn to the multifaceted problems now facing global politics, this holistic approach becomes more important still. Terrorism, for example, sits at the intersection of complex social, political, economic, and cultural processes. Research in sociology is highlighting the importance of social networks and media communications for terrorist organizations. Cultural theorists are pointing to the importance of not only religious beliefs but also martyr videos and other ritual practices in sustaining popular support for suicide bombing and terrorist operations. Scholars informed by political theory have identified the need to disentangle the presuppositions associated with secularism in the West before religious elements of political agency can be properly understood.[10] We are unlikely to comprehend the complex politics of terrorist organizations without connecting up discussions in security studies and foreign policy with insights from these fields. Transnational religious movements employing violence are—like Western humanitarian organizations who instead pursue liberal forms of advocacy—at once political, cultural, and normative projects that cannot be understood without attention to the way fluid circulations of affect unite their members and connect them to even broader audiences. While scholars may hold disciplinary conventions in great esteem, emotions that migrate across social settings, actors, and political issues generally do not.

Research in IR needs to take emotions seriously and can do so by paying greater attention to the social interactions and events giving rise to them. The macrolevel actors and problems traditionally studied in IR—whether states, cultural groups, or institutions—are products of microlevel, emotion-generating interactions. Indeed, circulations of affect render the micro/macro distinction more porous than convention suggests. By tapping knowledge in adjacent disciplines, scholars of global politics can develop multidimensional accounts of emotional processes affecting inter- and trans-national political behavior. Making sense of terrorism, global govern-ance, transnational advocacy, international conflict, diplomatic disputes, and other "big" topics in global politics will require looking down, as it were, at ground-level interactions that imbue politics with powerful emo-tion. Doing so does not undermine the importance to political outcomes of principled debates, deliberate policies, and heroic actions. But the behavior of leaders, entrepreneurs, activists, and insurgents is at once calculating *and* impassioned. Political endeavors rest on willful actions, but agency requires footholds in the everyday world of affect.

CHAPTER ONE

1. A number of IR scholars have studied aspects of emotion in IR; my hope is that this book will add to these conversations: Janice Bially Mattern, "A Practice Theory of Emotion for International Relations," in *International Practices*, ed. Emanuel Adler and Vincent Pouliot (New York: Cambridge University Press, 2011); Roland Bleiker and Emma Hutchison, "Fear No More: Emotions and World Politics," *Review of International Studies* 34 (2008): 115–35; Neta Crawford, "The Passion of World Politics: Propositions on Emotion and Emotional Relationships," *International Security* 24, no. 4 (2000): 116–56; Neta C. Crawford, "Human Nature and World Politics: Rethinking 'Man,'" *International Relations* 23, no. 2 (2009): 271–88; Todd H. Hall, "We Will Not Swallow This Bitter Fruit: Theorizing a Diplomacy of Anger," *Security Studies* 20, no. 4 (2011): 521–55; Richard Ned Lebow, *A Cultural Theory of International Relations* (New York: Cambridge University Press, 2008); Jonathan Mercer, "Emotional Beliefs," *International Organization* 64, no. 1 (2010): 1–31; Jonathan Mercer, "Rationality and Psychology in International Politics," *International Organization* 59, no. 1 (2005): 77–106; Brent E. Sasley, "Theorizing States' Emotions," *International Studies Review* 13, no. 3 (2011): 452–76; Paul Saurette, "You Dissin Me? Humiliation and Post 9/11 Global Politics," *Review of International Studies* 32, no. 3 (2006): 495–522.

2. On the challenges associated with applying neuroscience to theories in IR, see Rose McDermott, "Mutual Interests: The Case for Increasing Dialogue between Political Science and Neuroscience," *Political Research Quarterly* 62, no. 3 (2009): 571–83; Rose McDermott, "The Feeling of Rationality: The Meaning of Neuroscientific Advances for Political Science," *American Political Science Review* 2, no. 4 (2004): 692.

3. This neurosocial conceptualization of emotion is now recognized within the nascent field of "social neuroscience" or "neurosociology." See Ralph Adolphs, "Conceptual Challenges and Directions for Social Neuroscience," *Neuron* 65, no. 6 (2010): 752–67; David D. Franks, *Neurosociology: The Nexus between Neuroscience and Social Psychology* (New York: Springer, 2010); Eddie Harmon-Jones and Piotr Winkielman, *Social Neuroscience: Integrating Biological and Psychological Explanations of Social Behavior* (New York: Guilford Press, 2007); Gün R. Semin and Gerald Echterhoff, *Grounding Sociality: Neurons, Mind, and Culture* (New York: Psychology Press, 2011).

4. On the history of passion, see Philip Fisher, *The Vehement Passions* (Princeton, NJ: Princeton University Press, 2002); Thomas Dixon, *From Passions to Emotions: The Creation of a Secular Psychological Category* (New York: Cambridge University Press, 2003); Albert O. Hirschman, *The Passions and the Interests: Political Arguments for Capitalism before Its Triumph* (Princeton, NJ: Princeton University Press, 1996); Susan James, *Passion and Action: The Emotions in Seventeenth-Century Philosophy* (New York: Oxford University Press, 1997).

5. See William James, "What Is an Emotion?," *Mind* 9, no. 34 (1884): 188–205; William James, *The Principles of Psychology*, vol. 2 (New York: Dover Publications, 1950). I discuss these developments in Andrew A. G. Ross, "Coming in from the Cold: Constructivism and Emotions," *European Journal of International Relations* 12, no. 2 (2006): 197–222.

6. See, e.g., Andrew Ortony, Gerald L. Clore, and Allan Collins, *The Cognitive Structure of Emotions* (New York: Cambridge University Press, 1988).

7. Crawford, "Human Nature," 278.

8. See Ortony, Clore, and Collins, *Cognitive Structure*, 26.

9. Averill, quoted in ibid. On the blending of emotion, see also Nico H. Frijda, *The Emotions* (New York: Cambridge University Press, 1986), 253–54.

10. John Dewey, "What Are States of Mind?," in *John Dewey: The Middle Works, 1899–1924*, ed. Jo Ann Boydston (Carbondale: Southern Illinois Press, 1985), 37–38. Resisting the idea of "states of mind," Dewey saw emotions instead as responses to "a moving complex situation." In a similar vein, Nietzsche writes: "we set up a word at the point at which our ignorance begins." Friedrich Wilhelm Nietzsche, *The Will to Power*, trans. Walter Arnold Kaufmann and R. J. Hollingdale (New York: Random House, 1967), §482.

11. James, *Principles of Psychology*, 2:449.

12. William James, *Essays in Radical Empiricism* (Lincoln: University of Nebraska Press, 1976).

13. My approach is agnostic on whether "affect," embraced by many scholars in cultural studies and literary theory, or "emotion," more widely used in neuroscience, is the better term. My view is that the conceptualization of affect associated with the philosophy of Gilles Deleuze is compatible with certain insights and observations from psychology, microsociology, and neuroscience. For work committed to the term "affect" and closely inspired by Deleuze's writings, see the contributions in Melissa Gregg and Gregory J. Seigworth, eds., *The Affect Theory Reader* (Durham, NC: Duke University Press, 2010). Also see Brian Massumi, *Parables for the Virtual: Movement, Affect, Sensation* (Durham, NC: Duke University Press, 2002); William E. Connolly, *Neuropolitics: Thinking, Culture, Speed* (Minneapolis: University of Minnesota Press, 2002). For a critique, see Ruth Leys, "The Turn to Affect: A Critique," *Critical Inquiry* 37, no. 3 (2011): 434–72.

14. Prinz calls such an approach an "encompassing" theory. Jesse J. Prinz, *Gut Reactions: A Perceptual Theory of Emotion* (New York: Oxford University Press, 2004).

15. Antonio R. Damasio, *Looking for Spinoza: Joy, Sorrow, and the Feeling Brain* (New York: Harcourt, 2003), 37.

16. On these points, see Nico H. Frijda, "Varieties of Affect: Emotions and Episodes, Moods, and Sentiments," in *The Nature of Emotion: Fundamental Questions*, ed. Paul Ekman and Richard J. Davidson (New York: Oxford University Press, 1994), 60, 62; Frijda, *The Emotions*, 213.

17. Damasio, *Looking for Spinoza*, 43–45. On background emotions, see also Antonio R. Damasio, *Descartes' Error: Emotion, Reason, and the Human Brain* (New York: Putnam, 1994), 150–51.

18. For a kindred account of the "transmission of affect" combining psychoanalytic framings with an emphasis on entrainment through pheromones, see Teresa Brennan, *The Transmission of Affect* (Ithaca, NY: Cornell University Press, 2004).

19. My account of the social genesis of emotion bears strong affinities to Janice Bially Mattern's extraordinary theorization of "emotional practices." Bially Mattern, "Practice Theory of Emotion." While I am both persuaded by and indebted to her account, mine diverges on several key points. In order not to privilege established social practices over more episodic and emergent ones, my theorization avoids presenting "competency" as a prominent feature of emotional interactions. I also opt not to borrow Schatzki's Wittgensteinian emphasis on *human* ontology, which risks missing ways in which human interactions are interpenetrated with nonhuman elements—especially communications technologies.

20. By incorporating social dimensions of emotion, I aim to supplement research in IR that has taught us about the effects of emotion on individual attitudes and choices. For an excellent synthesis of that work, see Janice Gross Stein, "Psychological Explanations of International Decision Making and Collective Behavior," in *Handbook of International Relations*, ed. Walter Carlsnaes, Thomas Risse, and Beth A. Simmons (Thousand Oaks, CA: Sage, 2013). My account bears affinities with the idea that emotions comprise social "climates." See J. H. de Rivera, "Emotional Climate: Social Structure and Emotional Dynamics," in *International Review of Studies on Emotion*, ed. K. T. Strongman (New York: John Wiley and Sons, 1992). Crawford explores this idea in "Human Nature," 282.

21. The latter two are reciprocally connected, such that shared attention generates emotional experience, which in turn serves to entrench attention. Randall Collins, *Interaction Ritual Chains* (Princeton, NJ: Princeton University Press, 2004), 48. For Collins, we can legitimately posit the ubiquity of rituals as long as we guard against automatically imputing functionalist logics to them. Not all rituals serve to sustain social order; some are contingent interactions with relatively minimal impact on larger social structures, others are disruptive activities that undermine social order (15).

22. The framework overlaps with Adler and Pouliot's social practices, but also encompasses ad hoc meetings, communications, and other small group interactions not sustained by formal standards of competence. Social interactions such as spontaneous protests, isolated acts of violence, or experiments in popular justice are less formalized than Adler and Pouliot's "practices" and yet no less important for circulating affect. Emanuel Adler and Vincent Pouliot, "International Practices," *International Theory* 3, no. 1 (2011): 4–7. See also Vincent Pouliot, *International Security in Practice: The Politics of NATO-Russia Diplomacy* (New York: Cambridge University Press, 2010); Adler and Pouliot, eds., *International Practices*.

23. Collins, *Interaction Ritual Chains*, 119.

24. Charles Taylor, "Action as Expression," in *Intention and Intentionality: Essays in Honour of G.E.M. Anscombe*, ed. Cora Diamond and Jenny Teichman (Brighton: Harvester Press, 1979), 78, 80. On the importance of embodiment to sustaining "emotional practices," see Bially Mattern, "Practice Theory of Emotion."

25. Elaine Hatfield, John T. Cacioppo, and Richard L. Rapson, *Emotional Contagion* (New York: Cambridge University Press, 1994); Roland Neumann and Fritz Strack, "'Mood

Contagion': The Automatic Transfer of Mood between Persons," *Journal of Personality and Social Psychology* 79, no. 2 (2000): 211–23; Brian Parkinson and Gwenda Simons, "Affecting Others: Social Appraisal and Emotion Contagion in Everyday Decision Making," *Personality and Social Psychology Bulletin* 35, no. 8 (2009): 1071–84.

26. Gabriel de Tarde, *The Laws of Imitation*, trans. Elsie Clews Parsons (New York: Henry Holt and Company, 1903), xiii, 62, 197, 204. Tarde generally opted for the term "imitation," although he concedes that his use of it is inconsistent with conventional notions of imitation as deliberate copying.

27. Walt uses the term to describe such processes in Stephen M. Walt, "Fads, Fevers, and Firestorms," *Foreign Policy*, no. 121 (2000): 34–42.

28. Priscilla Wald, *Contagious: Cultures, Carriers, and the Outbreak Narrative* (Durham, NC: Duke University Press, 2008).

29. For a popular account of happiness as a property of social networks, see Nicholas A. Christakis and James H. Fowler, *Connected: The Surprising Power of Our Social Networks and How They Shape Our Lives* (New York: Little, Brown, 2009).

30. Gerben A. Van Kleef, "How Emotions Regulate Social Life: The Emotions as Social Information (EASI) Model," *Current Directions in Psychological Science* 18, no. 3 (2009): 185.

31. Van Kleef, "How Emotions Regulate Social Life," 185. Functionalist theories suggest further that emotional convergence of this kind benefits people by fostering "cohesion and longevity" of intimate relationships. Cameron Anderson, Dacher Keltner, and Oliver P. John, "Emotional Convergence between People over Time," *Journal of Personality and Social Psychology* 84, no. 5 (2003): 1065. See also Dacher Keltner and Jonathan Haidt, "Social Functions of Emotions at Four Levels of Analysis," *Cognition and Emotion* 13, no. 5 (1999): 505–21.

32. Keltner and Haidt, "Social Functions of Emotions," 511.

33. Quoted in Hatfield, Cacioppo, and Rapson, *Emotional Contagion*, 5.

34. See Neumann and Strack, "Mood Contagion," 212; Parkinson and Simons, "Affecting Others."

35. Ralph Adolphs, "Recognizing Emotion from Facial Expressions: Psychological and Neurological Mechanisms," *Behavioral and Cognitive Neuroscience Reviews* 1, no. 1 (2002): 29.

36. Damasio, *Looking for Spinoza*, 53–57.

37. James calls the body's status reports "organic reverberations"; Damasio calls them "body maps." James, *Principles of Psychology*, 2: 449; Damasio, *Descartes' Error*, 155–56; Damasio, *Looking for Spinoza*, 85–88. See also Antonio R. Damasio, "William James and the Modern Neurobiology of Emotion," in *Emotion, Evolution, and Rationality*, ed. Dylan Evans and Pierre Cruse (New York: Oxford University Press, 2004), 7.

38. Damasio, *Looking for Spinoza*, 115–16.

39. Christian Keysers and Valeria Gazzola, "Social Neuroscience: Mirror Neurons Recorded in Humans," *Current Biology* 20, no. 8 (2010): R353–54. For overviews of recent research on mirror neurons, see Marco Iacoboni, *Mirroring People: The New Science of How We Connect with Others* (New York: Farrar, Straus and Giroux, 2008), 106–26; Giacomo Rizzolatti and Corrado Sinigaglia, *Mirrors in the Brain: How Our Minds Share Actions and Emotions* (New York: Oxford University Press, 2008), 173–93.

40. J.A.C.J. Bastiaansen, M. Thioux, and C. Keysers, "Evidence for Mirror Systems in Emotions," *Philosophical Transactions of the Royal Society B: Biological Sciences* 364, no. 1528 (2009): 2391–404; Christian Keysers, *The Empathic Brain: How the Discovery of Mir-*

ror Neurons Changes Our Understanding of Human Nature ([Lexington, KY]: Christian Keysers, 2011), 91–117; Rizzolatti and Sinigaglia, *Mirrors in the Brain*, 173 93.

41. This study, by Wicker et al., is discussed in Rizzolatti and Sinigaglia, *Mirrors in the Brain*, 183–84.

42. Bastiaansen, Thioux, and Keysers, "Evidence for Mirror Systems," 2397, 2399.

43. Colin Allen, "Mirror, Mirror in the Brain, What's the Monkey Stand to Gain?," *Nous* 44, no. 2 (2010): 372–91; Shaun Gallagher, "Simulation Trouble," *Social Neuroscience* 2, nos. 3/4 (2007): 353–65; Gregory Hickok, "Eight Problems for the Mirror Neuron Theory of Action Understanding in Monkeys and Humans," *Journal of Cognitive Neuroscience* 21, no. 7 (2008): 1229–43; Rebecca Saxe, "Against Simulation: The Argument from Error," *Trends in Cognitive Sciences* 9, no. 4 (2005): 174–79; Victoria Southgate and Antonia F. de C. Hamilton, "Unbroken Mirrors: Challenging a Theory of Autism," *Trends in Cognitive Sciences* 12, no. 6 (2008): 225–29.

44. See, e.g., Ilan Dinstein, Cibu Thomas, Marlene Behrmann, and David J. Heeger, "A Mirror up to Nature," *Current Biology* 18, no. 1 (2008): R13–18; Bastiaansen, Thioux, and Keysers, "Evidence for Mirror Systems."

45. Iacoboni, *Mirroring People*, 120, emphasis in original.

46. Keysers, *Empathic Brain*, 117.

47. Bastiaansen, Thioux, and Keysers, "Evidence for Mirror Systems," 2399.

48. On the affinities between contemporary neuroscience and the early work of James, see Damasio, "William James"; Rizzolatti and Sinigaglia, *Mirrors in the Brain*, 189; Joseph E. LeDoux, *The Emotional Brain: The Mysterious Underpinnings of Emotional Life* (New York: Simon and Schuster, 1996), 42–72. See also my account in Ross, "Coming in from the Cold."

49. Keysers, *Empathic Brain*, 104; Rizzolatti and Sinigaglia, *Mirrors in the Brain*, 188–90; Iacoboni, *Mirroring People*, 119.

50. For work on these topics, see, respectively, Peter Totterdell, "Catching Moods and Hitting Runs: Mood Linkage and Subjective Performance in Professional Sports Teams," *Journal of Applied Psychology* 85, no. 6 (2000): 848–59; Sigal G. Barsade, "The Ripple Effect: Emotional Contagion and Its Influence on Group Behavior," *Administrative Science Quarterly* 47, no. 4 (2002): 644–75; J. E. Bono and R. Ilies, "Charisma, Positive Emotions and Mood Contagion," *Leadership Quarterly* 17, no. 4 (2006): 317–34.

51. Although scholars have considered the cultural manifestations of emotional contagion in a more speculative voice. See Hatfield, Cacioppo, and Rapson, *Emotional Contagion*, 104–26.

52. Ibid., 147. The broader phenomenon of emotional expressiveness is studied in Howard S. Friedman, Louise M. Prince, Ronald E. Riggio, and M. Robin DiMatteo, "Understanding and Assessing Nonverbal Expressiveness: The Affective Communication Test," *Journal of Personality and Social Psychology* 39, no. 2 (1980): 333–51.

53. Collins, *Interaction Ritual Chains*, 76.

54. Ibid.

55. Jonathan H. Turner, *Face-to-Face: Toward a Sociological Theory of Interpersonal Behavior* (Stanford, CA: Stanford University Press, 2002), 87.

56. Thomas J. Scheff, *Microsociology: Discourse, Emotion, and Social Structure* (Chicago: University of Chicago Press, 1990), 15–17.

57. For an application of Wittgenstein's account of "bodily doings," see Theodore R. Schatzki, *Social Practices: A Wittgensteinian Approach to Human Activity and the*

Social (New York: Cambridge University Press, 1996). See also Taylor, "Action as Expression."

58. Collins, *Interaction Ritual Chains*, xix, 64; Turner, *Face-to-Face*, 62.

59. For an explanation, see Collins, *Interaction Ritual Chains*, 54–64; Turner, *Face-to-Face*, 1.

60. Jeffrey R. Huntsinger, "Contagion without Contact: Anticipatory Mood Matching in Response to Affiliative Motivation," *Personality and Social Psychology Bulletin* 35, no. 7 (2009): 909–22.

61. Keysers, *Empathic Brain*, 101. Jennifer C. Britton, Stephan F. Taylor, Keith D. Sudheimer, and Israel Liberzon, "Facial Expressions and Complex IAPS Pictures: Common and Differential Networks," *NeuroImage* 31, no. 2 (2006): 906–19; Ahmad R. Hariri, Alessandro Tessitore, Venkata S. Mattay, Francesco Fera, and Daniel R. Weinberger, "The Amygdala Response to Emotional Stimuli: A Comparison of Faces and Scenes," *NeuroImage* 17, no. 1 (2002): 317–23.

62. Iacoboni, *Mirroring People*, 211. Adolphs speculates that the complex and dynamic nature of social settings may make "simulation-like mechanisms" especially well adapted to them. Adolphs, "Conceptual Challenges and Directions," 759.

63. In the 1970s, for example, Zillmann used his "excitation transfer theory" to study the affective impact of television and film. See Dolf Zillmann, "Excitation Transfer in Communication-Mediated Aggressive Behavior," *Journal of Experimental Social Psychology* 7, no. 4 (1971): 419–34; S. Shyam Sundar, "News Features and Learning," in *Communication and Emotion: Essays in Honor of Dolf Zillmann*, ed. Jennings Bryant, David R. Roskos-Ewoldsen, and Joanne Cantor (Mahwah, NJ: Lawrence Erlbaum Associates, 2003). Cantril's famous 1940 study suggested similar potential in radio broadcasts: Hadley Cantril, *The Invasion from Mars: A Study in the Psychology of Panic* (New Brunswick, NJ: Transaction Publishers, 2005).

64. Gabriel de Tarde, *Gabriel Tarde on Communication and Social Influence: Selected Papers*, ed. Terry N. Clark (Chicago: University of Chicago Press, 1969), 277–94.

65. Quoted in Anna Gibbs, "Panic! Affect Contagion, Mimesis and Suggestion in the Social Field," *Cultural Studies Review* 14, no. 2 (2008): 136.

66. On the structural changes created by al-Jazeera, see Marc Lynch, *Voices of the New Arab Public: Iraq, Al-Jazeera, and Middle East Politics Today* (New York: Columbia University Press, 2006).

67. John B. Thompson, *The Media and Modernity: A Social Theory of the Media* (Cambridge: Polity Press, 1995), 219. For a theorization of emotion and mass media, see Manuel Castells, *Communication Power* (New York: Oxford University Press, 2009), 137–65. Scollon's "mediated discourse analysis" extends Goffman's "with" interactions, which presuppose copresence, into "watch" interactions, which involve non-copresent audiences. Ronald Scollon, *Mediated Discourse as Social Interaction: A Study of News Discourse* (New York: Longman, 1998), 16, 89–94.

68. See the provocative study of the psychosocial impact of war memorials in Jenny Edkins, *Trauma and the Memory of Politics* (New York: Cambridge University Press, 2003).

69. For an effort to remedy these omissions, see Ty Solomon, "'I Wasn't Angry Because I Couldn't Believe It Was Happening': Affect and Discourse in Responses to 9/11," *Review of International Studies* 38, no. 4 (2012): 907–28.

70. See, e.g., Patrick N. Juslin and Klaus R. Scherer, "Vocal Expression of Affect," in *The New Handbook of Methods in Nonverbal Behavior Research*, ed. Jinni A. Harrigan, Robert Rosenthal, and Klaus R. Scherer (New York: Oxford University Press, 2005); B. de

Gelder and J. Vroomen, "The Perception of Emotions by Ear and by Eye," *Cognition and Emotion* 14, no. 3 (2000): 289–311.

71. For reasons discussed there, I regard a "circulation" as an open or flexible process rather than a dissemination of some fixed 'thing.' For a kindred use of the term in social theory, see Bruno Latour, *Reassembling the Social: An Introduction to Actor-Network-Theory* (New York: Oxford University Press, 2005), 17–18.

72. Emile Durkheim, *The Elementary Forms of the Religious Life*, trans. Joseph Ward Swain (Glencoe, IL: Free Press, 1954), 208–16.

73. Mercer, "Emotional Beliefs."

74. Hans Joas, *The Genesis of Values* (Chicago: University of Chicago Press, 2000), 17–19. See also Martha C. Nussbaum, *Upheavals of Thought: The Intelligence of Emotions* (New York: Cambridge University Press, 2001).

75. Emotions are thus central to what a growing literature in IR calls "ontological security." See Jennifer Mitzen, "Ontological Security in World Politics: State Identity and the Security Dilemma," *European Journal of International Relations* 12, no. 3 (2006): 341–70; Brent J. Steele, *Ontological Security in International Relations: Self-Identity and the IR State* (New York: Routledge, 2007). Ted Hopf's provocative and complementary account theorizes these norm-inspiring emotions as "habits": Ted Hopf, "The Logic of Habit in International Relations," *European Journal of International Relations* 16, no. 4 (2010): 539–61.

76. See Mark Mazower, *No Enchanted Palace: The End of Empire and the Ideological Origins of the United Nations* (Princeton, NJ: Princeton University Press, 2009), 2–3.

77. Lynn Hunt, *Inventing Human Rights: A History* (New York: W. W. Norton, 2007), 70–112.

78. See, e.g., the discussion of humiliation in Khaled Fattah and K. M. Fierke, "A Clash of Emotions: The Politics of Humiliation and Political Violence in the Middle East," *European Journal of International Relations* 15, no. 1 (2009): 67–93.

79. Tarde, *Laws of Imitation*, 204. See also Latour's elucidation of this point in Bruno Latour, "Gabriel Tarde and the End of the Social," in *The Social in Question: New Bearings in History and the Social Sciences*, ed. Patrick Joyce (New York: Routledge, 2002), 121.

80. On the attribution of emotions to groups as a problem of "scaling up," see Alexander Wendt, "*Social Theory* as Cartesian Science: An Auto-Critique from a Quantum Perspective," in *Constructivism in International Relations: Alexander Wendt and His Critics*, ed. Stefano Guzzini and Anna Leander (New York: Routledge, 2006), 184.

81. Collins, *Interaction Ritual Chains*, 6; Jeffrey C. Alexander, *Action and Its Environments: Toward a New Synthesis* (New York: Columbia University Press, 1988), 301–2.

82. Collins, *Interaction Ritual Chains*, 41. For my assessment of the emotional roots of such protest movements, see Andrew A. G. Ross, "Why They Don't Hate Us: Emotion, Agency and the Politics of 'Anti-Americanism,'" *Millennium: Journal of International Studies* 39, no. 1 (2010): 109–25.

83. Alison Brysk, *Global Good Samaritans: Human Rights as Foreign Policy* (New York: Oxford University Press, 2009); Amitav Acharya, "Ideas, Identity, and Institution-Building: From the 'ASEAN Way' to the 'Asia-Pacific Way'?," *Pacific Review* 10, no. 3 (1997): 319–46.

84. The assumption is evident in Wendt's statement: "To have an identity is simply to have certain ideas about who one is in a given situation." Alexander Wendt, *Social Theory of International Politics* (New York: Cambridge University Press, 1999), 170.

85. Pouliot, *International Security in Practice*; Hopf, "Logic of Habit."

86. Scott Straus, *The Order of Genocide: Race, Power, and War in Rwanda* (Ithaca, NY: Cornell University Press, 2006); Dominique Franche, *Rwanda: généalogie d'un génocide* (Paris: Editions Mille et une nuits, 1997).

87. Todd Hall, "Sympathetic States: State Strategies, Norms of Emotional Behavior, and the 9/11 Attacks," *Political Science Quarterly* 127, no. 3 (2012): 369–400.

CHAPTER TWO

1. Bially Mattern, "Practice Theory of Emotion," 72–80.

2. Stanley Schachter, "The Interaction of Cognitive and Physiological Determinants of Emotional State," in *Advances in Experimental Social Psychology*, ed. Leonard Berkowitz (New York: Academic Press, 1964). These results opened up later research into the social construction of emotion. James R. Averill, "A Constructivist View of Emotion," in *Emotion: Theory, Research, and Experience*, ed. Roberet Plutchik and Henry Kellerman (New York: Academic Press, 1980); Rom Harré, "An Outline of the Social Constructivist Viewpoint," in *The Social Construction of Emotions*, ed. Rom Harré (New York: Blackwell, 1986).

3. Sheila T. Murphy and R. B. Zajonc, "Affect, Cognition, and Awareness: Affective Priming with Optimal and Suboptimal Stimulus Exposures," *Journal of Personality and Social Psychology* 64, no. 5 (1993): 736. For more recent accounts, see Jennifer S. Lerner and Dacher Keltner, "Beyond Valence: Toward a Model of Emotion-Specific Influences on Judgement and Choice," *Cognition and Emotion* 14, no. 4 (2000): 473–93; Masanori Oikawa, Henk Aarts, and Haruka Oikawa, "There Is a Fire Burning in My Heart: The Role of Causal Attribution in Affect Transfer," *Cognition and Emotion* 25, no. 1 (2011): 156–63.

4. Dolf Zillmann, "Sequential Dependencies in Emotional Experience and Behavior," in *Emotion: Interdisciplinary Perspectives*, ed. Robert D. Kavanaugh, Betty Zimmerberg, and Steven Fein (Mahwah, NJ: Lawrence Erlbaum Associates, 1996), 251, 268.

5. Frijda, *The Emotions*, 59, 254–55; Zillmann, "Sequential Dependencies," 257.

6. Collins, *Interaction Ritual Chains*, 106–8, 81, 87. Jasper argues further that short-term emotions can disrupt long-term dispositions. James M. Jasper, *The Art of Moral Protest: Culture, Biography, and Creativity in Social Movements* (Chicago: University of Chicago Press, 1997), 111.

7. Sara Ahmed, *The Cultural Politics of Emotion* (New York: Routledge, 2004), 58–60, 66, 91–92.

8. Massumi, *Parables for the Virtual*, 35, 80–81.

9. Tarde, *Laws of Imitation*, 7.

10. See Elizabeth K. Gray and David Watson, "Assessing Positive and Negative Affect Via Self-Report," in *Handbook of Emotion Elicitation and Assessment*, ed. James A. Coan and John J. B. Allen (New York: Oxford University Press, 2007). For a summary and application of this work in political psychology, see George E. Marcus, W. Russell Neumen, and Michael MacKuen, *Affective Intelligence and Political Judgment* (Chicago: University of Chicago Press, 2000).

11. Théodule Ribot, *Essay on the Creative Imagination*, trans. Albert H. N. Baron (Chicago: Open Court Publishing, 1906), 37–38. Henri Bergson, *The Two Sources of Morality and Religion*, trans. R. Ashley Audra and Cloudesley Brereton (Garden City, NY: Doubleday, 1935), 46. Bergson does not deny that some emotions follow from intellectual ideas, but regards others as having a "supra-intellectual" quality.

12. Hans Joas, *The Creativity of Action* (Chicago: University of Chicago Press, 1996), 136. As he puts it, "action situations have to be *redefined* in a new and different way" (133).

13. On the significance of emotions for public events and of both for changing settled norms, see William H. Sewell Jr., *Logics of History: Social Theory and Social Transformation* (Chicago: University of Chicago Press, 2005), 249.

14. Fattah and Fierke, "A Clash of Emotions," 67–93.

15. Collins, *Interaction Ritual Chains*, 43.

16. Sewell, *Logics of History*, 225–28, 248–54.

17. John A. Bargh, "Auto-Motives: Preconscious Determinants of Social Interaction," in *Handbook of Motivation and Cognition: Foundations of Social Behavior*, vol. 2, ed. E. Tory Higgins and Richard M. Sorrentino (New York: Guilford Press, 1990), 118; Ran R. Hassin, John A. Bargh, and Shira Zimerman, "Automatic and Flexible: The Case of Nonconscious Goal Pursuit," *Social Cognition* 27, no. 1 (2009): 32.

18. Emanuel Adler and Vincent Pouliot, "International Practices: Introduction and Framework," in *International Practices*, ed. Adler and Pouliot, 3–34. Bially Mattern makes a similar point when she highlights Schatzki's insight that "a practitioner's competencies in one domain become his bodily excess in the next." Bially Mattern, "Practice Theory of Emotion," 122.

19. Ahmed, *Cultural Politics of Emotion*, 10. Regarding bare repetition as a necessary feature of "contagion," Ahmed elects to avoid the term.

20. Mahmood Mamdani, *Saviors and Survivors: Darfur, Politics, and the War on Terror* (New York: Doubleday, 2009).

21. Mustafa Emirbayer and Ann Mische, "What Is Agency?," *American Journal of Sociology* 103, no. 4 (1998): 963.

22. Daniel L. Schacter, *Searching for Memory: The Brain, the Mind, and the Past* (New York: Basic Books, 1996), 211; Henri Bergson, *Matter and Memory*, trans. N. M. Paul and W. S. Palmer (New York: Zone Books, 1991), 228, 240, 248. In Deleuze's influential account of the Bergsonian view, interaction occurs on a dense reserve of pre-existing or "virtual" affects. Gilles Deleuze, *Bergsonism*, trans. Hugh Tomlinson and Barbara Habberjam (New York: Zone Books, 1988), 67–71; Gilles Deleuze, *Difference and Repetition*, trans. Paul Patton (New York: Columbia University Press, 1994), 71–85.

23. Elizabeth A. Phelps and Laura A. Thomas, "Race, Behavior, and the Brain: The Role of Neuroimaging in Understanding Complex Social Behaviors," *Political Psychology* 24, no. 4 (2003): 752.

24. LeDoux, *The Emotional Brain*, 63.

25. Damasio, *Descartes' Error*, 146.

26. William James, *A Pluralistic Universe* (Cambridge, MA: Harvard University Press, 1977), 130; James, *Essays in Radical Empiricism*, 71, 141–42.

27. See Fisher, *The Vehement Passions*, 4; James, *Passion and Action*, 11. For an account of the historical reluctance to view passion as a form of activity, see Talal Asad, *Formations of the Secular: Christianity, Islam, Modernity* (Stanford, CA: Stanford University Press, 2003), 85.

28. *Oxford English Dictionary*, 2nd ed., s.v. "passion."

29. Joas argues that intentionalist theories unite action with will but, in doing so, artificially erect the latter as its precursor: "According to this view, which seems to assume that lethargy is the natural human state, action is initiated only after meaningful goals have been set in the cognized world and then—in a separate act of will—the decision to pursue such goals has been taken." Joas, *Creativity of Action*, 157.

30. Charles Taylor, *Human Agency and Language: Philosophical Papers I* (New York: Cambridge University Press, 1985), 15–20.

31. Joas, *Creativity of Action*, 17.

32. On the centrality of responsibility to agency in the Western tradition, see Asad, *Formations of the Secular*, 73–74.

33. Nicholas Onuf, *World of Our Making: Rules and Rule in Social Theory and International Relations* (Columbia: University of South Carolina Press, 1989), 51–52; and Friedrich V. Kratochwil, *Rules, Norms, and Decisions: On the Conditions of Practical and Legal Reasoning in International Relations and Domestic Affairs* (New York: Cambridge University Press, 1989), 55–56.

34. Adler and Pouliot, "International Practices" (in *International Theory*), 1–36; Pouliot, *International Security in Practice*; Hopf, "Logic of Habit," 539–61.

35. On the methodological challenges of studying the background knowledge informing social practices, see Pouliot, *International Security in Practice*, 52–91.

36. See, e.g., Damasio, *Descartes' Error*; Ronald de Sousa, *The Rationality of Emotion* (Cambridge, MA: MIT Press, 1987). Mercer offers a compelling application of these ideas to problems in IR. Mercer, "Rationality and Psychology in International Politics," 77–106.

37. Colin Wight, *Agents, Structures, and International Relations: Politics as Ontology* (New York: Cambridge University Press, 2006), 212, 214–15. For Wendt's contribution, see Alexander E. Wendt, "The Agent-Structure Problem in International Relations Theory," *International Organization* 41, no. 3 (1987): 337–38, and Wendt, *Social Theory of International Politics*. Doty calls Wendt's individualism solution a "leap of faith" that cannot not take into account the cultural and political contexts from which human agents became exposed to social structures in the first place. Roxanne Lynn Doty, "Aporia: A Critical Exploration of the Agent-Structure Problematique in International Relations Theory," *European Journal of International Relations* 3, no. 3 (1997): 384. On the agent-structure debate more generally, see also David Dessler, "What's at Stake in the Agent-Structure Debate?," *International Organization* 43, no. 3 (1989): 441–73.

38. Diana H. Coole, "Rethinking Agency: A Phenomenological Approach to Embodiment and Agentic Capacities," *Political Studies* 53, no. 1 (2005): 124–25.

39. Keysers, *Empathic Brain*, 117.

40. Tarde, *Laws of Imitation*, 145. On this point, see also Gilles Deleuze and Félix Guattari, *A Thousand Plateaus: Capitalism and Schizophrenia*, trans. Brian Massumi (Minneapolis: University of Minnesota Press, 1987), 218–19.

41. Bruno Latour, *Politics of Nature: How to Bring the Sciences into Democracy* (Cambridge, MA: Harvard University Press, 2004), 75–80. As Bennett puts it, actor-network-theory "affords natural-technological materialities a more active role": Jane Bennett, "The Agency of Assemblages and the North American Blackout," *Public Culture* 17, no. 3 (2005): 456. See also Jane Bennett, *Vibrant Matter: A Political Ecology of Things* (Durham, NC: Duke University Press, 2010).

42. Gilles Deleuze calls these quasi-groups "assemblages": polymorphic associations whose organizing principles are minimally salient and whose parts retain connection with other associations. Deleuze and Guattari, *A Thousand Plateaus*, esp. chaps. 9 and 12.

43. For a very compelling theory of diplomacy and foreign policy making along these lines, see Hall, "We Will Not Swallow This Bitter Fruit," 521–55.

44. Stuart Kaufman, for example, argues that we cannot understand the rise of Milošević without recognizing his ability to wield such symbols. Stuart J. Kaufman, *Modern Hatreds: The Symbolic Politics of Ethnic War* (Ithaca, NY: Cornell University Press, 2001).

45. They write: "Fascism is inseparable from a proliferation of molecular focuses of inter-action, which skip from point to point, *before* beginning to resonate together in the National Socialist State. Rural fascism and city or neighborhood fascism, youth fas-cism and war veteran's fascism, fascism of the Left and fascism of the Right, fascism of the couple, family, school, and office: every fascism is defined by a micro-black hole that stands on its own and communicates with the others, before resonating in a great, generalized central black hole." Deleuze and Guattari, *A Thousand Plateaus*, 230, 214.

46. Roger Dale Petersen, *Understanding Ethnic Violence: Fear, Hatred, and Resentment in Twentieth-Century Eastern Europe* (New York: Cambridge University Press, 2002), 25.

47. Mario Augusto Bunge, *Causality: The Place of the Causal Principle in Modern Science* (Cambridge, MA: Harvard University Press, 1959), 129.

48. William E. Connolly, "Method, Problem, Faith," in *Problems and Methods in the Study of Politics*, ed. Ian Shapiro, Rogers M. Smith, and Tarek E. Masoud (New York: Cam-bridge University Press, 2004), 332.

49. John R. Searle, *The Construction of Social Reality* (New York: Free Press, 1995), 144. He writes: "we acquire a set of cognitive abilities that are everywhere sensitive to intentional structure, and in particular to the rule structures of complex institutions" (145). This is why Wendt regards Searle as a proponent of "supervenient" model of group agency, in which an individual is pre-programmed to act as a member of a given group. Alexander Wendt, "The State as Person in International Theory," *Review of International Studies* 30, no. 2 (2004): 301.

50. For a discussion of emergent causality inspired in part by Deleuze, see Connolly, "Method, Problem, Faith," 342–43. See also Manuel De Landa, *A New Philosophy of Society: Assemblage Theory and Social Complexity* (New York: Continuum, 2006), 20.

51. I distinguish between "discourse about emotion" and the codes governing emotional expression uncovered by ethnographic research. In the latter vein, Lutz, for example, traces the "emotion concepts" and "emotion words" shaping emotional conduct. See Catherine Lutz, *Unnatural Emotions: Everyday Sentiments on a Micronesian Atoll and Their Challenge to Western Theory* (Chicago: University of Chicago Press, 1988).

52. Ross, "Why They Don't Hate Us," 109–25.

53. Das calls such a method a "descent into the ordinary." Veena Das, *Life and Words: Violence and the Descent into the Ordinary* (Berkeley: University of California Press, 2007).

54. For an important theorization of such processes, see Sasley, "Theorizing States' Emo-tions," 452–76.

CHAPTER THREE

1. See, e.g., John E. Mueller, *Overblown: How Politicians and the Terrorism Industry Inflate National Security Threats, and Why We Believe Them* (New York: Free Press, 2006); Diego Gambetta, "Reason and Terror: Has 9/11 Made It Hard to Think Straight?," *Boston Review* 29, no. 2 (2004): 32–36.

2. See, e.g., William J. Bennett, *Why We Fight: Moral Clarity and the War on Terrorism* (New York: Doubleday, 2002); Jean Bethke Elshtain, *Just War against Terror: The Burden of American Power in a Violent World* (New York: Basic Books, 2003).

3. Robert Putnam, "A Better Society in a Time of War," *New York Times*, October 19, 2001.

4. On fear and anxiety, see Leonie Huddy, Stanley Feldman, Charles Taber, and Gallya Lahav, "Threat, Anxiety, and Support of Antiterrorism Policies," *American Journal of*

Political Science 49, no. 3 (2005): 593–608; Chaim Kaufmann, "Threat Inflation and the Failure of the Marketplace of Ideas: The Selling of the Iraq War," *International Security* 29, no. 1 (2004): 46; Ronald R. Krebs and Chaim Kaufmann, "Correspondence: Selling the Market Short? The Marketplace of Ideas and the Iraq War," *International Security* 29, no. 4 (2005): 200; Robert L. Jervis, "The Confrontation between Iraq and the US: Implications for the Theory and Practice of Deterrence," *European Journal of International Relations* 9, no. 2 (2003): 317. On vengeance, see Peter Liberman, "An Eye for an Eye: Public Support for War against Evildoers," *International Organization* 60, no. 3 (2006): 687–722. On anti-Americanism, see, e.g., the essays in Peter J. Katzenstein and Robert O. Keohane, *Anti-Americanisms in World Politics* (Ithaca, NY: Cornell University Press, 2007).

5. John F. Harris, "Falwell Apologizes for Remarks," *Washington Post*, September 18, 2001.

6. I omit specific consideration of hatred in this chapter, since I have addressed it elsewhere. Ross, "Why They Don't Hate Us," 109–25.

7. On the former, see Stuart Croft, *Culture, Crisis and America's War on Terror* (New York: Cambridge University Press, 2006). On the purchase of flags, memorabilia, and other forms of memorialization, see Marita Sturken, *Tourists of History: Memory, Kitsch, and Consumerism from Oklahoma City to Ground Zero* (Durham, NC: Duke University Press, 2007).

8. For example, Croft, *Culture, Crisis, and America's War on Terror*; Richard Jackson, *Writing the War on Terrorism: Language, Politics, and Counter-Terrorism* (New York: Manchester University Press, 2005); Ronald R. Krebs and Jennifer K. Lobasz, "Fixing the Meaning of 9/11: Hegemony, Coercion, and the Road to War in Iraq," *Security Studies* 16, no. 3 (2007): 409–51.

9. Scollon, *Mediated Discourse as Social Interaction*.

10. See, e.g., Brigitte L. Nacos, Yaeli Bloch-Elkon, and Robert Y. Shapiro, *Selling Fear: Counterterrorism, the Media, and Public Opinion* (Chicago: University of Chicago Press, 2011).

11. Bernard Rime, Darío Paez, Nekane Basabe, and Francisco Martinez, "Social Sharing of Emotion, Post-Traumatic Growth, and Emotional Climate: Follow-up of Spanish Citizen's Response to the Collective Trauma of March 11th Terrorist Attacks in Madrid," *European Journal of Social Psychology* 40, no. 6 (2010): 1029–45.

12. Randall D. Marshall, Richard A. Bryant, Lawrence Amsel, S.U.H. Eun Jung, Joan M. Cook, and Yuval Neria, "The Psychology of Ongoing Threat: Relative Risk Appraisal, the September 11 Attacks, and Terrorism-Related Fears," *American Psychologist* 62, no. 4 (2007): 304–16.

13. Nacos, Bloch-Elkon, and Shapiro, *Selling Fear*, 3. See also J. Angstrom, "Mapping the Competing Historical Analogies of the War on Terrorism: The Bush Presidency," *International Relations* 25, no. 2 (2011): 224–42; T. Christopher Jespersen, "Analogies at War: Vietnam, the Bush Administration's War in Iraq, and the Search for a Usable Past," *Pacific Historical Review* 74, no. 3 (2005): 411–26; David Hoogland Noon, "Operation Enduring Analogy: World War II, the War on Terror, and the Uses of Historical Memory," *Rhetoric and Public Affairs* 7, no. 3 (2004): 339–65; Cynthia Weber, "Romantic Meditations of September 11," in *Rituals of Meditation: International Politics and Social Meaning*, ed. François Debrix and Cynthia Weber (Minneapolis: University of Minnesota Press, 2003).

14. On this argument, see Mueller, *Overblown*.

15. Yuen Foong Khong, *Analogies at War: Korea, Munich, Dien Bien Phu, and the Vietnam Decisions of 1965* (Princeton, NJ: Princeton University Press, 1992), 7.

16. Emily S. Rosenberg, *A Date Which Will Live: Pearl Harbor in American Memory* (Durham, NC: Duke University Press, 2003), 3.

17. Connolly, *Neuropolitics*, 36. On the emotional dimension of analogies, see also Roland Paris, "Kosovo and the Metaphor War," *Political Science Quarterly* 117, no. 3 (2002): 428; Michael C. Desch, "The Myth of Abandonment: The Use and Abuse of the Holocaust Analogy," *Security Studies* 15, no. 1 (2006): 111.

18. Rosenberg, *A Date Which Will Live*, 2, 113–25, 163–68. See also Noon, "Operation Enduring Analogy," 344; Geoffrey M. White, "National Subjects: September 11 and Pearl Harbor," *American Ethnologist* 31, no. 3 (2004): 293–310.

19. Both quoted in Noon, "Operation Enduring Analogy," 350.

20. Ibid., 346, 355. For a more nuanced account, see John E. Bodnar, *The "Good War" in American Memory* (Baltimore: Johns Hopkins University Press, 2010).

21. Collins, *Interaction Ritual Chains*, 37. White argues that memorialization practices coupled personal emotions with national unity and collective memory. White, "National Subjects."

22. Susan Willis, "Anthrax 'R' Us," *Social Text* 20, no. 4 (2002): 25; Scott Shane, "Portrait Emerges of Anthrax Suspect's Troubled Life," *New York Times*, January 4, 2009.

23. David Brown, "How Do We Treat This Outbreak of Uncertainty?," *Washington Post*, November 4, 2001; Willis, "Anthrax 'R' Us," 19.

24. Mueller, *Overblown*, 21–22.

25. Leonie Huddy, Nadia Khatib, and Theresa Capelos, "The Polls—Trends: Reactions to the Terrorist Attacks of September 11, 2001," *Public Opinion Quarterly* 66, no. 3 (2002): 423; Dante Chinni and Mark Sappenfield, "Coping with Fear," *Christian Science Monitor*, October 30, 2001.

26. Willis, "Anthrax 'R' Us," 19; Richard Cohen, "Our Forgotten Panic," *Washington Post*, July 22, 2004; Huddy, Khatib, and Capelos, "The Polls," 423, 440.

27. See Cohen, "Our Forgotten Panic"; Glenn Greenwald, "The Unresolved Story of ABC News' False Saddam-Anthrax Reports," *Salon*, April 9, 2007, http://www.salon.com/opinion/greenwald/2007/04/09/abc_anthrax.

28. Croft, for example, argues that the discourse of terrorism as a foreign threat perpetrated by al Qaeda against innocent Americans supplied a "template to be placed over events" such as the anthrax scare. Croft, *Culture, Crisis, and America's War on Terror*, 110.

29. Pew Forum on Religion and Public Life and Pew Research Center for the People and the Press (hereinafter Pew Forum), "Post 9/11 Attitudes: Religion More Prominent, Muslim-Americans More Accepted," Pew Research Center, Washington, DC, 2001. See also Croft, *Culture, Crisis, and America's War on Terror*, 103.

30. For a detailed discussion of these and other American perceptions toward the Middle East, see Douglas Little, *American Orientalism: The United States and the Middle East since 1945*, 3rd ed. (Chapel Hill: University of North Carolina Press, 2008).

31. George W. Bush, "Remarks by President Upon Arrival," Whitehouse.gov, September 16, 2001, http://www.whitehouse.gov/news/releases/2001/09/20010916-2.html (accessed July 24, 2006).

32. George W. Bush, "'Islam Is Peace,' Says President," Whitehouse.gov, September 17, 2001, http://www.whitehouse.gov/news/releases/2001/09/20010917-11.html (accessed July 24, 2006).

33. Bernard Lewis, "The Roots of Muslim Rage," *Atlantic Monthly*, September 1990; Samuel P. Huntington, *The Clash of Civilizations and the Remaking of World Order* (New York: Simon and Schuster, 1996). On the history of this idea in America, see also Zachary Lockman, *Contending Visions of the Middle East: The History and Politics of Orientalism* (New York: Cambridge University Press, 2004).

34. The news media was especially enthusiastic: Philip Seib, "The News Media and 'the Clash of Civilizations,'" in *Media and Conflict in the Twenty-First Century*, ed. Philip Seib (New York: Palgrave, 2005), 217–34.

35. George W. Bush, "Remarks by the President to United Nations General Assembly," U.S. Mission to the U.N. website, November 10, 2001, http://www.un.int/usa/01_162.htm (accessed July 25, 2006).

36. See, e.g., Jack G. Shaheen, "Reel Bad Arabs: How Hollywood Vilifies a People," *Annals of the American Academy of Political and Social Sciences* 588 (2003): 171–93.

37. One author argues that 9/11 "consolidated the conflation of the categories 'Arab,' 'Middle Eastern,' and 'Muslim' and the notion of an 'Arab/Middle Eastern/Muslim enemy of the nation." Nadine Naber, "Introduction," in *Race and Arab Americans before and after 9/11: From Invisible Citizens to Visible Subjects*, ed. Jamal Amaney and Nadine Naber (Syracuse, NY: Syracuse University Press, 2008), 38.

38. Patricia J. Williams, *Seeing a Color-Blind Future: The Paradox of Race* (New York: Noonday Press, 1998).

39. Ahmed makes this point in a provocative discussion that influenced my analysis in this section. Ahmed, *Cultural Politics of Emotion*, 75–79.

40. Louise Cainkar, "The Impact of the September 11 Attacks on Arab and Muslim Communities in the United States," in *The Maze of Fear: Security and Migration after 9/11*, ed. John Tirman (New York: New Press, 2004), 215; Salah D. Hassan, "Arabs, Race and the Post–September 11 National Security State," *Middle East Report*, no. 224 (2002): 16–21; Amnesty International, "Threat and Humiliation: Racial Profiling, Domestic Security, and Human Rights in the United States," Amnesty International, New York, 2004.

41. Nadine Naber, "Race, Gender, and the Culture of Fear among Arab Immigrants in San Francisco Post-9/11," *Cultural Dynamics* 18, no. 3 (2006): 247.

42. Leti Volpp, "The Citizen and the Terrorist," in *September 11 in History: A Watershed Moment?*, ed. Mary L. Dudziak (Durham, NC: Duke University Press, 2003), 150.

43. Naber, "Culture of Fear," 251, 253, 256.

44. Erik Love, "Confronting Islamophobia in the United States: Framing Civil Rights Activism among Middle Eastern Americans," in *Anti-Muslim Prejudice: Past and Present*, ed. Maleiha Malik (New York: Routledge, 2010), 202; Ervand Abrahamian, "The US Media, Huntington and September 11," *Third World Quarterly* 24, no. 3 (2003): 538; Associated Press, "Muhammad a Terrorist to Falwell," *New York Times*, October 4, 2002.

45. Huddy et al., "Threat, Anxiety, and Support of Antiterrorism Policies," 602.

46. Hussein Ibish and Anne Stewart, "Report of Hate Crimes and Discrimination against Arab Americans: The Post–September 11 Backlash, September 11, 2001–October 11, 2002," American-Arab Anti-Discrimination Committee, Washington, DC, 2003; Applied Research Center, "The Public's Truth: Stories of Racial Profiling and the Attack on Civil Liberties," Applied Research Center, Oakland, CA, 2003; Human Rights Watch, "'We Are Not the Enemy': Hate Crimes against Arabs, Muslims, and Those Perceived to Be Arab or Muslim after September 11," Human Rights Watch, New

York, 2002; Council on American-Islamic Relations, "The Status of Muslim Civil Rights in the United States, 2005," CAIR, Washington, DC, 2005, 41–42.

47. Ibish and Stewart, "Report of Hate Crimes," 21–29; Volpp, "Citizen and the Terrorist," 152; Mary Beth Sheridan, "Backlash Changes Form, Not Function; Sept. 11 Aftereffects Include Less-Visible Discrimination Cases," *Washington Post*, March 2, 2002. Passengers' comments quoted in Council on American-Islamic Relations, "Status of Muslim Civil Rights," 55.

48. Damasio, *Looking for Spinoza*, 57, and *Descartes' Error*, 173–98; Phelps and Thomas, "Race, Behavior, and the Brain," 747–58; Joan Y. Chiao, Tetsuya Iidaka, Heather L. Gordon, Junpei Nogawa, Moshe Bar, Elissa Aminoff, Norihiro Sadato, and Nalini Ambady, "Cultural Specificity in Amygdala Response to Fear Faces," *Journal of Cognitive Neuroscience* 20, no. 12 (2008): 2167–74; Joan Y. Chiao and Vani A. Mathur, "Intergroup Empathy: How Does Race Affect Empathic Neural Responses?," *Current Biology* 20, no. 11 (2010): R478–80.

49. Park Jaihyun, Karla Felix, and Grace Lee, "Implicit Attitudes toward Arab-Muslims and the Moderating Effects of Social Information," *Basic and Applied Social Psychology* 29, no. 1 (2007): 35–45; Connolly, *Neuropolitics*, 46–48.

50. Phelps and Thomas, "Race Behavior," 751; Pew Forum, "Post 9/11 Attitudes."

51. As Ahmed notes, the "metonymy" of affect "can stick words like 'terrorist' and 'Islam' together—even when arguments are made that seem to unmake those links." Ahmed, *Cultural Politics of Emotion*, 76.

52. On torture, see, e.g., Jutta Brunnée and Stephen J. Toope, *Legitimacy and Legality in International Law: An Interactional Account* (New York: Cambridge University Press, 2010), 220. On the use of force, see: Michael Barnett, *Empire of Humanity: A History of Humanitarianism* (Ithaca, NY: Cornell University Press, 2011); Martha Finnemore, *The Purpose of Intervention: Changing Beliefs about the Use of Force* (Ithaca, NY: Cornell University Press, 2003).

53. Giorgio Agamben, *State of Exception* (Chicago: University of Chicago Press, 2005), 25. While Agamben insists on the "biopolitical" and "mystical" roots of sovereign authority, his philosophical account focuses on parsing the general logic of legal exception rather than exploring the social, psychological, or cultural conditions sustaining specific moments of it.

54. David Luban, "Eight Fallacies about Liberty and Security," in *Human Rights in the "War on Terror,"* ed. Richard Ashby Wilson (New York: Cambridge University Press, 2005), 243. On cultural discriminations in US law, see Sumi Cho and Gil Gott, "The Racial Sovereign," in *Sovereignty, Emergency, Legality*, ed. Austin Sarat (New York: Cambridge University Press, 2010). In international law, see Antony Anghie, *Imperialism, Sovereignty, and the Making of International Law* (New York: Cambridge University Press, 2007).

55. George W. Bush, *U.S. National Security Strategy* (Washington: White House, August 2002), 13–16; George W. Bush, "President Bush Outlines Iraqi Threat," White House website, October 7, 2002, http://georgewbush-whitehouse.archives.gov/news/releases/2002/10/print/20021007–8.html (accessed February 7, 2010); George W. Bush, "President Says Saddam Hussein Must Leave Iraq within 48 Hours," White House website, March 17, 2003, http://georgewbush-whitehouse.archives.gov/news/releases/2003/03/20030317–7.html (accessed November 11, 2009).

56. Stephen D. Krasner, *Sovereignty: Organized Hypocrisy* (Princeton, NJ: Princeton University Press, 1999).

57. As Cramer notes, a domestic norm of "militarized patriotism" ultimately trumped the global norm of nonintervention. Jane Kellett Cramer, "Militarized Patriotism: Why the U.S. Marketplace of Ideas Failed before the Iraq War," *Security Studies* 16, no. 3 (2007): 491. On "norm regress," see Ryder McKeown, "Norm Regress: US Revisionism and the Slow Death of the Torture Norm," *International Relations* 23, no. 1 (2009): 5–25.

58. Finnemore, *Purpose of Intervention,* 154–55. This is also an important dimension of Crawford's argument on decolonization in Neta C. Crawford, *Argument and Change in World Politics: Ethics, Decolonization, and Humanitarian Intervention* (New York: Cambridge University Press, 2002).

59. For this argument, see the essay by Murphy in Jeffrie G. Murphy and Jean Hampton, *Forgiveness and Mercy* (New York: Cambridge University Press, 1988).

60. Mueller, *Overblown,* 51.

61. Elshtain, *Just War against Terror;* Oded Löwenheim and Gadi Heimann, "Revenge in International Politics," *Security Studies* 17, no. 4 (2008): 685–724; Robert C. Solomon, *A Passion for Justice: Emotions and the Origins of the Social Contract* (Reading, MA: Addison-Wesley, 1990), 32, 197.

62. Raj Chari, "The 2004 Spanish Election: Terrorism as a Catalyst for Change?," *West European Politics* 27, no. 5 (2004): 954–63; Enrique Gil Calvo, *11/14-M: El cambio trágico: de la masacre al vuelco electoral* (Madrid: Adhara, 2005), 85–86; Enric Ordeix i Rigo, "Aznar's Political Failure or Punishment for Supporting the Iraq War?: Hypotheses about the Causes of the 2004 Spanish Election Results," *American Behavioral Scientist* 49, no. 4 (2005): 610–15; Ingrid Van Biezen, "Terrorism and Democratic Legitimacy: Conflicting Interpretations of the Spanish Elections," *Mediterranean Politics* 10, no. 1 (2005): 99–108.

63. The PP's political rhetoric accused Spanish voters of being duped by Al Qaeda, with officials describing "a frightened and disorientated electorate voted with a knee-jerk reaction." "An Election Bombshell," *Economist,* March 20, 2004, http://www.economist.com/node/2521089.

64. Susana Conejero and Itziar Etxebarria, "The Impact of the Madrid Bombing on Personal Emotions, Emotional Atmosphere and Emotional Climate," *Journal of Social Issues* 63, no. 2 (2007): 283; Ian Burkitt, "Powerful Emotions: Power Government and Opposition in the 'War on Terror,'" *Sociology* 39, no. 4 (2005): 692.

65. Elaine Sciolino, "Grieving Crowds in Spain Seethe at Train Attacks," *New York Times,* March 12, 2004; Lizette Alvarez and Elaine Sciolino, "Spain Grapples with Notion That Terrorism Trumped Democracy," *New York Times,* March 16, 2004.

66. Elaine Sciolino, Doreen Carvajal, and Lizette Alvarez, "Spain Struggles to Cope as the Equation of Terror Changes in an Instant," *New York Times,* March 11, 2004; Angelique Chrisafis, "Sick, Afraid, Defiant, They Marched in Their Millions: Angelique Chrisafis in Madrid on the Turmoil of Emotion That Gripped a Nation in Mourning," *The Guardian,* March 13, 2004; Peter Popham, "'We Are Shocked. We Can't Understand What Has Happened to Us,'" *The Independent,* March 13, 2004; Casimiro García-Abadillo, *11-M: La venganza* (Madrid: Esfera de los Libros, 2005), 72, my translation; Tim Gaynor, "Thousands on Streets in Pain and Grief," *The Independent,* March 12, 2004; Burkitt, "Powerful Emotions," 691.

67. Castells, *Communication Power,* 360, 352; Sandra L. Suárez, "Mobile Democracy: Text Messages, Voter Turnout and the 2004 Spanish General Election," *Representation* 42, no. 2 (2006): 122; Angelique Chrisafis, "Madrid Aftermath: Angry Voters Demand to Know the Truth Behind Carnage," *The Guardian,* March 15, 2004; Gil Calvo, *Cambio*

tragico, 153, my translation. Another observer notes a "growing climate of backlash." García-Abadillo, *La venganza*, 108.

68. Cristina Flesher Fominaya, "The Madrid Bombings and Popular Protest: Misinformation, Counter-Information, Mobilisation and Elections after '11-M,'" *Contemporary Social Science* 6, no. 3 (2011): 290; Castells, *Communication Power*, 363.

69. Castells, *Communication Power*, 355. As one account suggests, the demonstrations of March 13 "helped to unite the anger of the anti-war mobilizations of 2002–2003 with a wider desire to oust Aznar's PP from government." Isis Sánchez Estellés, "The Political-Opportunity Structure of the Spanish Anti-War Movement (2002–2004) and Its Impact," *Sociological Review* 58, suppl. S2 (2010): 255.

70. Tom Dannenbaum, "Bombs, Ballots, and Coercion: The Madrid Bombings, Electoral Politics, and Terrorist Strategy," *Security Studies* 20, no. 3 (2011): 321–22; "From A to Z: Mr. Aznar Suffered a Shakespearean Ending. Mr. Zapatero Has Made a More Quixotic Start," *Economist*, June 24, 2004, http://www.economist.com/node/2521089; i Rigo, "Aznar's Political Failure," 612.

71. Narciso Michavila, "War, Terrorism and Elections: Electoral Impact of the Islamist Terror Attacks on Madrid," Real Instituto Elcano de Estudios Internacionales y Estratégicos, Madrid, 2005, 18.

72. Wyn Rees and Richard J. Aldrich, "Contending Cultures of Counterterrorism: Transatlantic Divergence or Convergence?," *International Affairs* 81, no. 5 (2005): 912, 914–15.

73. Associated Press, "Bin Laden Tape Is Probably Authentic, CIA Says," *Washington Post*, October 21, 2003; Dannenbaum, "Bombs Ballots," 312.

74. Media reports suggest that the attacks also did not precipitate the kind of tensions between Muslim and non-Muslim citizens visible in the United States. Elaine Sciolino, "Spain Is Riven by the Sorrows of March," *New York Times*, March 11, 2005, 4.

75. Anthony N. Celso, "Spanish Post-3/11 Antiterror Policy: Zapatero's Tyranny of Circumstance and the Dashing of Good Intentions," *Mediterranean Quarterly* 20, no. 2 (2009): 16.

76. Alejandro Colás, "An Exceptional Response? Security, Development and Civil Society in Spanish Policy after 11-M," *Development and Change* 41, no. 2 (2010): 320–28.

77. Anthony Celso, "The Tragedy of Al-Andalus: The Madrid Terror Attacks and the Islamization of Spanish Politics," *Mediterranean Quarterly* 16, no. 3 (2005): 86–101.

78. See: Bennett, *Why We Fight*; Elshtain, *Just War*; Lance Morrow, "The Case for Rage and Retribution," *Time*, September 14, 2001. Al Gore, for example, argued in a September 2002 speech that nothing should be permitted "to diminish our focus on the necessity for avenging the 3,000 Americans who were murdered." Quoted in Croft, *Culture, Crisis, and America's War on Terror*, 163.

79. Cramer, "Militarized Patriotism."

CHAPTER FOUR

1. Huntington, *Clash of Civilizations and the Remaking of World Order*; Robert D. Kaplan, *Balkan Ghosts: A Journey through History* (New York: Vintage Books, 1994), 32; Robert D. Kaplan, *The Coming Anarchy: Shattering the Dreams of the Post Cold War* (New York: Random House, 2000), 34.

2. See, e.g., Norman M. Naimark, *Fires of Hatred: Ethnic Cleansing in Twentieth-Century Europe* (Cambridge, MA: Harvard University Press, 2001). Kaufman and Petersen offer a more sustained interrogation of "hatred," although both find the category to be of enduring value. Kaufman, *Modern Hatreds*; Petersen, *Understanding Ethnic Violence*.

From a constructivist perspective, Wilmer, for example, argues that elites sought to arouse fear in addition to hatred, but considers both as tightly bound to the politics of identity. As she puts it, leaders "rallied emotions against a clear idea of the enemy." Franke Wilmer, *The Social Construction of Man, the State, and War: Identity, Conflict, and Violence in Former Yugoslavia* (New York: Routledge, 2002), 260.

3. Straus, *Order of Genocide*, 132; see also 14, 27–34, 73; Lee Ann Fujii, *Killing Neighbors: Webs of Violence in Rwanda* (Ithaca, NY: Cornell University Press, 2009), 4–7, 77, 183; see Stef Jansen, "'Why Do They Hate Us?' Everyday Serbian Nationalist Knowledge of Muslim Hatred," *Journal of Mediterranean Studies* 13, no. 2 (2003): 215–37.

4. Recognizing that hatred has been overestimated does not mean embracing a utopian fantasy that, beneath the machinations of power politics, people in conflicted societies are magically committed to peace. Ethnic conflicts are too often seen through a polarized opposition between well-entrenched hatreds and romanticized pluralism. See, for example, the response to Jansen and others in Robert M. Hayden, "Moral Vision and Impaired Insight: The Imagining of Other Peoples' Communities in Bosnia," *Current Anthropology* 48, no. 1 (2007): 105–31.

5. My study does not address directly participation in genocidal killing itself, although these social interactions likely had emotional effects of their own. Fujii offers a very compelling account of the participative dimension of the *Interahamwe* militias, arguing that group identity and social networks lowered resistance to killing. Fujii, *Killing Neighbors*, 154–79.

6. As Fujii suggests in her conclusion, scholars need to regard violent conflict "as a creative, not just destructive, process." Ibid., 188.

7. Franche, *Rwanda*, 60 (my translation). I generally agree with Franche when he describes Hutus and Tutsis as "communities of fear" rather than ethnic groups. My point is that when fear forged allegiances and stimulated memories in the early 1990s, it did so as a contingent and creative force rather than a repetitive one.

8. Mahmood Mamdani, *When Victims Become Killers: Colonialism, Nativism, and the Genocide in Rwanda* (Princeton, NJ: Princeton University Press, 2001), 191. Even detailed historical work represents violence as the product of pent-up hatred needing release. One historian describes the response to the 1963 invasions: "Popular participation in violence created a kind of collective catharsis through which years of pent-up hatred suddenly seemed to find an outlet." René Lemarchand, *Rwanda and Burundi* (Washington, DC: Praeger, 1970), 224.

9. Danielle de Lame, "Mighty Secrets, Public Commensality, and the Crisis of Transparency: Rwanda through the Looking Glass," *Canadian Journal of African Studies* 38, no. 2 (2004): 279–317.

10. She offers a functionalist interpretation of these developments, arguing that the demonization of Tutsis and the preparation for genocide "provided anxious parts of the population with an alternative order, preventing a fall into complete chaos." Ibid., 307.

11. Mamdani, *When Victims Become Killers*, 190, 231–32. The idea that Tutsis were a foreign race rather than a domestic ethnic group was part of a larger hypothesis developed by Western observers during the nineteenth century to account for the traces of civilization in Africa. In this case, the Tutsis were seen to be a kind of proto-European cultural vanguard within Africa (79–87). See also Franche, *Rwanda*, 25–48, and Gérard Prunier, *The Rwanda Crisis: History of a Genocide* (New York: Columbia University Press, 1995), 5–9.

12. de Lame, "Mighty Secrets," 306; Christopher C. Taylor, *Sacrifice as Terror: The Rwan-*

dan Genocide of 1994 (New York: Berg, 1999), 161; Claudine Vidal, *Sociologie des passions: Rwanda, Côte D'Ivoire* (Paris: Karthala, 1991), 40. See also the brief discussion in *Prosecutor v. Ferdinand Nahimana, Jean-Bosco Barayagwiza, and Hassan Ngeze*, ICTR-99–52-T, Judgment and Sentence of Trial Chamber I, December 3, 2003, para. 1079 (hereinafter *Prosecutor v. Nahimana*).

13. On this point, see Adam Jones, "Gender and Genocide in Rwanda," *Journal of Genocide Research* 4, no. 1 (2002): 65–94.

14. Taylor, *Sacrifice as Terror*, 174.

15. Straus, *Order of Genocide*, 199, 173. Straus does not explain the difference between understanding insecurity and uncertainty as rationales (he writes "the aim [of the perpetrators] was 'security' in a context of acute insecurity") and regarding them as "climates" (7, 172).

16. Tone Bringa, "Averted Gaze: Genocide in Bosnia-Herzegovina 1992–1995," in *Annihilating Difference: The Anthropology of Genocide*, ed. Alex Laban Hinton (Berkeley: University of California Press, 2002), 212.

17. See Laura Silber and Allan Little, *Yugoslavia: Death of a Nation* (New York: Penguin Books, 1997), 31–33; Lenard J. Cohen, *Serpent in the Bosom: The Rise and Fall of Slobodan Milošević*, rev. ed. (Boulder, CO: Westview Press, 2002), 102–6; and Branimir Anzulovic, *Heavenly Serbia: From Myth to Genocide* (New York: New York University Press, 1999), 114–18.

18. Silber and Little, *Yugoslavia*, 31.

19. Barry R. Posen, "The Security Dilemma and Ethnic Conflict," *Survival* 35, no. 1 (1993): 29–35; Jack Snyder and Robert Jervis, "Civil War and the Security Dilemma," in *Civil Wars, Insecurity, and Intervention*, ed. Barbara F. Walter (New York: Columbia University Press, 1999); Chaim Kaufmann, "Possible and Impossible Solutions to Ethnic Civil Wars," *International Security* 20, no. 4 (1996): 136–75; and David A. Lake and Donald Rothchild, "Containing Fear: The Origins and Management of Ethnic Conflict," *International Security* 21, no. 2 (1996): 41–75.

20. Fujii, *Killing Neighbors*, 184.

21. Robert M. Hayden, "Recounting the Dead: The Discovery and Redefinition of Wartime Massacres in Late- and Post-Communist Yugoslavia," in *Memory, History, and Opposition under State Socialism*, ed. Rubie S. Watson (Santa Fe, NM: School of American Research Press, 1994), 178. On the debate over how many were killed during World War II, see Anzulovic, *Heavenly Serbia*, 103–4; and Sabrina P. Ramet, *Balkan Babel: The Disintegration of Yugoslavia from the Death of Tito to the Fall of Milošević*, 4th ed. (Boulder, CO: Westview Press, 2002), 53.

22. See Bette Denich, "Dismembering Yugoslavia: Nationalist Ideologies and the Symbolic Revival of Genocide," *American Ethnologist* 21, no. 2 (1994): 367–90; and Hayden, "Recounting the Dead."

23. Kaufman, *Modern Hatreds*, 173.

24. Katherine Verdery, *The Political Lives of Dead Bodies: Reburial and Postsocialist Change* (New York: Columbia University Press, 1999), 28.

25. Kaufman, *Modern Hatreds*, 173.

26. Hayden, "Recounting the Dead," 168, 174.

27. Verdery, *Political Lives*, 97, 107, 99. See also Bringa, who argues that the absence of memorialization intensified, rather than diminished, the emotional power of the mass graves: "Averted Gaze," 211.

28. Verdery, *Political Lives*, 100.

29. Denich, "Dismembering Yugoslavia," 371.

30. Verdery, *Political Lives*, 110 (my emphasis).

31. Robert D. Kaplan, "A Reader's Guide to the Balkans," *New York Times*, April 18, 1993. For Kaplan, "history" in this traditional society has failed to evolve into the mature, linear form it takes in the West. See Kaplan, *Balkan Ghosts*, 58.

32. Michael Ignatieff, *The Warrior's Honor: Ethnic War and the Modern Conscience* (New York: Penguin, 1998), 186. In a similar vein, Judah writes: "Every village in Croatia and Bosnia was now beginning to remember what the neighbours had done fifty years before." Tim Judah, *The Serbs: History, Myth, and the Destruction of Yugoslavia*, 2nd ed. (New Haven, CT: Yale University Press, 2000), 284.

33. Daniel Schacter calls this "mood-congruent retrieval": *Searching for Memory*, 211–12.

34. Ibid., 9, 161–91; Deleuze, *Bergsonism*, 55–61; Bergson, *Matter and Memory*, 228, 240.

35. Damasio calls these "availability errors," betraying his commitment to an abstract standard of emotional conduct: *Descartes' Error*, 192. See also Schacter, *Searching for Memory*, 192–217.

36. Maurice Halbwachs and Lewis A. Coser, *On Collective Memory* (Chicago: University of Chicago Press, 1992), 52.

37. Verdery, *Political Lives*, 108.

38. United Nations Security Council, Statute of the International Criminal Tribunal for Rwanda, art. 2(3)(e), S.C. Res. 955, UNSCOR, 49th Sess., 3453th mtg., Annex, UN Doc. S/RES/955 (1994), reprinted in 33 I.L.M. 1598 (1994).

39. *Prosecutor v. Nahimana*, paras. 32, 141, 45, 58, 985.

40. All citations from the speech are from a translation used by a Canadian federal court of appeals, the proceedings of which I discuss below. *Mugesera v. Canada* (*Minister of Citizenship and Immigration*), [2003] F.C.A. 325 (Federal Ct. of Appeals), at para. 17 (hereinafter *Mugesera v. Canada* [F.C.A.]).

41. See Alison Des Forges, *"Leave None to Tell the Story": Genocide in Rwanda* (New York: Human Rights Watch and International Federation of Human Rights, 1999), 86.

42. *Mugesera v. Canada* (F.C.A.), para. 54.

43. Ultimately, the court is powerless to consider the full context of the speech, since it is concerned only with "whether a crime would have been committed in Canada," were the speech to have been delivered there (ibid., para. 200.) The case is an appeal from a federal court's review of an internal adjudication by the Ministry of Citizenship and Immigration.

44. *Mugesera v. Canada (Minister of Citizenship and Immigration)*, [2005] 2 S.C.R. 100, 2005 SCC 40, para. 103 (hereinafter *Mugesera v. Canada* [S.C.C.]).

45. *Mugesera v. Canada* (F.C.A.), para. 173.

46. See the translation included in ibid., para. 17.

47. *Mugesera v. Canada* (S.C.C.), p. 8; *Mugesera v. Canada* (F.C.A.), para. 183.

48. *Prosecutor v. Nahimana*, para. 1022.

49. David McNeill, ed., *Language and Gesture* (New York: Cambridge University Press, 2000); Brenda Farnell, "Rethinking 'Verbal' and 'Non-Verbal' in Discursive Performance," *Textus* 14 (2001): 401–20.

50. Judy Reilly and Judy Seibert, "Language and Emotion," in *Handbook of Affective Sciences*, ed. Richard J. Davidson, Klaus R. Scherer, and H. Hill Goldsmith (New York: Oxford University Press, 2002), 538.

51. Ralph Adolphs, "Social Cognition: Feeling Voices to Recognize Emotions," *Current Biology* 20, no. 24 (2010): R1071–72; Ralph Adolphs, "Neural Systems for Recognizing Emotion," *Current Opinion in Neurobiology* 12, no. 2 (2002): 169–77; J. S. Morris,

S. K. Scott, and R. J. Dolan, "Saying It with Feeling: Neural Responses to Emotional Vocalizations," *Neuropsychologia* 37, no. 10 (1999): 1155–63. There is, however, some disagreement on whether prosody stimulates the mirror neurons discussed in chapter 1. Compare Adolphs, "Social Cognition," R1072 and Iacoboni, *Mirroring People*, 105.

52. Quoted in *Prosecutor v. Nahimana*, 45.
53. For an extensive catalogue of statements from the Rwandan media, see Jean-Pierre Chrétien, *Rwanda, Les médias du génocide* (Paris: Karthala, 1995).
54. Straus, *Order of Genocide*, 130, 49, 148.
55. Indeed, Straus addresses this problem himself. Ibid., 123.
56. Prunier, *Rwanda Crisis*, 189; and Christine L. Kellow and H. Leslie Steves, "The Role of Radio in the Rwandan Genocide," *Journal of Communication* 48, no. 3 (1998): 116. See also Bill Berkeley, "Sounds of Violence," *New Republic*, August 24, 1994, 18; and African Rights, *Rwanda: Death, Despair, and Defiance*, rev. ed. (London: African Rights, 1995), 1010.
57. Richard Vokes, "Charisma, Creativity, and Cosmopolitanism: A Perspective on the Power of the New Radio Broadcasting in Uganda and Rwanda," *Journal of the Royal Anthropological Institute* 13, no. 4 (2007): 817.
58. Quoted in Des Forges, *Leave None to Tell the Story*, 70.
59. de Lame, "Mighty Secrets," 311.
60. *Prosecutor v. Nahimana*, para. 1031.
61. Quoted in Des Forges, *Leave None to Tell the Story*, 70.
62. See Vokes for an account of the microsociology of radio listening in the Great Lakes Region. Vokes, "Charisma, Creativity, and Cosmopolitanism."
63. With the votes of representatives from Serbia, Vojvodina, Kosovo, and Montenegro, Milošević virtually controlled the eight-vote power-sharing structure left behind by Tito. Were Slovenia to succeed, his control would be complete.
64. On the historical significance of Kosovo and the so-called Kosovo myth, see Anzulovic, *Heavenly Serbia*, chapter 4.
65. There has been much discussion of the role of economic factors in the rise of nationalism in Yugoslavia. Its economy during the 1980s experienced decreasing reliance on export of manufactured goods; IMF austerity policies beginning in the late 1970s; layoffs, increasing unemployment, and wage restrictions; and price increases and consumer goods shortages. See Susan L. Woodward, *Balkan Tragedy: Chaos and Dissolution after the Cold War* (Washington, DC: Brookings Institution, 1995), 50–51 and passim; Branka Magaš, *The Destruction of Yugoslavia: Tracking the Break-up 1980–92* (New York: Verso, 1993), 94–96.
66. Ger Duijzings, *History and Reminders in East Bosnia* (Amsterdam: Netherlands Institute for War Documentation, 2003), 30–31.
67. Maliqi, quoted in Howard Clark, *Civil Resistance in Kosovo* (Sterling, VA: Pluto Press, 2000), 48. See also Shkëlzen Maliqi, *Kosova: Separate Worlds: Reflections and Analyses, 1989–1998* (Pristina: MM, 1998); Magaš, *Destruction of Yugoslavia*, 179–90.
68. Magaš, *Destruction of Yugoslavia*, 188.
69. Ahmed, *Cultural Politics of Emotion*, 45.
70. This was the claim of Milošević's wife, Mirjana Marković. See Cohen, *Serpent in the Bosom*, 132.
71. Silber and Little, *Yugoslavia*, 66.
72. Ivan Čolović, *The Politics of Symbol in Serbia: Essays in Political Anthropology*, trans. Celia Hawkesworth (London: Hurst and Co., 2002), 269.

73. See, e.g., the discussion of the Albanian protests in Maliqi, *Kosova*, 86; and Silber and Little, *Yugoslavia*, 63.
74. One observer wrote: "Far from being spontaneous, the recent mass rallies in Serbia were in fact little more than an instrument of inner-party struggle." Magaš, *Destruction of Yugoslavia*, 171. Many critics of Milošević and his tactics have been quick to point out that demonstrators were frequently given monetary reward for their participation, especially at the November 19 rally in Belgrade. See Silber and Little, *Yugoslavia*, 63–64.
75. On the Kosovo Polje meeting, see Cohen, *Serpent in the Bosom*, 106–9; Tim Judah, *Kosovo: War and Revenge*, 2nd ed. (New Haven: Yale University Press, 2002), 52–53; Noel Malcolm, *Kosovo: A Short History* (London: Macmillan, 1998), 341–42; Louis Sell, *Slobodan Milošević and the Destruction of Yugoslavia* (Durham, NC: Duke University Press, 2002), 1–3; and Silber and Little, *Yugoslavia*, 37–38.
76. Silber and Little, *Yugoslavia*, 40, 38. Protest organizers later admitted to having supplied a truck full of stones.
77. Quoted in ibid.
78. Sell, *Slobodan Milošević*, 1; Cohen, *Serpent in the Bosom*, 107; Angus Macqueen and Paul Mitchell, "The Cracks Appear," in *Yugoslavia: Death of a Nation* (New York: Discovery Channel Video, 1996); Magaš, *Destruction of Yugoslavia*, 201.
79. Cohen, *Serpent in the Bosom*, 144.
80. Crowd size estimates varied dramatically. Milošević personally estimated 1.5 million; the Belgrade media reported 2 million.
81. On this aspect of the speech, see Cohen, *Serpent in the Bosom*, 146, 57.
82. The Tribunal translated the statement as: "They are not armed battles, though even ones of that kind have not been excluded." *Prosecutor v. Milošević*, Case no. IT-02-54, Transcript no. 02–02–14-IT of the Trial Chamber, February 14, 2002, 273, 271.
83. Teofil Pancic, "Sex in the City, Sloba and the Hague," *Helsinki Charter* 49 (2002).
84. Cohen, *Serpent in the Bosom*, 146.

CHAPTER FIVE

1. See, e.g., Stuart J. Kaufman, "Escaping the Symbolic Politics Trap: Reconciliation Initiatives and Conflict Resolution in Ethnic Wars," *Journal of Peace Research* 43, no. 2 (2006): 201–18.
2. See, e.g., Stef Jansen, "Troubled Locations: Return, the Life Course, and Transformations of 'Home' in Bosnia-Herzegovina," *Focaal: The European Journal of Anthropology*, no. 49 (2007): 15–30; and David Newbury, "Returning Refugees: Four Historical Patterns of 'Coming Home,' to Rwanda," *Comparative Studies in Society and History* 47, no. 2 (2005): 252–85.
3. My argument echoes the call for legal institutions to develop a greater understanding of the cultural and emotional contexts in which they are engaged. See Jodi Halpern and Harvey M. Weinstein, "Rehumanizing the Other: Empathy and Reconciliation," *Human Rights Quarterly* 26 (2004): 561–83; Martha Minow, "Institutions and Emotions: Redressing Mass Violence," in *The Passions of Law*, ed. Susan A. Bandes (New York: New York University Press, 1999); and Eric Stover and Harvey M. Weinstein, "Introduction: Conflict, Justice, and Reclamation," in *My Neighbor, My Enemy: Justice and Community in the Aftermath of Mass Atrocity*, ed. Stover and Weinstein (New York: Cambridge University Press, 2004); Laurel E. Fletcher and Harvey M. Weinstein, "Violence and Social Repair: Rethinking the Contribution of Justice to Reconciliation," *Human Rights Quarterly* 24, no. 3 (2002): 573–639. My approach also differs

from this work by contesting the assumption that postconflict societies are characterized by cycles of hatred and other identity-bound emotions, regarding emotions as necessary features of social life and potential resources in the pursuit of justice, and, finally, moving from a narrow range of privileged emotions, such as forgiveness or empathy, to a range of possible emotions deserving expression in a public and participative process aimed at building trust.

4. James C. McKinley Jr., "As Crowds Vent Their Rage, Rwanda Publicly Executes 22," *New York Times*, April 25, 1998.

5. Minow, "Institutions and Emotions," 268.

6. Martha Minow and Nancy L. Rosenblum, *Breaking the Cycles of Hatred: Memory, Law, and Repair* (Princeton, NJ: Princeton University Press, 2002).

7. As Vamik Volkan explains, the traumatic experience is then "transgenerationally-transmitted." Quoted in Vanessa Pupavac, "The Emotionology of the New International Security Paradigm," *European Journal of Social Theory* 7, no. 4 (2004): 157.

8. Ibid., 149, 150 and passim.

9. On the aversion to emotional influences in the legal domain, see Susan A. Bandes, "Introduction," in *The Passions of Law*, ed. Susan A. Bandes (New York: New York University Press, 1999).

10. For an account of the West's racialization of African political culture, see Siba N. Grovogui, "Come to Africa: A Hermeneutics of Race in International Theory," *Alternatives: Global, Local, Political* 26, no. 4 (2001): 425–48.

11. Gary Jonathan Bass, *Stay the Hand of Vengeance: The Politics of War Crimes Tribunals* (Princeton, NJ: Princeton University Press, 2000).

12. Martha Minow, *Between Vengeance and Forgiveness: Facing History after Genocide and Mass Violence* (Boston: Beacon Press, 1998), 26.

13. See, e.g., Priscilla B. Hayner, *Unspeakable Truths: Facing the Challenge of Truth Commissions* (New York: Routledge, 2001); Minow, *Between Vengeance*, 52–90.

14. Minow, "Institutions and Emotions," 267, 271.

15. Mark Osiel, *Mass Atrocity, Collective Memory, and the Law* (New Brunswick, NJ: Transaction Publishers, 1997), 17.

16. Martha C. Nussbaum, "'Secret Sewers of Vice': Disgust, Bodies, and the Law," in *Passions of Law*, ed. Bandes, 19–62; Solomon, *Passion for Justice*; William Ian Miller, *Eye for an Eye* (New York: Cambridge University Press, 2006).

17. Hirschman, *Passions and the Interests*, 64–66.

18. Gilles Deleuze, *Empiricism and Subjectivity: An Essay on Hume's Theory of Human Nature*, trans. Constantin V. Boundas (New York: Columbia University Press, 1991), 43.

19. Austin Sarat, "Vengeance, Victims and the Identities of Law," *Social and Legal Studies* 6, no. 2 (1997): 169; Bandes, "Introduction," 11.

20. Dan Saxon, "Exporting Justice: Perceptions of the ICTY among the Serbian, Croatian, and Muslim Communities in the Former Yugoslavia," *Journal of Human Rights* 4, no. 4 (2005): 559.

21. Fletcher and Weinstein, "Violence and Social Repair," 604–5; Tim Judah, "The Fog of Justice," *New York Review of Books* 51, no. 1 (2004): 25; Elizabeth Neuffer, *The Key to My Neighbor's House: Seeking Justice in Bosnia and Rwanda* (New York: Picador, 2001), 181–82, 211, 302–3, 353–55, 376.

22. After flocking to The Hague for what had been touted as the most important war crimes trial since Nuremberg, reporters were left uninspired by an overly technical prosecution of a low-ranking Serb soldier. Bass, *Stay the Hand of Vengeance*, 257;

and John Hagan, *Justice in the Balkans: Prosecuting War Crimes in the Hague Tribunal* (Chicago: University of Chicago Press, 2003), 81.

23. Neuffer, *Neighbor's House*, 181.
24. Saxon, "Exporting Justice," 566; Hagan, *Justice in the Balkans*; Neuffer, *Neighbor's House*, 353–55.
25. Several years later, the Rwandan government codified rape as a crime equal in severity to the planning of genocide.
26. See Neuffer, *Neighbor's House*, 271–92; Catherine Newbury and Hannah Baldwin, "Aftermath: Women in Postgenocide Rwanda," Working Paper no. 303, USAID, Washington, DC, 2000, 4–5. Engle argues that the advocacy surrounding rape as genocide inadvertently reified ethnic identities. Karen Engle, "Feminism and Its (Dis)Contents: Criminalizing Wartime Rape in Bosnia and Herzegovina," *American Journal of International Law* 99, no. 4 (2005): 778–816.
27. Alison Des Forges and Timothy Longman, "Legal Responses to Genocide in Rwanda," in *My Neighbor, My Enemy*, ed. Stover and Weinstein, 57; Timothy Longman, Phuong Pham, and Harvey M. Weinstein, "Connecting Justice to Human Experience: Attitudes toward Accountability and Reconciliation in Rwanda," in *My Neighbor, My Enemy*, ed. Stover and Weinstein, 219. On perceptions of the ICTY, see Dina Corkalo, Dean Ajdukovic, Harvey M. Weinstein, Eric Stover, Dino Djipa, and Miklos Biro, "Neighbors Again? Intercommunity Relations after Ethnic Cleansing," in *My Neighbor, My Enemy*, ed. Stover and Weinstein, 143–61; and Saxon, "Exporting Justice," 562.
28. Peter Uvin and Charles Mironko, "Western and Local Approaches to Justice in Rwanda," *Global Governance* 9, no. 2 (2003): 221, 222.
29. Kamari Maxine Clarke, *Fictions of Justice: The International Criminal Court and the Challenges of Legal Pluralism in Sub-Saharan Africa* (New York: Cambridge University Press, 2009), 14.
30. Samantha Power, *A Problem from Hell: America and the Age of Genocide* (New York: Basic Books, 2002), 386.
31. United Nations Secretary-General, "Secretary-General, in 'Mission of Healing' to Rwanda, Pledges Support of United Nations for Country's Search for Peace and Progress," United Nations, New York, May 6, 1998, 1.
32. See, e.g., Stephen Buckley, "Mass Slaughter Was Avoidable, General Says; Ex-Leader of Peacekeepers Testifies at Rwandan's Trial," *Washington Post*, February 26, 1998; Lara Santoro, "Rwanda Massacres Were Avoidable, General Says," *Christian Science Monitor*, February 27, 1998; David Beresford, "General Sobs at Memory of Rwandan Genocide," *Guardian*, February 26, 1998.
33. Uvin and Mironko, "Western and Local Approaches to Justice," 220.
34. For an overview of these arguments, see Minow, *Between Vengeance*, 52–90. See also Hayner, *Unspeakable Truths*.
35. For a general overview of debates over the rationale behind truth and reconciliation, see the essays in Robert I. Rotberg and Dennis F. Thompson, eds., *Truth v. Justice: The Morality of Truth Commissions* (Princeton, NJ: Princeton University Press, 2000).
36. Alex Boraine, *A Country Unmasked: Inside South Africa's Truth and Reconciliation Commission* (New York: Oxford University Press, 2001), 99. On the issue of how the commission defined "gross violations," see 106–7.
37. The HRVC was eventually forced to discontinue this practice. Many observers felt this form of solicitation effectively made forgiveness into a demand rather than a gesture of generosity. See Richard A. Wilson, *The Politics of Truth and Reconciliation in*

South Africa: Legitimizing the Post-Apartheid State (New York: Cambridge University Press, 2001), 119.

38. Robert I. Rotberg, "Truth Commissions and the Provision of Truth, Justice, and Reconciliation," in *Truth v. Justice*, ed. Rotberg and Thompson, 5.

39. For an account of this critique, see Rajeev Bhargava, "Restoring Decency to Barbaric Societies," in *Truth v. Justice*, ed. Rotberg and Thompson, 52–53.

40. Mahmood Mamdani, "The Truth According to the TRC," in *The Politics of Memory: Truth, Healing, and Social Justice*, ed. Ifi Amadiume and Abdullahi An-Na'im (London: Zed Books, 2000), 182.

41. Wilson, *Politics of Truth*, 111.

42. Antjie Krog, *Country of My Skull: Guilt, Sorrow, and the Limits of Forgiveness in the New South Africa*, 1st U.S. ed. (New York: Three Rivers Press, 2000).

43. Fletcher and Weinstein, "Violence and Social Repair," 622; Das, *Life and Words*, 15.

44. See ibid. and Arjun Appadurai, "The Capacity to Aspire: Culture and the Terms of Recognition," in *Culture and Public Action*, ed. Vijayendra Rao and Michael Walton (Stanford, CA: Stanford University Press, 2004).

45. Roberto Mangabeira Unger, *Democracy Realized: The Progressive Alternative* (New York: Verso, 1998), 260.

46. John Mutamba and Jeanne Izabiliza, *The Role of Women in Reconciliation and Peace Building in Rwanda: Ten Years after Genocide 1994–2004: Contributions, Challenges and Way Forward* (Kigali: National Unity and Reconciliation Commission, 2005), 37–45, 23.

47. Elizabeth Powley, "Strengthening Governance: The Role of Women in Rwanda's Transition," Hunt Alternatives Fund, Boston, 2003, 2; Newbury and Baldwin, "Aftermath," 6; and Laura Fraser, "Coffee, and Hope, Grow in Rwanda," *New York Times*, August 6, 2006. My concern here is not with questions relating to gender consciousness, equality, and political participation, although there has been much discussion of these topics in this case. See, e.g., African Rights, "Women Taking a Lead: Progress Towards Empowerment and Gender Equity in Rwanda," Discussion Paper no. 12, African Rights, Kigali, 2004; Powley, "Strengthening Governance"; and Marc Lacey, "Women's Voices Rise as Rwanda Reinvents Itself," *New York Times*, February 26, 2005, A1.

48. See, e.g., Newbury and Baldwin, "Aftermath," 3–8.

49. Erin K. Baines, "Les Femmes Aux Mille Bras: Building Peace in Rwanda," in *Gender, Conflict, and Peacekeeping*, ed. Dyan Imazurana, Angela Raven-Roberts, and Jane L. Parpart (Lanham, MD: Rowman and Littlefield, 2005), 226, 231.

50. See Johan Pottier, *Re-Imagining Rwanda: Conflict, Survival and Disinformation in the Late Twentieth Century* (New York: Cambridge University Press, 2002), 130–50.

51. Halpern and Weinstein, "Rehumanizing the Other," 582; Bert Ingelaere, "'Does the Truth Pass across the Fire without Burning?' Locating the Short Circuit in Rwanda's Gacaca Courts," *Journal of Modern African Studies* 47, no. 4 (2009): 515; Appadurai, "Capacity to Aspire," 75–78.

52. Collins, *Interaction Ritual Chains*, xiv. See also the discussion of Giddens's theory in Mitzen, "Ontological Security in World Politics," 341–70.

53. Hoffman offers such a view in the context of interstate relations. Aaron Hoffman, "A Conceptualization of Trust in International Relations," *European Journal of International Relations* 8, no. 3 (2002): 375–401. Mercer recognizes the emotional dimension of trust but nevertheless treats it epistemologically, as a form of "certainty beyond observable evidence." Mercer, "Rationality and Psychology in International Politics," 95.

54. Pouliot, *International Security in Practice*, 40; Ralph Adolphs, "Trust in the Brain," *Nature Neuroscience* 5, no. 3 (2002): 192–93; Antonio R. Damasio, *The Feeling of What Happens: Body and Emotion in the Making of Consciousness* (New York: Harcourt Brace, 1999), 66–67.

55. Collins, *Interaction Ritual Chains*, 119.

56. See Claudine Vidal, "Les commémorations du génocide au Rwanda," *Les Temps Modernes* 613 (2001): 1–46; Timothy Longman and Théonèste Rutagengwa, "Memory, Identity, and Community in Rwanda," in *My Neighbor, My Enemy*, ed. Stover and Weinstein, 166; Jennie E. Burnet, "The Injustice of Local Justice: Truth, Reconciliation, and Revenge in Rwanda," *Genocide Studies and Prevention* 3, no. 2 (2008): 173–93; Longman and Rutagengwa, "Memory, Identity, and Community"; Lars Waldorf, "Mass Justice for Mass Atrocity: Rethinking Local Justice as Transitional Justice," *Temple Law Review* 79, no. 1 (2006): 1–87.

57. Rwanda, Office of the President, *The Unity of Rwandans: Before the Colonial Period and under the Colonial Rule, under the First Republic* (Kigali: Republic of Rwanda, Office of the President of the Republic, 1999).

58. Longman and Rutagengwa, "Memory, Identity, and Community," 176.

59. Quoted in ibid.

60. Mahmood Mamdani, "Reconciliation without Justice," in *Religion and Media*, ed. Hent de Vries (Stanford, CA: Stanford University Press, 1999), 383.

61. Das, *Life and Words*, 97–100.

62. Longman and Rutagengwa, "Memory, Identity, and Community," 176.

63. She argues that acts of censorship may perpetuate the "force" of an expression merely by marking it as part of a restricted discourse. Judith Butler, *Excitable Speech: A Politics of the Performative* (New York: Routledge, 1997), 130.

64. Vidal, "Commémorations du génocide," 22; Waldorf, "Mass Justice."

65. See, e.g., Scott Straus, "Origins and Aftermaths: The Dynamics of Genocide and Their Post-Crime Implications," in *After Mass Crime: Rebuilding States and Communities*, ed. Béatrice Pouligny, Simon Chesterman, and Albrecht Schnabel (New York: United Nations University Press, 2007).

66. William Schabas, "Genocide Trials and Gacaca Courts," *Journal of International Criminal Justice* 3 (2005): 881; Urusaro Alice Karekezi, Alphonse Nshimiyamana, and Beth Mutamba, "Localizing Justice: Gacaca Courts in Post-Genocide Rwanda," in *My Neighbor, My Enemy*, ed. Stover and Weinstein, 73. Most scholars discussed here agree that the *gacaca* system implemented by the Rwandan government during the 2000s was less a resort to a "traditional" institution than a strategic appropriation and extensive modification of customary legal practices.

67. Republic of Rwanda, Departement des Juridictions Gacaca, "Les Juridictions Gacaca comme solution alternative au reglement du contentieux du genocide," Departement des Juridictions Gacaca, Kigali, 2003, 8.

68. For discussions of these problems, see Burnet, "Injustice of Local Justice"; Amnesty International, *Rwanda—Gacaca: A Question of Justice* (London: Amnesty International, International Secretariat, 2002); Schabas, "Genocide Trials and Gacaca Courts"; Lars Waldorf, "Remnants and Remains: Narratives of Suffering in Post-Genocide Rwanda's Gacaca Courts," in *Humanitarianism and Suffering: The Mobilization of Empathy*, ed. Richard A. Wilson and Richard D. Brown (New York: Cambridge University Press, 2008); Waldorf, "Mass Justice." For a response to these criticisms, see Philip Clark, *The Gacaca Courts, Post-Genocide Justice and Reconciliation in Rwanda: Justice without Lawyers* (New York: Cambridge University Press, 2010); Ariel Meyer-

stein, "Between Law and Culture: Rwanda's Gacaca and Postcolonial Legality," *Law and Social Inquiry* 32 (2007): 467–508.

69. Clark, for example, argues that attendance rates fluctuated throughout the process and did not drop off in the linear form suggested by critics. Clark, *Gacaca Courts,* 148.

70. Ibid., 133.

71. Karen Brouneus, "The Trauma of Truth Telling: Effects of Witnessing in the Rwandan Gacaca Courts on Psychological Health," *Journal of Conflict Resolution* 54, no. 3 (2010): 408–37; Burnet, "Injustice of Local Justice"; Clark, *Gacaca Courts,* 149.

72. Longman, Pham, and Weinstein, "Connecting Justice," 219.

73. S. Gabisirege and S. Babalola, "Perceptions about the Gacaca Law in Rwanda: Evidence from a Multi-Method Study," Special Publication no. 19, Johns Hopkins University School of Public Health, Center for Communications Programs, Baltimore, 2001, 14.

74. Uvin and Mironko, "Western and Local Approaches," 227–28. Even a study conducted after the trials were well underway confirms that Rwandans, though fearful of how it was being implemented in practice, regarded the *gacaca* process as a "step towards reconciliation." Ingelaere, "Does the Truth Pass across the Fire," 511.

75. Neuffer, *Neighbor's House,* 377; and Longman and Rutagengwa, "Memory, Identity, and Community," 173.

76. Several observers question the authenticity of confessions, which were viewed by some genocide suspects as the best hope for release from prison. Waldorf, "Mass Justice," 72.

77. Clark, *Gacaca Courts,* 281–92, 66.

78. Ingelaere, "Does the Truth Pass across the Fire," 517.

79. Osiel, *Mass Atrocity,* 42.

80. Ingelaere, "Does the Truth Pass across the Fire."

81. Clark, *Gacaca Courts,* 139.

82. Nancy L. Rosenblum, "Justice and the Experience of Injustice," in *Breaking the Cycles of Hatred: Violence, Memory, Repair,* ed. Nancy L. Rosenblum (Princeton, NJ: Princeton University Press, 2003).

83. Das writes: "the idea that the reenactment of the past at the collective level is a *compulsion to repeat* seems to short-circuit the complex ways in which we might understand how particular regions of the past are actualized through mediums of rumor, or in the singularity of individual lives as they knit together relations that have become frayed." Das, *Life and Words,* 102.

84. Minow, "Institutions and Emotions," 277.

CONCLUSION

1. Benedict Anderson, *Imagined Communities: Reflections on the Origin and Spread of Nationalism,* rev. and extended ed. (New York: Verso, 1991).

2. I discuss this idea further in Andrew A. G. Ross, "Realism, Emotion, and Dynamic Allegiances in Global Politics," *International Theory* 5, no. 2 (2013): 273–99.

3. See, e.g., Clifford Bob, The Marketing of Rebellion: Insurgents, Media, and International Activism (New York: Cambridge University Press, 2005); R. Charli Carpenter, "Studying Issue (Non)-Adoption in Transnational Advocacy Networks," *International Organization* 61, no. 3 (2007): 643–67.

4. Price distinguishes between grafting as a self-conscious strategy of norm entrepreneurs and grafting as a factual matter of historical context. The emotional ingredients

of historical context—what he calls "genealogical heritage"—are what I believe remain undertheorized in the study of global politics. Richard Price, "Reversing the Gun Sights: Transnational Civil Society Targets Land Mines," *International Organization* 52, no. 3 (1998): 613–44.

5. Mamdani offers an account that gestures in this direction. Mamdani, *Saviors and Survivors*.

6. See, e.g., Clifford Bob, *The Global Right Wing and the Clash of World Politics* (New York: Cambridge University Press, 2012).

7. See, e.g., Crawford, *Argument and Change in World Politics*; Jennifer Mitzen, "Reading Habermas in Anarchy: Multilateral Diplomacy and Global Public Spheres," American Political Science Review 99, no. 3 (2005): 401–17; Thomas Risse, "'Let's Argue!': Communicative Action in World Politics," *International Organization* 54, no. 1 (2000): 1–39.

8. Cass Sunstein, "On the Divergent American Reactions to Terrorism and Climate Change," *Columbia Law Review* 107 (2007): 503–57.

9. Jacques E. C. Hymans, *The Psychology of Nuclear Proliferation: Identity, Emotions, and Foreign Policy* (New York: Cambridge University Press, 2006).

10. See, respectively, Karin Knorr Cetina, "Complex Global Microstructures: The New Terrorist Societies," Theory, Culture and Society 22, no. 5 (2005): 213–34; Faisal Devji, *Landscapes of the Jihad: Militancy, Morality, Modernity* (Ithaca, NY: Cornell University Press, 2005); and Elizabeth Shakman Hurd, The Politics of Secularism in International Relations (Princeton, NJ: Princeton University Press, 2008).

BIBLIOGRAPHY

Abrahamian, Ervand. "The US Media, Huntington and September 11." *Third World Quarterly* 24, no. 3 (2003): 529–44.

Acharya, Amitav. "Ideas, Identity, and Institution-Building: From the 'ASEAN Way' to the 'Asia-Pacific Way'?" *Pacific Review* 10, no. 3 (1997): 319–46.

Adler, Emanuel, and Vincent Pouliot, eds. *International Practices*. New York: Cambridge University Press, 2011.

———. "International Practices." *International Theory* 3, no. 1 (2011): 1–36.

———. "International Practices: Introduction and Framework." In *International Practices*, ed. Emanuel Adler and Vincent Pouliot, 3–34. New York: Cambridge University Press, 2011.

Adolphs, Ralph. "Conceptual Challenges and Directions for Social Neuroscience." *Neuron* 65, no. 6 (2010): 752–67.

———. "Neural Systems for Recognizing Emotion." *Current Opinion in Neurobiology* 12, no. 2 (2002): 169–77.

———. "Recognizing Emotion from Facial Expressions: Psychological and Neurological Mechanisms." *Behavioral and Cognitive Neuroscience Reviews* 1, no. 1 (2002): 21–62.

———. "Social Cognition: Feeling Voices to Recognize Emotions." *Current Biology* 20, no. 24 (2010): R1071–72.

———. "Trust in the Brain." *Nature Neuroscience* 5, no. 3 (2002): 192–93.

African Rights. *Rwanda: Death, Despair, and Defiance*. Rev. ed. London: African Rights, 1995.

———. "Women Taking a Lead: Progress Towards Empowerment and Gender Equity in Rwanda." Discussion Paper no. 12. African Rights, Kigali, 2004.

Agamben, Giorgio. *State of Exception*. Chicago: University of Chicago Press, 2005.

Ahmed, Sara. *The Cultural Politics of Emotion*. New York: Routledge, 2004.

Alexander, Jeffrey C. *Action and Its Environments: Toward a New Synthesis*. New York: Columbia University Press, 1988.

Allen, Colin. "Mirror, Mirror in the Brain, What's the Monkey Stand to Gain?" *Nous* 44, no. 2 (2010): 372–91.

Amnesty International. *Rwanda—Gacaca: A Question of Justice*. London: Amnesty International, International Secretariat, 2002.

———. "Threat and Humiliation: Racial Profiling, Domestic Security, and Human Rights in the United States." Amnesty International, New York, 2004.

Anderson, Benedict. *Imagined Communities: Reflections on the Origin and Spread of Nationalism.* Rev. and extended ed. New York: Verso, 1991.

Anderson, Cameron, Dacher Keltner, and Oliver P. John. "Emotional Convergence between People over Time." *Journal of Personality and Social Psychology* 84, no. 5 (2003): 1054–68.

Anghie, Antony. *Imperialism, Sovereignty, and the Making of International Law.* New York: Cambridge University Press, 2007.

Angstrom, J. "Mapping the Competing Historical Analogies of the War on Terrorism: The Bush Presidency." *International Relations* 25, no. 2 (2011): 224–42.

Anzulovic, Branimir. *Heavenly Serbia: From Myth to Genocide.* New York: New York University Press, 1999.

Appadurai, Arjun. "The Capacity to Aspire: Culture and the Terms of Recognition." In *Culture and Public Action,* ed. Vijayendra Rao and Michael Walton, 59–84. Stanford, CA: Stanford University Press, 2004.

Applied Research Center. "The Public's Truth: Stories of Racial Profiling and the Attack on Civil Liberties." Applied Research Center, Oakland, CA, 2003.

Asad, Talal. *Formations of the Secular: Christianity, Islam, Modernity.* Stanford, CA: Stanford University Press, 2003.

Averill, James R. "A Constructivist View of Emotion." In *Emotion: Theory, Research, and Experience,* ed. Roberet Plutchik and Henry Kellerman, 305–39. New York: Academic Press, 1980.

Baines, Erin K. "Les Femmes Aux Mille Bras: Building Peace in Rwanda." In *Gender, Conflict, and Peacekeeping,* ed. Dyan Imazurana, Angela Raven-Roberts and Jane L. Parpart, 220–41. Lanham, MD: Rowman and Littlefield, 2005.

Bandes, Susan A. "Introduction." In *The Passions of Law,* ed. Susan A. Bandes, 1–15. New York: New York University Press, 1999.

Bargh, John A. "Auto-Motives: Preconscious Determinants of Social Interaction." In *Handbook of Motivation and Cognition: Foundations of Social Behavior,* vol. 2, ed. E. Tory Higgins and Richard M. Sorrentino, 93–130. New York: Guilford Press, 1990.

Barnett, Michael N. *Empire of Humanity: A History of Humanitarianism.* Ithaca, NY: Cornell University Press, 2011.

Barsade, Sigal G. "The Ripple Effect: Emotional Contagion and Its Influence on Group Behavior." *Administrative Science Quarterly* 47, no. 4 (2002): 644–75.

Bass, Gary Jonathan. *Stay the Hand of Vengeance: The Politics of War Crimes Tribunals.* Princeton, NJ: Princeton University Press, 2000.

Bastiaansen, J. A. C. J., M. Thioux, and C. Keysers. "Evidence for Mirror Systems in Emotions." *Philosophical Transactions of the Royal Society B: Biological Sciences* 364, no. 1528 (2009): 2391–404.

Bennett, Jane. "The Agency of Assemblages and the North American Blackout." *Public Culture* 17, no. 3 (2005): 445–65.

———. *Vibrant Matter: A Political Ecology of Things.* Durham, NC: Duke University Press, 2010.

Bennett, William J. *Why We Fight: Moral Clarity and the War on Terrorism.* New York: Doubleday, 2002.

Bergson, Henri. *Matter and Memory.* Translated by N. M. Paul and W. S. Palmer. New York: Zone Books, 1991.

———. *The Two Sources of Morality and Religion.* Translated by R. Ashley Audra and Cloudesley Brereton. Garden City, NY: Doubleday, 1935.

Bhargava, Rajeev. "Restoring Decency to Barbaric Societies." In *Truth v. Justice: The Morality of Truth Commissions*, ed. Robert I. Rotberg and Dennis F. Thompson, 45–67. Princeton, NJ: Princeton University Press, 2000.

Bially Mattern, Janice. "A Practice Theory of Emotion for International Relations." In *International Practices*, ed. Emanuel Adler and Vincent Pouliot, 63–86. New York: Cambridge University Press, 2011.

Bleiker, Roland, and Emma Hutchison. "Fear No More: Emotions and World Politics." *Review of International Studies* 34 (2008): 115–35.

Bob, Clifford. *The Global Right Wing and the Clash of World Politics.* New York: Cambridge University Press, 2012.

———. *The Marketing of Rebellion: Insurgents, Media, and International Activism.* New York: Cambridge University Press, 2005.

Bodnar, John E. *The "Good War" in American Memory.* Baltimore: Johns Hopkins University Press, 2010.

Bono, J. E., and R. Ilies. "Charisma, Positive Emotions and Mood Contagion." *Leadership Quarterly* 17, no. 4 (2006): 317–34.

Boraine, Alex. *A Country Unmasked: Inside South Africa's Truth and Reconciliation Commission.* New York: Oxford University Press, 2001.

Brennan, Teresa. *The Transmission of Affect.* Ithaca, NY: Cornell University Press, 2004.

Bringa, Tone. "Averted Gaze: Genocide in Bosnia-Herzegovina 1992–1995." In *Annihilating Difference: The Anthropology of Genocide*, ed. Alex Laban Hinton, 194–225. Berkeley: University of California Press, 2002.

Britton, Jennifer C., Stephan F. Taylor, Keith D. Sudheimer, and Israel Liberzon. "Facial Expressions and Complex IAPS Pictures: Common and Differential Networks." *NeuroImage* 31, no. 2 (2006): 906–19.

Brouneus, Karen. "The Trauma of Truth Telling: Effects of Witnessing in the Rwandan Gacaca Courts on Psychological Health." *Journal of Conflict Resolution* 54, no. 3 (2010): 408–37.

Brunnée, Jutta, and Stephen J. Toope. *Legitimacy and Legality in International Law: An Interactional Account.* New York: Cambridge University Press, 2010.

Brysk, Alison. *Global Good Samaritans: Human Rights as Foreign Policy.* New York: Oxford University Press, 2009.

Bunge, Mario Augusto. *Causality: The Place of the Causal Principle in Modern Science.* Cambridge, MA: Harvard University Press, 1959.

Burkitt, Ian. "Powerful Emotions: Power Government and Opposition in the 'War on Terror.'" *Sociology* 39, no. 4 (2005): 679–95.

Burnet, Jennie E. "The Injustice of Local Justice: Truth, Reconciliation, and Revenge in Rwanda." *Genocide Studies and Prevention* 3, no. 2 (2008): 173–93.

Bush, George W. *The National Security Strategy of the United States of America.* Washington, DC: The White House, 2002.

Butler, Judith. *Excitable Speech: A Politics of the Performative.* New York: Routledge, 1997.

Cainkar, Louise. "The Impact of the September 11 Attacks on Arab and Muslim Communities in the United States." In *The Maze of Fear: Security and Migration after 9/11*, ed. John Tirman, 215–39. New York: New Press, 2004.

Cantril, Hadley. *The Invasion from Mars: A Study in the Psychology of Panic.* New Brunswick, NJ: Transaction Publishers, 2005.

Carpenter, R. Charli. "Studying Issue (Non)-Adoption in Transnational Advocacy Networks." *International Organization* 61, no. 3 (2007): 643–67.

Castells, Manuel. *Communication Power*. New York: Oxford University Press, 2009.

Celso, Anthony. "The Tragedy of Al-Andalus: The Madrid Terror Attacks and the Islamization of Spanish Politics." *Mediterranean Quarterly* 16, no. 3 (2005): 86–101.

Celso, Anthony N. "Spanish Post-3/11 Antiterror Policy: Zapatero's Tyranny of Circumstance and the Dashing of Good Intentions." *Mediterranean Quarterly* 20, no. 2 (2009): 11–25.

Cetina, Karin Knorr. "Complex Global Microstructures: The New Terrorist Societies." *Theory, Culture and Society* 22, no. 5 (2005): 213–34.

Chari, Raj. "The 2004 Spanish Election: Terrorism as a Catalyst for Change?" *West European Politics* 27, no. 5 (2004): 954–63.

Chiao, Joan Y., Tetsuya Iidaka, Heather L. Gordon, Junpei Nogawa, Moshe Bar, Elissa Aminoff, Norihiro Sadato, and Nalini Ambady. "Cultural Specificity in Amygdala Response to Fear Faces." *Journal of Cognitive Neuroscience* 20, no. 12 (2008): 2167–74.

Chiao, Joan Y., and Vani A. Mathur. "Intergroup Empathy: How Does Race Affect Empathic Neural Responses?" *Current Biology* 20, no. 11 (2010): R478–80.

Cho, Sumi, and Gil Gott. "The Racial Sovereign." In *Sovereignty, Emergency, Legality*, ed. Austin Sarat, 182–227. New York: Cambridge University Press, 2010.

Chrétien, Jean-Pierre. *Rwanda, les médias du génocide*. Paris: Karthala, 1995.

Christakis, Nicholas A., and James H. Fowler. *Connected: The Surprising Power of Our Social Networks and How They Shape Our Lives*. New York: Little, Brown, 2009.

Clark, Howard. *Civil Resistance in Kosovo*. Sterling, VA: Pluto Press, 2000.

Clark, Philip. *The Gacaca Courts, Post-Genocide Justice and Reconciliation in Rwanda: Justice without Lawyers*. New York: Cambridge University Press, 2010.

Clarke, Kamari Maxine. *Fictions of Justice: The International Criminal Court and the Challenges of Legal Pluralism in Sub-Saharan Africa*. New York: Cambridge University Press, 2009.

Cohen, Lenard J. *Serpent in the Bosom: The Rise and Fall of Slobodan Milošević*. Rev. ed. Boulder, CO: Westview Press, 2002.

Colás, Alejandro. "An Exceptional Response? Security, Development and Civil Society in Spanish Policy after 11-M." *Development and Change* 41, no. 2 (2010): 313–33.

Collins, Randall. *Interaction Ritual Chains*. Princeton, NJ: Princeton University Press, 2004.

Čolović, Ivan. *The Politics of Symbol in Serbia: Essays in Political Anthropology*. Translated by Celia Hawkesworth. London: Hurst and Co., 2002.

Conejero, Susana, and Itziar Etxebarria. "The Impact of the Madrid Bombing on Personal Emotions, Emotional Atmosphere and Emotional Climate." *Journal of Social Issues* 63, no. 2 (2007): 273–87.

Connolly, William E. "Method, Problem, Faith." In *Problems and Methods in the Study of Politics*, ed. Ian Shapiro, Rogers M. Smith and Tarek E. Masoud, 332–49. New York: Cambridge University Press, 2004.

———. *Neuropolitics: Thinking, Culture, Speed*. Minneapolis: University of Minnesota Press, 2002.

Coole, Diana H. "Rethinking Agency: A Phenomenological Approach to Embodiment and Agentic Capacities." *Political Studies* 53, no. 1 (2005): 124–42.

Corkalo, Dina, Dean Ajdukovic, Harvey M. Weinstein, Eric Stover, Dino Djipa, and Miklos Biro. "Neighbors Again? Intercommunity Relations after Ethnic Cleansing." In *My Neighbor, My Enemy*, ed. Stover and Weinstein, 143–61.

Council on American-Islamic Relations. "The Status of Muslim Civil Rights in the United States, 2005." Council on American-Islamic Relations, Washington, DC, 2005.

Cramer, Jane Kellett. "Militarized Patriotism: Why the U.S. Marketplace of Ideas Failed before the Iraq War." *Security Studies* 16, no. 3 (2007): 489–524.

Crawford, Neta C. *Argument and Change in World Politics: Ethics, Decolonization, and Humanitarian Intervention.* New York: Cambridge University Press, 2002.

———. "Human Nature and World Politics: Rethinking 'Man.'" *International Relations* 23, no. 2 (2009): 271–88.

———. "The Passion of World Politics: Propositions on Emotion and Emotional Relationships." *International Security* 24, no. 4 (2000): 116–56.

Croft, Stuart. *Culture, Crisis and America's War on Terror.* New York: Cambridge University Press, 2006.

Damasio, Antonio R. *Descartes' Error: Emotion, Reason, and the Human Brain.* New York: Putnam, 1994.

———. *The Feeling of What Happens: Body and Emotion in the Making of Consciousness.* New York: Harcourt Brace, 1999.

———. *Looking for Spinoza: Joy, Sorrow, and the Feeling Brain.* New York: Harcourt, 2003.

———. "William James and the Modern Neurobiology of Emotion." In *Emotion, Evolution, and Rationality,* ed. Dylan Evans and Pierre Cruse, 3–12. New York: Oxford University Press, 2004.

Dannenbaum, Tom. "Bombs, Ballots, and Coercion: The Madrid Bombings, Electoral Politics, and Terrorist Strategy." *Security Studies* 20, no. 3 (2011): 303–49.

Das, Veena. *Life and Words: Violence and the Descent into the Ordinary.* Berkeley: University of California Press, 2007.

de Gelder, B., and J. Vroomen. "The Perception of Emotions by Ear and by Eye." *Cognition and Emotion* 14, no. 3 (2000): 289–311.

de Lame, Danielle. "Mighty Secrets, Public Commensality, and the Crisis of Transparency: Rwanda through the Looking Glass." *Canadian Journal of African Studies* 38, no. 2 (2004): 279–317.

DeLanda, Manuel. *A New Philosophy of Society: Assemblage Theory and Social Complexity.* New York: Continuum, 2006.

de Rivera, J. H. "Emotional Climate: Social Structure and Emotional Dynamics." In *International Review of Studies on Emotion,* ed. K. T. Strongman, 197–218. New York: John Wiley and Sons, 1992.

de Sousa, Ronald. *The Rationality of Emotion.* Cambridge, MA: MIT Press, 1987.

Deleuze, Gilles. *Bergsonism.* Translated by Hugh Tomlinson and Barbara Habberjam. New York: Zone Books, 1988.

———. *Difference and Repetition.* Translated by Paul Patton. New York: Columbia University Press, 1994.

———. *Empiricism and Subjectivity: An Essay on Hume's Theory of Human Nature.* Translated by Constantin V. Boundas. New York: Columbia University Press, 1991.

Deleuze, Gilles, and Félix Guattari. *A Thousand Plateaus: Capitalism and Schizophrenia.* Translated by Brian Massumi. Minneapolis: University of Minnesota Press, 1987.

Denich, Bette. "Dismembering Yugoslavia: Nationalist Ideologies and the Symbolic Revival of Genocide." *American Ethnologist* 21, no. 2 (1994): 367–90.

Des Forges, Alison. *"Leave None to Tell the Story": Genocide in Rwanda.* New York: Human Rights Watch and International Federation of Human Rights, 1999.

Des Forges, Alison, and Timothy Longman. "Legal Responses to Genocide in Rwanda." In *My Neighbor, My Enemy,* ed. Stover and Weinstein, 49–68.

Desch, Michael C. "The Myth of Abandonment: The Use and Abuse of the Holocaust Analogy." *Security Studies* 15, no. 1 (2006): 106–45.

Dessler, David. "What's at Stake in the Agent-Structure Debate?" *International Organization* 43, no. 3 (1989): 441–73.

Devji, Faisal. *Landscapes of the Jihad: Militancy, Morality, Modernity*. Ithaca, NY: Cornell University Press, 2005.

Dewey, John. "What Are States of Mind?" In *John Dewey: The Middle Works, 1899–1924*, ed. Jo Ann Boydston, 31–43. Carbondale: Southern Illinois Press, 1985.

Dinstein, Ilan, Cibu Thomas, Marlene Behrmann, and David J. Heeger. "A Mirror Up to Nature." *Current Biology* 18, no. 1 (2008): R13–18.

Dixon, Thomas. *From Passions to Emotions: The Creation of a Secular Psychological Category*. New York: Cambridge University Press, 2003.

Doty, Roxanne Lynn. "Aporia: A Critical Exploration of the Agent-Structure Problematique in International Relations Theory." *European Journal of International Relations* 3, no. 3 (1997): 365–92.

Duijzings, Ger. *History and Reminders in East Bosnia*. Amsterdam: Netherlands Institute for War Documentation, 2003.

Durkheim, Emile. *The Elementary Forms of the Religious Life*. Translated by Joseph Ward Swain. Glencoe, IL: Free Press, 1954.

Edkins, Jenny. *Trauma and the Memory of Politics*. New York: Cambridge University Press, 2003.

Elshtain, Jean Bethke. *Just War against Terror: The Burden of American Power in a Violent World*. New York: Basic Books, 2003.

Emirbayer, Mustafa, and Ann Mische. "What Is Agency?" *American Journal of Sociology* 103, no. 4 (1998): 962–1023.

Engle, Karen. "Feminism and Its (Dis)Contents: Criminalizing Wartime Rape in Bosnia and Herzegovina." *American Journal of International Law* 99, no. 4 (2005): 778–816.

Estellés, Isis Sánchez. "The Political-Opportunity Structure of the Spanish Anti-War Movement (2002–2004) and Its Impact." *Sociological Review* 58, suppl. S2 (2010): 246–69.

Farnell, Brenda. "Rethinking 'Verbal' and 'Non-Verbal' in Discursive Performance." *Textus* 14 (2001): 401–20.

Fattah, Khaled, and K. M. Fierke. "A Clash of Emotions: The Politics of Humiliation and Political Violence in the Middle East." *European Journal of International Relations* 15, no. 1 (2009): 67–93.

Finnemore, Martha. *The Purpose of Intervention: Changing Beliefs about the Use of Force*. Ithaca, NY: Cornell University Press, 2003.

Fisher, Philip. *The Vehement Passions*. Princeton, NJ: Princeton University Press, 2002.

Fletcher, Laurel E., and Harvey M. Weinstein. "Violence and Social Repair: Rethinking the Contribution of Justice to Reconciliation." *Human Rights Quarterly* 24, no. 3 (2002): 573–639.

Fominaya, Cristina Flesher. "The Madrid Bombings and Popular Protest: Misinformation, Counter-Information, Mobilisation and Elections after '11-M.'" *Contemporary Social Science* 6, no. 3 (2011): 289–307.

Franche, Dominique. *Rwanda: généalogie d'un génocide*. Paris: Editions mille et une nuits, 1997.

Franks, David D. *Neurosociology: The Nexus between Neuroscience and Social Psychology*. New York: Springer, 2010.

Friedman, Howard S., Louise M. Prince, Ronald E. Riggio, and M. Robin DiMatteo. "Understanding and Assessing Nonverbal Expressiveness: The Affective Communication Test." *Journal of Personality and Social Psychology* 39, no. 2 (1980): 333–51.

Frijda, Nico H. *The Emotions*. New York: Cambridge University Press, 1986.

———. "Varieties of Affect: Emotions and Episodes, Moods, and Sentiments." In *The Nature of Emotion: Fundamental Questions*, ed. Paul Ekman and Richard J. Davidson, 59–67. New York: Oxford University Press, 1994.

Fujii, Lee Ann. *Killing Neighbors: Webs of Violence in Rwanda*. Ithaca, NY: Cornell University Press, 2009.

Gabisirege, S., and S. Babalola. "Perceptions about the Gacaca Law in Rwanda: Evidence from a Multi-Method Study." Special Publication no. 19. Johns Hopkins University School of Public Health, Center for Communications Programs, Baltimore, 2001.

Gallagher, Shaun. "Simulation Trouble." *Social Neuroscience* 2, nos. 3/4 (2007): 353–65.

Gambetta, Diego. "Reason and Terror: Has 9/11 Made It Hard to Think Straight?" *Boston Review* 29, no. 2 (2004): 32–36.

García-Abadillo, Casimiro. *11-M: la venganza*. Madrid: Esfera de los Libros, 2005.

Gibbs, Anna. "Panic! Affect Contagion, Mimesis and Suggestion in the Social Field." *Cultural Studies Review* 14, no. 2 (2008): 130–45.

Gil Calvo, Enrique. *11/14-M: El cambio trágico: De la masacre al vuelco electoral*. Madrid: Adhara, 2005.

Gray, Elizabeth K., and David Watson. "Assessing Positive and Negative Affect Via Self-Report." In *Handbook of Emotion Elicitation and Assessment*, ed. James A. Coan and John J. B. Allen, 171–83. New York: Oxford University Press, 2007.

Gregg, Melissa, and Gregory J. Seigworth, eds. *The Affect Theory Reader*. Durham, NC: Duke University Press, 2010.

Gross Stein, Janice. "Psychological Explanations of International Decision Making and Collective Behavior." In *Handbook of International Relations*, ed. Walter Carlsnaes, Thomas Risse, and Beth A. Simmons, 195–219. Thousand Oaks, CA: Sage, 2013.

Grovogui, Siba N. "Come to Africa: A Hermeneutics of Race in International Theory." *Alternatives: Global, Local, Political* 26, no. 4 (2001): 425–48.

Hagan, John. *Justice in the Balkans: Prosecuting War Crimes in the Hague Tribunal*. Chicago: University of Chicago Press, 2003.

Halbwachs, Maurice, and Lewis A. Coser. *On Collective Memory*. Chicago: University of Chicago Press, 1992.

Hall, Todd. "Sympathetic States: State Strategies, Norms of Emotional Behavior, and the 9/11 Attacks." *Political Science Quarterly* 127, no. 3 (2012): 369–400.

Hall, Todd H. "We Will Not Swallow This Bitter Fruit: Theorizing a Diplomacy of Anger." *Security Studies* 20, no. 4 (2011): 521–55.

Halpern, Jodi, and Harvey M. Weinstein. "Rehumanizing the Other: Empathy and Reconciliation." *Human Rights Quarterly* 26 (2004): 561–83.

Hariri, Ahmad R., Alessandro Tessitore, Venkata S. Mattay, Francesco Fera, and Daniel R. Weinberger. "The Amygdala Response to Emotional Stimuli: A Comparison of Faces and Scenes." *NeuroImage* 17, no. 1 (2002): 317–23.

Harmon-Jones, Eddie, and Piotr Winkielman. *Social Neuroscience: Integrating Biological and Psychological Explanations of Social Behavior*. New York: Guilford Press, 2007.

Harré, Rom. "An Outline of the Social Constructivist Viewpoint." In *The Social Construction of Emotions*, ed. Rom Harré, 2–14. New York: Blackwell, 1986.

Hassan, Salah D. "Arabs, Race and the Post-September 11 National Security State." *Middle East Report*, no. 224 (2002): 16–21.

Hassin, Ran R., John A. Bargh, and Shira Zimerman. "Automatic and Flexible: The Case of Nonconscious Goal Pursuit." *Social Cognition* 27, no. 1 (2009): 20–36.

Hatfield, Elaine, John T. Cacioppo, and Richard L. Rapson. *Emotional Contagion*. New York: Cambridge University Press, 1994.

Hayden, Robert M. "Moral Vision and Impaired Insight: The Imagining of Other Peoples' Communities in Bosnia." *Current Anthropology* 48, no. 1 (2007): 105–31.

———. "Recounting the Dead: The Discovery and Redefinition of Wartime Massacres in Late- and Post-Communist Yugoslavia." In *Memory, History, and Opposition under State Socialism,* ed. Rubie S. Watson, 167–84. Santa Fe, NM: School of American Research Press, 1994.

Hayner, Priscilla B. *Unspeakable Truths: Facing the Challenge of Truth Commissions.* New York: Routledge, 2001.

Hickok, Gregory. "Eight Problems for the Mirror Neuron Theory of Action Understanding in Monkeys and Humans." *Journal of Cognitive Neuroscience* 21, no. 7 (2008): 1229–43.

Hirschman, Albert O. *The Passions and the Interests: Political Arguments for Capitalism before Its Triumph.* Princeton, NJ: Princeton University Press, 1996.

Hoffman, Aaron. "A Conceptualization of Trust in International Relations." *European Journal of International Relations* 8, no. 3 (2002): 375–401.

Hopf, Ted. "The Logic of Habit in International Relations." *European Journal of International Relations* 16, no. 4 (2010): 539–61.

Huddy, Leonie, Stanley Feldman, Charles Taber, and Gallya Lahav. "Threat, Anxiety, and Support of Antiterrorism Policies." *American Journal of Political Science* 49, no. 3 (2005): 593–608.

Huddy, Leonie, Nadia Khatib, and Theresa Capelos. "The Polls—Trends: Reactions to the Terrorist Attacks of September 11, 2001." *Public Opinion Quarterly* 66, no. 3 (2002): 418–50.

Human Rights Watch. "'We Are Not the Enemy': Hate Crimes against Arabs, Muslims, and Those Perceived to Be Arab or Muslim after September 11." Human Rights Watch, New York, 2002.

Hunt, Lynn. *Inventing Human Rights: A History.* New York: W. W. Norton, 2007.

Huntington, Samuel P. *The Clash of Civilizations and the Remaking of World Order.* New York: Simon & Schuster, 1996.

Huntsinger, Jeffrey R. "Contagion without Contact: Anticipatory Mood Matching in Response to Affiliative Motivation." *Personality and Social Psychology Bulletin* 35, no. 7 (2009): 909–22.

Hurd, Elizabeth Shakman. *The Politics of Secularism in International Relations.* Princeton, NJ: Princeton University Press, 2008.

Hymans, Jacques E. C. *The Psychology of Nuclear Proliferation: Identity, Emotions, and Foreign Policy.* New York: Cambridge University Press, 2006.

i Rigo, Enric Ordeix. "Aznar's Political Failure or Punishment for Supporting the Iraq War?: Hypotheses about the Causes of the 2004 Spanish Election Results." *American Behavioral Scientist* 49, no. 4 (2005): 610–15.

Iacoboni, Marco. *Mirroring People: The New Science of How We Connect with Others.* New York: Farrar, Straus and Giroux, 2008.

Ibish, Hussein, and Anne Stewart. "Report of Hate Crimes and Discrimination against Arab Americans: The Post-September 11 Backlash, September 11, 2001–October 11, 2002." American-Arab Anti-Discrimination Committee, Washington, DC, 2003.

Ignatieff, Michael. *The Warrior's Honor: Ethnic War and the Modern Conscience.* New York: Penguin, 1998.

Ingelaere, Bert. "'Does the Truth Pass across the Fire without Burning?' Locating the Short Circuit in Rwanda's Gacaca Courts." *Journal of Modern African Studies* 47, no. 4 (2009): 507–28.

Jackson, Richard. *Writing the War on Terrorism: Language, Politics, and Counter-Terrorism.* New York: Manchester University Press, 2005.

Jaihyun, Park, Karla Felix, and Grace Lee. "Implicit Attitudes toward Arab-Muslims and the Moderating Effects of Social Information." *Basic and Applied Social Psychology* 29, no. 1 (2007): 35–45.

James, Susan. *Passion and Action: The Emotions in Seventeenth-Century Philosophy.* New York: Oxford University Press, 1997.

James, William. *Essays in Radical Empiricism.* Lincoln: University of Nebraska Press, 1976.

———. *A Pluralistic Universe.* Cambridge, MA: Harvard University Press, 1977.

———. *The Principles of Psychology.* Vol. 2. New York: Dover Publications, 1950.

———. "What Is an Emotion?" *Mind* 9, no. 34 (1884): 188–205.

Jansen, Stef. "Troubled Locations: Return, the Life Course, and Transformations of 'Home' in Bosnia-Herzegovina." *Focaal: The European Journal of Anthropology* no. 49 (2007): 15–30.

———. "'Why Do They Hate Us?' Everyday Serbian Nationalist Knowledge of Muslim Hatred." *Journal of Mediterranean Studies* 13, no. 2 (2003): 215–37.

Jasper, James M. *The Art of Moral Protest: Culture, Biography, and Creativity in Social Movements.* Chicago: University of Chicago Press, 1997.

Jervis, Robert L. "The Confrontation between Iraq and the US: Implications for the Theory and Practice of Deterrence." *European Journal of International Relations* 9, no. 2 (2003): 315–37.

Jespersen, T. Christopher. "Analogies at War: Vietnam, the Bush Administration's War in Iraq, and the Search for a Usable Past." *Pacific Historical Review* 74, no. 3 (2005): 411–26.

Joas, Hans. *The Creativity of Action.* Chicago: University of Chicago Press, 1996.

———. *The Genesis of Values.* Chicago: University of Chicago Press, 2000.

Jones, Adam. "Gender and Genocide in Rwanda." *Journal of Genocide Research* 4, no. 1 (2002): 65–94.

Judah, Tim. "The Fog of Justice." *New York Review of Books* 51, no. 1 (2004): 23–25.

———. *Kosovo: War and Revenge.* 2nd ed. New Haven, CT: Yale University Press, 2002.

———. *The Serbs: History, Myth, and the Destruction of Yugoslavia.* 2nd ed. New Haven, CT: Yale University Press, 2000.

Juslin, Patrick N., and Klaus R. Scherer. "Vocal Expression of Affect." In *The New Handbook of Methods in Nonverbal Behavior Research,* ed. Jinni A. Harrigan, 65–136. New York: Oxford University Press, 2005.

Kaplan, Robert D. *Balkan Ghosts: A Journey through History.* New York: Vintage Books, 1994.

———. *The Coming Anarchy: Shattering the Dreams of the Post Cold War.* New York: Random House, 2000.

Karekezi, Urusaro Alice, Alphonse Nshimiyamana, and Beth Mutamba. "Localizing Justice: Gacaca Courts in Post-Genocide Rwanda." In *My Neighbor, My Enemy,* ed. Stover and Weinstein, 69–84.

Katzenstein, Peter J., and Robert O. Keohane. *Anti-Americanisms in World Politics.* Ithaca, NY: Cornell University Press, 2007.

Kaufman, Stuart J. "Escaping the Symbolic Politics Trap: Reconciliation Initiatives and Conflict Resolution in Ethnic Wars." *Journal of Peace Research* 43, no. 2 (2006): 201–18.

———. *Modern Hatreds: The Symbolic Politics of Ethnic War.* Ithaca, NY: Cornell University Press, 2001.

Kaufmann, Chaim. "Possible and Impossible Solutions to Ethnic Civil Wars." *International Security* 20, no. 4 (1996): 136–75.

———. "Threat Inflation and the Failure of the Marketplace of Ideas: The Selling of the Iraq War." *International Security* 29, no. 1 (2004): 5–48.

Kellow, Christine L., and H. Leslie Steves. "The Role of Radio in the Rwandan Genocide." *Journal of Communication* 48, no. 3 (1998): 107–28.

Keltner, Dacher, and Jonathan Haidt. "Social Functions of Emotions at Four Levels of Analysis." *Cognition and Emotion* 13, no. 5 (1999): 505–21.

Keysers, Christian. *The Empathic Brain: How the Discovery of Mirror Neurons Changes Our Understanding of Human Nature.* [Lexington, KY]: Christian Keysers, 2011.

Keysers, Christian, and Valeria Gazzola. "Social Neuroscience: Mirror Neurons Recorded in Humans." *Current Biology* 20, no. 8 (2010): R353–54.

Khong, Yuen Foong. *Analogies at War: Korea, Munich, Dien Bien Phu, and the Vietnam Decisions of 1965.* Princeton, NJ: Princeton University Press, 1992.

Krasner, Stephen D. *Sovereignty: Organized Hypocrisy.* Princeton, NJ: Princeton University Press, 1999.

Kratochwil, Friedrich V. *Rules, Norms, and Decisions: On the Conditions of Practical and Legal Reasoning in International Relations and Domestic Affairs.* New York: Cambridge University Press, 1989.

Krebs, Ronald R., and Chaim Kaufmann. "Correspondence: Selling the Market Short? The Marketplace of Ideas and the Iraq War." *International Security* 29, no. 4 (2005): 196–207.

Krebs, Ronald R., and Jennifer K. Lobasz. "Fixing the Meaning of 9/11: Hegemony, Coercion, and the Road to War in Iraq." *Security Studies* 16, no. 3 (2007): 409–51.

Krog, Antjie. *Country of My Skull: Guilt, Sorrow, and the Limits of Forgiveness in the New South Africa.* 1st U.S. ed. New York: Three Rivers Press, 2000.

Lake, David A., and Donald Rothchild. "Containing Fear: The Origins and Management of Ethnic Conflict." *International Security* 21, no. 2 (1996): 41–75.

Latour, Bruno. "Gabriel Tarde and the End of the Social." In *The Social in Question: New Bearings in History and the Social Sciences*, ed. Patrick Joyce, 117–32. New York: Routledge, 2002.

———. *Politics of Nature: How to Bring the Sciences into Democracy.* Cambridge, MA: Harvard University Press, 2004.

———. *Reassembling the Social: An Introduction to Actor-Network-Theory.* New York: Oxford University Press, 2005.

Lebow, Richard Ned. *A Cultural Theory of International Relations.* New York: Cambridge University Press, 2008.

LeDoux, Joseph E. *The Emotional Brain: The Mysterious Underpinnings of Emotional Life.* New York: Simon and Schuster, 1996.

Lemarchand, René. *Rwanda and Burundi.* Washington, DC: Praeger, 1970.

Lerner, Jennifer S., and Dacher Keltner. "Beyond Valence: Toward a Model of Emotion-Specific Influences on Judgement and Choice." *Cognition and Emotion* 14, no. 4 (2000): 473–93.

Lewis, Bernard. "The Roots of Muslim Rage." *Atlantic Monthly*, September 1990, 47–60.

Leys, Ruth. "The Turn to Affect: A Critique." *Critical Inquiry* 37, no. 3 (2011): 434–72.

Liberman, Peter. "An Eye for an Eye: Public Support for War against Evildoers." *International Organization* 60, no. 3 (2006): 687–722.

Little, Douglas. *American Orientalism: The United States and the Middle East since 1945.* 3rd ed. Chapel Hill: University of North Carolina Press, 2008.

Lockman, Zachary. *Contending Visions of the Middle East: The History and Politics of Orientalism.* New York: Cambridge University Press, 2004.

Longman, Timothy, Phuong Pham, and Harvey M. Weinstein. "Connecting Justice to Human Experience: Attitudes toward Accountability and Reconciliation in Rwanda." In *My Neighbor, My Enemy*, ed. Stover and Weinstein, 206–25.

Longman, Timothy, and Théonèste Rutagengwa. "Memory, Identity, and Community in Rwanda." In *My Neighbor, My Enemy*, ed. Stover and Weinstein, 162–82.

Love, Erik. "Confronting Islamophobia in the United States: Framing Civil Rights Activism among Middle Eastern Americans." In *Anti-Muslim Prejudice: Past and Present*, ed. Maleiha Malik, 191–215. New York: Routledge, 2010.

Löwenheim, Oded, and Gadi Heimann. "Revenge in International Politics." *Security Studies* 17, no. 4 (2008): 685–724.

Luban, David. "Eight Fallacies about Liberty and Security." In *Human Rights in the "War on Terror,"* ed. Richard Ashby Wilson, 242–57. New York: Cambridge University Press, 2005.

Lutz, Catherine. *Unnatural Emotions: Everyday Sentiments on a Micronesian Atoll and Their Challenge to Western Theory*. Chicago: University of Chicago Press, 1988.

Lynch, Marc. *Voices of the New Arab Public: Iraq, Al-Jazeera, and Middle East Politics Today*. New York: Columbia University Press, 2006.

Macqueen, Angus, and Paul Mitchell. "The Cracks Appear." In *Yugoslavia: Death of a Nation*. New York: Discovery Channel Video, 1996.

Magaš, Branka. *The Destruction of Yugoslavia: Tracking the Break-up, 1980–92*. New York: Verso, 1993.

Malcolm, Noel. *Kosovo: A Short History*. London: Macmillan, 1998.

Maliqi, Shkëlzen. *Kosova: Separate Worlds: Reflections and Analyses, 1989–1998*. Pristina: MM, 1998.

Mamdani, Mahmood. "Reconciliation without Justice." In *Religion and Media*, ed. Hent de Vries, 376–87. Stanford, CA: Stanford University Press, 1999.

———. *Saviors and Survivors: Darfur, Politics, and the War on Terror*. New York: Doubleday, 2009.

———. "The Truth According to the TRC." In *The Politics of Memory: Truth, Healing, and Social Justice*, ed. Ifi Amadiume and Abdullahi An-Na'im, 176–83. London: Zed Books, 2000.

———. *When Victims Become Killers: Colonialism, Nativism, and the Genocide in Rwanda*. Princeton, NJ: Princeton University Press, 2001.

Marcus, George E., W. Russell Neumen, and Michael MacKuen. *Affective Intelligence and Political Judgment*. Chicago: University of Chicago Press, 2000.

Marshall, Randall D., Richard A. Bryant, Lawrence Amsel, S.U.H. Eun Jung, Joan M. Cook, and Yuval Neria. "The Psychology of Ongoing Threat: Relative Risk Appraisal, the September 11 Attacks, and Terrorism-Related Fears." *American Psychologist* 62, no. 4 (2007): 304–16.

Massumi, Brian. *Parables for the Virtual: Movement, Affect, Sensation*. Durham, NC: Duke University Press, 2002.

Mazower, Mark. *No Enchanted Palace: The End of Empire and the Ideological Origins of the United Nations*. Princeton, NJ: Princeton University Press, 2009.

McDermott, Rose. "The Feeling of Rationality: The Meaning of Neuroscientific Advances for Political Science." *American Political Science Review* 2, no. 4 (2004): 691–706.

———. "Mutual Interests: The Case for Increasing Dialogue between Political Science and Neuroscience." *Political Research Quarterly* 62, no. 3 (2009): 571–83.

McKeown, Ryder. "Norm Regress: US Revisionism and the Slow Death of the Torture Norm." *International Relations* 23, no. 1 (2009): 5–25.

McNeill, David, ed. *Language and Gesture.* New York: Cambridge University Press, 2000.

Mercer, Jonathan. "Emotional Beliefs." *International Organization* 64, no. 1 (2010): 1–31.

———. "Rationality and Psychology in International Politics." *International Organization* 59, no. 1 (2005): 77–106.

Meyerstein, Ariel. "Between Law and Culture: Rwanda's Gacaca and Postcolonial Legality." *Law and Social Inquiry* 32 (2007): 467–508.

Michavila, Narciso. "War, Terrorism and Elections: Electoral Impact of the Islamist Terror Attacks on Madrid." Real Instituto Elcano de Estudios Internacionales y Estratégicos, Madrid, 2005.

Miller, William Ian. *Eye for an Eye.* New York: Cambridge University Press, 2006.

Minow, Martha. *Between Vengeance and Forgiveness: Facing History after Genocide and Mass Violence.* Boston: Beacon Press, 1998.

———. "Institutions and Emotions: Redressing Mass Violence." In *The Passions of Law*, ed. Susan A. Bandes, 265–81. New York: New York University Press, 1999.

Minow, Martha, and Nancy L. Rosenblum. *Breaking the Cycles of Hatred: Memory, Law, and Repair.* Princeton, NJ: Princeton University Press, 2002.

Mitzen, Jennifer. "Ontological Security in World Politics: State Identity and the Security Dilemma." *European Journal of International Relations* 12, no. 3 (2006): 341–70.

———. "Reading Habermas in Anarchy: Multilateral Diplomacy and Global Public Spheres." *American Political Science Review* 99, no. 3 (2005): 401–17.

Morris, J. S., S. K. Scott, and R. J. Dolan. "Saying It with Feeling: Neural Responses to Emotional Vocalizations." *Neuropsychologia* 37, no. 10 (1999): 1155–63.

Mueller, John E. *Overblown: How Politicians and the Terrorism Industry Inflate National Security Threats, and Why We Believe Them.* New York: Free Press, 2006.

Mugesera v. Canada (Minister of Citizenship and Immigration), [2003] F.C.A. 325 (Federal Ct. of Appeals).

Mugesera v. Canada (Minister of Citizenship and Immigration), [2005] 2 S.C.R. 100 (S.C.C.).

Murphy, Jeffrie G., and Jean Hampton. *Forgiveness and Mercy.* New York: Cambridge University Press, 1988.

Murphy, Sheila T., and R. B. Zajonc. "Affect, Cognition, and Awareness: Affective Priming with Optimal and Suboptimal Stimulus Exposures." *Journal of Personality and Social Psychology* 64, no. 5 (1993): 723–39.

Mutamba, John, and Jeanne Izabiliza. *The Role of Women in Reconciliation and Peace Building in Rwanda: Ten Years after Genocide 1994–2004: Contributions, Challenges and Way Forward.* Kigali: National Unity and Reconciliation Commission, 2005.

Naber, Nadine. "Introduction." In *Race and Arab Americans before and after 9/11: From Invisible Citizens to Visible Subjects*, ed. Jamal Amaney and Nadine Naber, 1–45. Syracuse, NY: Syracuse University Press, 2008.

———. "Race, Gender, and the Culture of Fear among Arab Immigrants in San Francisco Post-9/11." *Cultural Dynamics* 18, no. 3 (2006): 235–67.

Nacos, Brigitte L., Yaeli Bloch-Elkon, and Robert Y. Shapiro. *Selling Fear: Counterterrorism, the Media, and Public Opinion.* Chicago: University of Chicago Press, 2011.

Naimark, Norman M. *Fires of Hatred: Ethnic Cleansing in Twentieth-Century Europe.* Cambridge, MA: Harvard University Press, 2001.

Neuffer, Elizabeth. *The Key to My Neighbor's House: Seeking Justice in Bosnia and Rwanda.* New York: Picador, 2001.

Neumann, Roland, and Fritz Strack. "'Mood Contagion': The Automatic Transfer of Mood between Persons." *Journal of Personality and Social Psychology* 79, no. 2 (2000): 211–23.

Newbury, Catherine, and Hannah Baldwin. "Aftermath: Women in Postgenocide Rwanda." Working Paper no. 303. USAID, Washington, DC, 2000.

Newbury, David. "Returning Refugees: Four Historical Patterns of 'Coming Home,' to Rwanda." *Comparative Studies in Society and History* 47, no. 2 (2005): 252–85.

Nietzsche, Friedrich Wilhelm. *The Will to Power*. Translated by Walter Arnold Kaufmann and R. J. Hollingdale. New York: Random House, 1967.

Noon, David Hoogland. "Operation Enduring Analogy: World War II, the War on Terror, and the Uses of Historical Memory." *Rhetoric and Public Affairs* 7, no. 3 (2004): 339–65.

Nussbaum, Martha C. "'Secret Sewers of Vice': Disgust, Bodies, and the Law." In *The Passions of Law*, ed. Susan A. Bandes, 19–62. New York: New York University Press, 1999.

———. *Upheavals of Thought: The Intelligence of Emotions*. New York: Cambridge University Press, 2001.

Oikawa, Masanori, Henk Aarts, and Haruka Oikawa. "There Is a Fire Burning in My Heart: The Role of Causal Attribution in Affect Transfer." *Cognition and Emotion* 25, no. 1 (2011): 156–63.

Onuf, Nicholas. *World of Our Making: Rules and Rule in Social Theory and International Relations*. Columbia: University of South Carolina Press, 1989.

Ortony, Andrew, Gerald L. Clore, and Allan Collins. *The Cognitive Structure of Emotions*. New York: Cambridge University Press, 1988.

Osiel, Mark. *Mass Atrocity, Collective Memory, and the Law*. New Brunswick, NJ: Transaction Publishers, 1997.

Pancic, Teofil. "Sex in the City, Sloba and the Hague." *Helsinki Charter* 49 (2002).

Paris, Roland. "Kosovo and the Metaphor War." *Political Science Quarterly* 117, no. 3 (2002): 423–50.

Parkinson, Brian, and Gwenda Simons. "Affecting Others: Social Appraisal and Emotion Contagion in Everyday Decision Making." *Personality and Social Psychology Bulletin* 35, no. 8 (2009): 1071–84.

Petersen, Roger Dale. *Understanding Ethnic Violence: Fear, Hatred, and Resentment in Twentieth-Century Eastern Europe*. New York: Cambridge University Press, 2002.

Phelps, Elizabeth A., and Laura A. Thomas. "Race, Behavior, and the Brain: The Role of Neuroimaging in Understanding Complex Social Behaviors." *Political Psychology* 24, no. 4 (2003): 747–58.

Posen, Barry R. "The Security Dilemma and Ethnic Conflict." *Survival* 35, no. 1 (1993): 29–35.

Pottier, Johan. *Re-Imagining Rwanda: Conflict, Survival and Disinformation in the Late Twentieth Century*. New York: Cambridge University Press, 2002.

Pouliot, Vincent. *International Security in Practice: The Politics of NATO-Russia Diplomacy*. New York: Cambridge University Press, 2010.

Power, Samantha. *A Problem from Hell: America and the Age of Genocide*. New York: Basic Books, 2002.

Powley, Elizabeth. "Strengthening Governance: The Role of Women in Rwanda's Transition." Hunt Alternatives Fund, Boston, 2003.

Price, Richard. "Reversing the Gun Sights: Transnational Civil Society Targets Land Mines." *International Organization* 52, no. 3 (1998): 613–44.

Prinz, Jesse J. *Gut Reactions: A Perceptual Theory of Emotion*. New York: Oxford University Press, 2004.

Prosecutor v. Milošević (Trial Transcript) IT-02-54. Transcript no. 02-02-14-IT of the ICTY Trial Chamber (February 14, 2002).

Prosecutor v. Ferdinand Nahimana, Jean-Bosco Barayagwiza, and Hassan Ngeze. ICTR-99-52-T, Judgment and Sentence of the ICTR Trial Chamber I (December 3, 2003).

Prunier, Gérard. *The Rwanda Crisis: History of a Genocide.* New York: Columbia University Press, 1995.

Pupavac, Vanessa. "The Emotionology of the New International Security Paradigm." *European Journal of Social Theory* 7, no. 4 (2004): 149–70.

Ramet, Sabrina P. *Balkan Babel: The Disintegration of Yugoslavia from the Death of Tito to the Fall of Milošević.* 4th ed. Boulder, CO: Westview Press, 2002.

Rees, Wyn, and Richard J. Aldrich. "Contending Cultures of Counterterrorism: Transatlantic Divergence or Convergence?" *International Affairs* 81, no. 5 (2005): 905–23.

Reilly, Judy, and Judy Seibert. "Language and Emotion." In *Handbook of Affective Sciences*, ed. Richard J. Davidson, Klaus R. Scherer and H. Hill Goldsmith, 535–59. New York: Oxford University Press, 2002.

Republic of Rwanda, Departement des Juridictions Gacaca. "Les Juridictions Gacaca comme solution alternative au reglement du contentieux du genocide." Departement des Juridictions Gacaca, Kigali, 2003.

Ribot, Théodule. *Essay on the Creative Imagination.* Translated by Albert H. N. Baron. Chicago: Open Court Publishing, 1906.

Rime, Bernard, Darío Paez, Nekane Basabe, and Francisco Martinez. "Social Sharing of Emotion, Post-Traumatic Growth, and Emotional Climate: Follow-up of Spanish Citizen's Response to the Collective Trauma of March 11th Terrorist Attacks in Madrid." *European Journal of Social Psychology* 40, no. 6 (2010): 1029–45.

Risse, Thomas. "'Let's Argue!': Communicative Action in World Politics." *International Organization* 54, no. 1 (2000): 1–39.

Rizzolatti, Giacomo, and Corrado Sinigaglia. *Mirrors in the Brain: How Our Minds Share Actions and Emotions.* New York: Oxford University Press, 2008.

Rosenberg, Emily S. *A Date Which Will Live: Pearl Harbor in American Memory.* Durham, NC: Duke University Press, 2003.

Rosenblum, Nancy L. "Justice and the Experience of Injustice." In *Breaking the Cycles of Hatred: Violence, Memory, Repair,* ed. Nancy L. Rosenblum, 77–106. Princeton, NJ: Princeton University Press, 2003.

Ross, Andrew A. G. "Coming in from the Cold: Constructivism and Emotions." *European Journal of International Relations* 12, no. 2 (2006): 197–222.

———. "Realism, Emotion, and Dynamic Allegiances in Global Politics." *International Theory* 5, no. 2 (2013): 273–99.

———. "Why They Don't Hate Us: Emotion, Agency and the Politics of 'Anti-Americanism.'" *Millennium: Journal of International Studies* 39, no. 1 (2010): 109–25.

Rotberg, Robert I. "Truth Commissions and the Provision of Truth, Justice, and Reconciliation." In *Truth v. Justice: The Morality of Truth Commissions,* ed. Robert I. Rotberg and Dennis F. Thompson, 3–21. Princeton, NJ: Princeton University Press, 2000.

Rotberg, Robert I., and Dennis F. Thompson, eds. *Truth v. Justice: The Morality of Truth Commissions.* Princeton, NJ: Princeton University Press, 2000.

Rwanda. Office of the President. *The Unity of Rwandans: Before the Colonial Period and under the Colonial Rule, under the First Republic.* Kigali: Republic of Rwanda, Office of the President of the Republic, 1999.

Sarat, Austin. "Vengeance, Victims and the Identities of Law." *Social and Legal Studies* 6, no. 2 (1997): 163–89.

Sasley, Brent E. "Theorizing States' Emotions." *International Studies Review* 13, no. 3 (2011): 452–76.

Saurette, Paul. "You Dissin Me? Humiliation and Post 9/11 Global Politics." *Review of International Studies* 32, no. 3 (2006): 495–522.

Saxe, Rebecca. "Against Simulation: The Argument from Error." *Trends in Cognitive Sciences* 9, no. 4 (2005): 174–79.

Saxon, Dan. "Exporting Justice: Perceptions of the ICTY among the Serbian, Croatian, and Muslim Communities in the Former Yugoslavia." *Journal of Human Rights* 4, no. 4 (2005): 559–72.

Schabas, William. "Genocide Trials and Gacaca Courts." *Journal of International Criminal Justice* 3 (2005): 879–95.

Schachter, Stanley. "The Interaction of Cognitive and Physiological Determinants of Emotional State." In *Advances in Experimental Social Psychology*, ed. Leonard Berkowitz, 49–80. New York: Academic Press, 1964.

Schacter, Daniel L. *Searching for Memory: The Brain, the Mind, and the Past.* New York: Basic Books, 1996.

Schatzki, Theodore R. *Social Practices: A Wittgensteinian Approach to Human Activity and the Social.* New York: Cambridge University Press, 1996.

Scheff, Thomas J. *Microsociology: Discourse, Emotion, and Social Structure.* Chicago: University of Chicago Press, 1990.

Scollon, Ronald. *Mediated Discourse as Social Interaction: A Study of News Discourse.* New York: Longman, 1998.

Searle, John R. *The Construction of Social Reality.* New York: Free Press, 1995.

Seib, Philip. "The News Media and 'the Clash of Civilizations.'" In *Media and Conflict in the Twenty-First Century*, ed. Philip Seib, 217–34. New York: Palgrave, 2005.

Sell, Louis. *Slobodan Milosevic and the Destruction of Yugoslavia.* Durham, NC: Duke University Press, 2002.

Semin, Gün R., and Gerald Echterhoff. *Grounding Sociality: Neurons, Mind, and Culture.* New York: Psychology Press, 2011.

Sewell, William H., Jr. *Logics of History: Social Theory and Social Transformation.* Chicago: University of Chicago Press, 2005.

Shaheen, Jack G. "Reel Bad Arabs: How Hollywood Vilifies a People." *Annals of the American Academy of Political and Social Sciences* 588 (2003): 171–93.

Silber, Laura, and Allan Little. *Yugoslavia: Death of a Nation.* New York: Penguin Books, 1997.

Snyder, Jack, and Robert Jervis. "Civil War and the Security Dilemma." In *Civil Wars, Insecurity, and Intervention*, ed. Barbara F. Walter, 15–37. New York: Columbia University Press, 1999.

Solomon, Robert C. *A Passion for Justice: Emotions and the Origins of the Social Contract.* Reading, MA: Addison-Wesley, 1990.

Solomon, Ty. "'I Wasn't Angry Because I Couldn't Believe It Was Happening': Affect and Discourse in Responses to 9/11." *Review of International Studies* 38, no. 4 (2012): 907–28.

Southgate, Victoria, and Antonia F. de C. Hamilton. "Unbroken Mirrors: Challenging a Theory of Autism." *Trends in Cognitive Sciences* 12, no. 6 (2008): 225–29.

Steele, Brent J. *Ontological Security in International Relations: Self-Identity and the IR State.* New York: Routledge, 2007.

Stover, Eric, and Harvey M. Weinstein. "Introduction: Conflict, Justice, and Reclamation." In *My Neighbor, My Enemy*, ed. Stover and Weinstein, 1–28.

Stover, Eric, and Harvey M. Weinstein, eds. *My Neighbor, My Enemy: Justice and Community in the Aftermath of Mass Atrocity.* New York: Cambridge University Press, 2004.

Straus, Scott. *The Order of Genocide: Race, Power, and War in Rwanda*. Ithaca, NY: Cornell University Press, 2006.

———. "Origins and Aftermaths: The Dynamics of Genocide and Their Post-Crime Implications." In *After Mass Crime: Rebuilding States and Communities*, ed. Béatrice Pouligny, Simon Chesterman and Albrecht Schnabel, 122–41. New York: United Nations University Press, 2007.

Sturken, Marita. *Tourists of History: Memory, Kitsch, and Consumerism from Oklahoma City to Ground Zero*. Durham, NC: Duke University Press, 2007.

Suárez, Sandra L. "Mobile Democracy: Text Messages, Voter Turnout and the 2004 Spanish General Election." *Representation* 42, no. 2 (2006): 117–28.

Sundar, S. Shyam. "News Features and Learning." In *Communication and Emotion: Essays in Honor of Dolf Zillmann*, ed. Jennings Bryant, David R. Roskos-Ewoldsen and Joanne Cantor, 275–96. Mahwah, NJ: Lawrence Erlbaum Associates, 2003.

Sunstein, Cass. "On the Divergent American Reactions to Terrorism and Climate Change." *Columbia Law Review* 107 (2007): 503–57.

Tarde, Gabriel de. *Gabriel Tarde on Communication and Social Influence: Selected Papers*. Edited by Terry N. Clark. Chicago: University of Chicago Press, 1969.

———. *The Laws of Imitation*. Translated by Elsie Clews Parsons. New York: Henry Holt, 1903.

Taylor, Charles. "Action as Expression." In *Intention and Intentionality: Essays in Honour of G.E.M. Anscombe*, ed. Cora Diamond and Jenny Teichman, 73–89. Brighton: Harvester Press, 1979.

———. *Human Agency and Language: Philosophical Papers I*. New York: Cambridge University Press, 1985.

Taylor, Christopher C. *Sacrifice as Terror: The Rwandan Genocide of 1994*. New York: Berg, 1999.

Thompson, John B. *The Media and Modernity: A Social Theory of the Media*. Cambridge: Polity Press, 1995.

Totterdell, Peter. "Catching Moods and Hitting Runs: Mood Linkage and Subjective Performance in Professional Sports Teams." *Journal of Applied Psychology* 85, no. 6 (2000): 848–59.

Turner, Jonathan H. *Face-to-Face: Toward a Sociological Theory of Interpersonal Behavior*. Stanford, CA: Stanford University Press, 2002.

Unger, Roberto Mangabeira. *Democracy Realized: The Progressive Alternative*. New York: Verso, 1998.

United Nations Secretary-General. "Secretary-General, in 'Mission of Healing' to Rwanda, Pledges Support of United Nations for Country's Search for Peace and Progress." United Nations, New York, May 6, 1998.

United Nations Security Council. "Statute of the International Criminal Tribunal for Rwanda." UNSCR 955, U.N. SCOR, 49th, 3453th mtg., U.N. Doc. S/RES/955 (1994), 1994.

Uvin, Peter, and Charles Mironko. "Western and Local Approaches to Justice in Rwanda." *Global Governance* 9, no. 2 (2003): 219–31.

Van Biezen, Ingrid. "Terrorism and Democratic Legitimacy: Conflicting Interpretations of the Spanish Elections." *Mediterranean Politics* 10, no. 1 (2005): 99–108.

Van Kleef, Gerben A. "How Emotions Regulate Social Life: The Emotions as Social Information (EASI) Model." *Current Directions in Psychological Science* 18, no. 3 (2009): 184–88.

Verdery, Katherine. *The Political Lives of Dead Bodies: Reburial and Postsocialist Change*. New York: Columbia University Press, 1999.

Vidal, Claudine. "Les commémorations du génocide au Rwanda." *Les Temps Modernes* 613 (2001): 1–46.

———. *Sociologie des passions: Rwanda, Côte D'ivoire.* Paris: Karthala, 1991.

Vokes, Richard. "Charisma, Creativity, and Cosmopolitanism: A Perspective on the Power of the New Radio Broadcasting in Uganda and Rwanda." *Journal of the Royal Anthropological Institute* 13, no. 4 (2007): 805–24.

Volpp, Leti. "The Citizen and the Terrorist." In *September 11 in History: A Watershed Moment?*, ed. Mary L. Dudziak, 147–62. Durham, NC: Duke University Press, 2003.

Wald, Priscilla. *Contagious: Cultures, Carriers, and the Outbreak Narrative.* Durham, NC: Duke University Press, 2007.

Waldorf, Lars. "Mass Justice for Mass Atrocity: Rethinking Local Justice as Transitional Justice." *Temple Law Review* 79, no. 1 (2006): 1–87.

———. "Remnants and Remains: Narratives of Suffering in Post-Genocide Rwanda's Gacaca Courts." In *Humanitarianism and Suffering: The Mobilization of Empathy*, ed. Richard A. Wilson and Richard D. Brown, 285–305. New York: Cambridge University Press, 2008.

Walt, Stephen M. "Fads, Fevers, and Firestorms." *Foreign Policy*, no. 121 (2000): 34–42.

Weber, Cynthia. "Romantic Meditations of September 11." In *Rituals of Meditation: International Politics and Social Meaning*, ed. François Debrix and Cynthia Weber, 173–88. Mineapolis: University of Minnesota Press, 2003.

Wendt, Alexander. "*Social Theory* as Cartesian Science: An Auto-Critique from a Quantum Perspective." In *Constructivism in International Relations: Alexander Wendt and His Critics*, ed. Stefano Guzzini and Anna Leander, 181–219. New York: Routledge, 2006.

———. *Social Theory of International Politics.* New York: Cambridge University Press, 1999.

———. "The State as Person in International Theory." *Review of International Studies* 30, no. 2 (2004): 289–316.

Wendt, Alexander E. "The Agent-Structure Problem in International Relations Theory." *International Organization* 41, no. 3 (1987): 335–70.

White, Geoffrey M. "National Subjects: September 11 and Pearl Harbor." *American Ethnologist* 31, no. 3 (2004): 293–310.

Wight, Colin. *Agents, Structures, and International Relations: Politics as Ontology.* New York: Cambridge University Press, 2006.

Williams, Patricia J. *Seeing a Color-Blind Future: The Paradox of Race.* New York: Noonday Press, 1998.

Willis, Susan. "Anthrax 'R' Us." *Social Text* 20, no. 4 (2002): 19–28.

Wilmer, Franke. *The Social Construction of Man, the State, and War: Identity, Conflict, and Violence in Former Yugoslavia.* New York: Routledge, 2002.

Wilson, Richard A. *The Politics of Truth and Reconciliation in South Africa: Legitimizing the Post-Apartheid State.* New York: Cambridge University Press, 2001.

Woodward, Susan L. *Balkan Tragedy: Chaos and Dissolution after the Cold War.* Washington, DC: Brookings Institution, 1995.

Zillmann, Dolf. "Excitation Transfer in Communication-Mediated Aggressive Behavior." *Journal of Experimental Social Psychology* 7, no. 4 (1971): 419–34.

———. "Sequential Dependencies in Emotional Experience and Behavior." In *Emotion: Interdisciplinary Perspectives*, ed. Robert D. Kavanaugh, Betty Zimmerberg, and Steven Fein, 243–72. Mahwah, NJ: Lawrence Erlbaum Associates, 1996.

INDEX

ACLU. *See* American Civil Liberties Union (ACLU)
actor-network-theory, 55, 172n41
ADC. *See* American-Arab Anti-Discrimination Committee (ADC)
Adler, Emanuel, 48, 53, 165n22
affect: vs. emotion, 20, 164n13. *See also* circulations of affect; emotions
affective transfer. *See* contagion
Afghanistan War, 70, 72, 75, 84
Agamben, Giorgio, 83, 177n53
agency: and agentic capacities, 54–55; and circulations of affect, 32; and communications technologies, 54–55; and creativity, 42, 49, 157; definition of, 52; and emotions, 51–56; in global politics, 51, 54–56, 162; and structure, 53–54, 172n37; and will, 52, 171n29. *See also* collective agency
Ahmed, Sara, 44, 48, 115
Akayesu, Prosecutor v., 99, 131
al Qaeda, 83, 86–87, 88, 89, 90, 91, 156, 157
ambiguity: and contagion, 32, 44, 46, 48, 64, 157; and creativity, 10, 121, 157; of emotions, 18, 19, 41, 56, 60, 144; and fear, 18, 92; in political speeches, 95, 108–9, 112, 120; and reburials, 102
American-Arab Anti-Discrimination Committee (ADC), 80, 81
American Civil Liberties Union (ACLU), 80, 81
amygdala, 50
analogies. *See* historical analogies

Anderson, Benedict, 155
anger: connections with other emotions, 2, 19, 21, 58, 154; and contagion, 28, 39; after the Madrid bombings, 11–12, 69–70, 86–90, 91–92, 179n69; after 9/11, 11–12, 15, 42, 67–68, 69, 70, 71, 75, 85–86, 91; in Rwanda, 63, 145; in South Africa, 43; and terrorism, 85–90; and transitional justice, 147, 148
anthrax threats, 68, 70, 73–76, 91
anti-Americanism, 9, 42, 61
anxiety, 51, 67, 154
Appadurai, Arjun, 139
Arab Spring, 9, 15, 156
assemblages, 55, 155–56, 158, 172n42
Aznar, José María, 86

beliefs, 10, 16, 33, 34–35, 42, 47, 52, 54, 60, 70, 97
Benedict XVI, 36
Bennett, Jane, 55, 172n41
Bergson, Henri, 2, 40, 46, 49, 105, 141, 157
Bhaskar, Roy, 53, 54
Bially Mattern, Janice, 41–42, 165n19
bin Laden, Osama, 89
bioterrorism, 74–75. *See also* anthrax threats
body maps, 50, 166n37
Bourdieu, Pierre, 53
Britain, 44
Bush, George W., 8, 36, 63, 72, 77, 78, 80, 82–83, 84, 92
Bush Doctrine, 84, 158
Butler, Judith, 142

CAIR. *See* Council on American-Islamic Relations (CAIR)
Canada, Mugesera, trial in, 107–10
carryover, 43, 48–49, 75, 91. *See also* contagion
Castells, Manuel, 87, 88
causality, 10, 57–60
China, 37
circulation, definition of, 169n71
circulations of affect: and collective agency, 35–37, 63, 65, 94, 155; and communications technologies, 5; and creativity, 16–17; definition of, 21, 37–38, 153; and discourse, 63; and elites, 6, 56; and ethnic conflict, 12, 124; and ethnic nationalism, 115; existence of, 62; fear as, 96–101; and identity, 13, 33; and individuality, 21, 32, 41; and institutions, 13, 33; after 9/11, 70–81; and norms, 13, 33; and political impact, 32–34, 38; and social interactions, 1–2, 4, 10, 16, 21–22, 38, 39, 40, 41, 62, 64–65, 94, 119, 121, 148, 153, 160. *See also* contagion
civilizations, clash of, 77–78, 93
Clarke, Kamari Maxine, 133
Clinton, Bill, 134
Cold War, 157
collective agency: and circulations of affect, 17, 35–37, 55, 63, 65, 94, 96, 155; and communications technologies, 9; and contagion, 28, 155; and ethnic conflict, 37, 154–55; and identity, 8, 36–37, 119; and terrorism, 36, 37
collective effervescence, 44
Collins, Randall, 22, 24, 28, 30, 32, 36, 44, 47–48, 73, 75, 139, 165n21
communications technologies: and agency, 9, 54–55; and circulations of affect, 5; and communities, 155; and contagion, 28–31, 45, 51; Internet, 30; and 9/11, 5, 71; radio broadcasts, 4, 5, 30, 31, 63, 94, 95, 96, 110–12, 113; and social interactions, 5, 6, 16, 28–31; social networks, 30; and Spanish political protests, 88; television broadcasts, 5, 30, 96
compassion, 40, 149
compassion fatigue, 43
Connolly, William E., 58, 82
constructivism: and agency, 52, 53–54; and constitutive causality, 59–60; on end of Cold War, 157; on hatred, 18, 93; on

identity, 7, 10, 55, 59, 63, 64, 96, 152, 160, 180n2; on norms, 10, 59, 63, 84–85, 152, 160; on war, 160–61
contagion: clinical research on, 27–28; and collective agency, 28, 155; and communications technologies, 28–31, 45, 51; and creativity, 10, 40–42, 45–51, 56–57, 62, 64, 156–57; definition of, 22–23; and discourse, 31; durability of, 42–43; and individuality, 32; mechanisms of, 23–25, 48–49; and microsociology, 28–29; and 9/11, 75; nonconscious, 40, 43; primitive emotional contagion, 24–25; properties of, 41–45; sites of, 28; and social interactions, 2, 40, 44, 45, 49–51. *See also* circulations of affect; interconnectedness of emotions
Coole, Diana, 54
copresence, 22, 28–29
Council on American-Islamic Relations (CAIR), 80, 81
Cramer, Jane Kellett, 92
Crawford, Neta C., 18, 163n1
creativity: and agency, 42, 157; Bergson on, 2, 40, 46, 49, 157; and contagion, 10, 17, 40–42, 45–51, 56–57, 62, 64, 156–57; definition of, 46; and ethnic conflict, 120–21; James on, 2, 50, 58, 157; and the Madrid bombings, 92; and memory, 45, 49; and nationalism, 95–96; Ribot on, 40, 46, 49, 157
cultural theory, 2, 44, 161
cycles of hatred, 12, 19, 61, 97, 104, 121, 123, 125–29, 148, 154, 185n3. *See also* discourse about emotion

Dallaire, Roméo, 134
Damasio, Antonio, 20–21, 25, 50–51
Darfur, 9, 48–49, 156, 158
Darwin, Charles: *The Expression of Emotions in Man and Animals*, 21
Das, Veena, 137, 141, 189n83
de Lame, Danielle, 97, 111
Deleuze, Gilles, 44, 56, 105, 115, 130, 141, 164n13, 172n42, 173n45
desires, 54
Dewey, John, 19, 47, 164n10
disappointment, 28, 147
discourse, 11, 64, 159; about emotion, 8–9, 42, 61–62, 91, 154; and contagion, 31,

42; emotional, 31, 62–64, 94; after 9/11, 70–71; and social interactions, 160, 168n67. *See also* anti-Americanism; cycles of hatred; political speeches
Doty, Roxanne Lynn, 172n37
Durkheim, Emile, 22, 33, 44, 47

Egypt, 15, 30
elites, 5–6; and circulations of affect, 6, 56; and emotional symbols, 6, 56, 172n44; mobilization by, 5, 116–19, 120; and popular emotion, 55–57, 95, 116–19, 156
Elshtain, Jean, 85–86
emergence, 60, 64, 148, 155–56, 159, 165n19, 173n50
emotional contagion. *See* contagion
emotional escalation, 43
emotional recognition, 25–27
emotional symbols, 10, 56, 71–73, 96, 102–3, 117, 172n44
emotions: background, 20–21, 28, 152, 154, 165n17; basic, 19, 21; cognitive makeup of, 17–18; complexities of, 61, 154; durability of, 20, 42–46, 62, 73; interconnectedness of, 2, 19, 20–21, 39, 43, 57–59, 68, 149, 153–54, 157; long- vs. short-term, 44–45, 62, 73; nonconscious, 3, 61, 160; prior, 32; psychology of, 17–20; sociology of, 16, 22; taxonomic approach to, 2, 17, 19, 149; vs. affect, 20, 164n13; vs. feelings, 20–21. *See also* affect; circulations of affect; *individual emotions*; moods
empathy, 2, 26–27, 147, 149
Engle, Karen, 186n25–26
enthusiasm, 20, 44, 51, 59, 154
envy, 21
ETA, 86–87
ethnic cleansing, 100
ethnic conflict: and circulations of affect, 12, 124; and collective agency, 37, 154–55; and creativity, 120–21; and emotional symbols, 56; role of fear in, 94–95, 96–101, 119; role of hatred in, 6, 8–9, 12, 57, 61, 93–94, 121, 180n4; and identity, 18, 34, 37, 96, 119, 149; research on, 15–16. *See also* Rwanda; Yugoslavia
ethnographic research, 63, 173n50
excitation transfer, 43–46, 49, 58, 75, 95, 115, 157, 168n63. *See also* contagion

Expression of Emotions in Man and Animals, The (Darwin), 21

facial expressions, 29, 110
Falwell, Jerry, 68, 80
fascism, 56, 173n45
fear: of anthrax attacks, 73–76; as a circulation of affect, 96–101; connections with other emotions, 2, 21, 39, 58, 68, 154, 157; and creativity, 51; and ethnic conflict, 94–95, 96–101, 119; experienced by Arab and Muslim Americans, 79; and militancy, 59; after 9/11, 11–12, 32, 67–69, 70, 71, 75, 85, 91, 92; and racial difference, 81, 82; realist approach to, 18; role of elites in creating, 94–95; in Rwanda, 18, 37, 96–99, 108, 110, 111, 119, 156, 180n7; and security dilemma, 18, 101, 151; and social norms, 47; in Yugoslavia, 99–101
feelings, 34–35, 160; vs. emotions, 20–21
flexibility, 2, 10, 46, 48, 49, 60, 95, 121, 157
football matches, 96, 116
forgiveness, 12, 128, 135–36, 145, 147, 149, 150, 186n37
Franche, Dominique, 97, 180n7
Freud, Sigmund, 61, 104
Frijda, Nico, 44
frustration, 96, 116, 117, 125, 127, 128, 136, 142, 154
Fujii, Lee Ann, 94, 101, 180n5

gacaca courts, 125, 143–48, 189n74
Geneva Conventions, 83
gender, 98, 187n47. *See also* women in Rwanda
genocide: and fear, 97; incitement to, 106–12; participation in, 180n5; and rape, 99. *See also* Rwanda
Genocide Convention, 106
Germany: National Socialism, 56, 173n45
Giddens, Anthony, 53, 139
global warming, 159
Goffman, Erving, 22, 28
grief, 19, 87, 103–4, 134
Guattari, Félix, 56, 173n45
guilt, 21, 125, 134
Gulf War, 76

habits, 17, 37, 46–47, 59, 81–83, 96, 97, 99, 105, 141, 169n75

Habyarimana, Juvenal, 107
Halbwachs, Maurice, 105
Hall, Todd, 37, 163n1
hand gestures, 31, 110
hate crimes, 4, 5, 44, 80–81
hatred: ancient, 8–9, 12, 42, 61, 93, 96, 126–27, 154; anti-West, 61, 67; connections with other emotions, 21, 58, 68, 157; constructivist approach to, 18, 93; cycles of, 12, 19, 61, 104, 125–29, 154, 185n3; and ethnic conflict, 6, 8–9, 12, 57, 61, 93–94, 121, 180n4; identity-based, 18–19; and incitement, 106–7; and 9/11, 67–68; racial, 31; in Rwanda, 6, 18, 31, 63, 93–94, 111, 156; and transitional justice, 19, 93, 123, 125–29, 148; in Yugoslavia, 6, 18, 94
historical analogies, 71–73, 86, 91, 95
HIV/AIDS, 98
Holocaust, 72, 158; Holocaust Memorial Museum, 31
hope, 21, 51, 63, 147
Hopf, Ted, 53, 169n75
HRVC. See South Africa Human Rights Violations Committee (HRVC)
Human Rights Watch, 80
Hume, David, 130
humiliation, 19, 39, 47, 51, 116
Huntington, Samuel, 77, 78, 93
Hussein, Saddam, 74, 76, 84, 91, 156
Hutu Power movement, 97

ICTR. See International Criminal Tribunal for Rwanda (ICTR)
ICTY. See International Criminal Tribunal for former Yugoslavia (ICTY)
identity: and anti-Americanism, 9; and circulations of affect, 16, 33, 42; constructivism on, 7, 10, 55, 59, 63, 64, 96, 152, 160, 180n2; and emotions, 8–9, 10, 12, 33, 47, 60, 94, 123–24; ethnic, 98, 100, 103, 105, 120, 140–42, 147; and ethnic conflict, 8, 18, 34, 37, 95–96, 119, 149; and hatred, 18–19, 126, 185n3; analytical limitations of, 8–9, 12, 18, 36–37, 40, 55, 60, 94, 96, 102, 119, 126, 139; theories of, 7–9, 12, 36–37, 55, 96, 149; and the media, 70; national, 34, 95–96, 102–5; racial, 78–79, 98, 141; and reconciliation, 18, 127, 139–42, 147; in Rwanda, 155; and social interactions,

60; suppression of, 141–42; and terrorism, 8, 36–37, 48, 69, 78–79
identity politics, 7
Ignatieff, Michael, 104
imitation, 166n26
incitement to genocide, 60, 106–12, 116
India, 139, 141
individuality, 21, 32, 41
Ingelaere, Bert, 139, 146
institutions, 33
intentionality, 13, 53–54, 152
interaction rituals. See rituals, interaction; social interaction
interconnectedness of emotions, 2, 19, 20–21, 39, 43, 57–59, 68, 149, 153–54, 157. See also contagion
International Covenant on Civil and Political Rights, 106
International Criminal Court (ICC), 133
International Criminal Tribunal for former Yugoslavia (ICTY), 32, 118, 120, 125, 130–31, 134
International Criminal Tribunal for Rwanda (ICTR), 99, 106, 109, 111–12, 120, 125, 130–32, 134, 154
International law, 2, 59, 83, 84, 107; customary international law, 82
international relations (IR), 18, 19, 36–37, 53, 57, 151–52, 154, 160–61. See also constructivism; realism
Internet, 30
Iranian hostage crisis, 76
Iraq War, 11, 70, 72, 74–76, 84, 88–89, 156
Israel, 36, 47, 76

James, William, 2, 17, 19–20, 25, 27, 40, 46, 47, 50, 58, 149, 157
Jasenovac, 101–2
Joas, Hans, 46–47, 171n29
joy, 2
Judah, Tim, 182n32

Kangura, 110, 111
Kant, Immanuel, 52
Kaplan, Robert, 93, 104
Kaufman, Stuart, 172n44
Kaufmann, Chaim, 102–3
Krasner, Stephen, 84
Kratochwil, Friedrich, 53
Kyoto Protocol, 159

Latour, Bruno, 55
law: and emotions, 129–30, 147; trials as public rituals, 16, 129–34, 143–48; legal exceptions, 82–85, 92. See also transitional justice
leaders. See elites
legal exceptions, 82–85, 92
levels of analysis, 4–7, 16, 34–36, 155
Lewis, Bernard, 77, 78
liberalism, 127–28
love, 19
Luban, David, 83
Lutz, Catherine, 173n50

Madrid bombings, 4, 11–12, 62, 69–70, 86–90, 91–92, 179n69
Mamdani, Mahmood, 49, 97, 98, 136, 141
Mandela, Nelson, 43
Massumi, Brian, 44–45
Mead, George Herbert, 47
media: after 9/11, 5, 70–71; radio broadcasts, 4, 5, 30, 31, 63, 94, 95, 96, 110–12, 113; television broadcasts, 5, 30, 96, 113, 115. See also communications technologies
memory: Bergson on, 49, 105, 141; creativity of, 10, 45, 49, 73, 104, 106, 129, 145; collective, 93, 102–6, 142, 175n21; and emotions, 25, 40, 45, 49, 104–6; of Pearl Harbor, 60, 71–73; as a product of social interaction, 105–6; and repression, 104; in Rwanda, 97, 138, 141–42; and transitional justice, 135–36; virtual, 141–42; of World War II, 71–73, 103–6; in Yugoslavia, 101–6, 118, 182n32
Mercer, Jonathan, 33, 163n1
methodology, 58, 60–62, 152, 160
microsociology, 3, 10, 21, 28–29, 152, 157
military force, 82–83
Milošović, Slobodan, 62, 95, 113, 115, 116–19, 120, 156, 172n44, 183n63
Minow, Martha, 126, 128, 149
mirror neurons, 25–27, 54, 183n51
moods, 20, 21, 24, 29, 44, 49, 62, 152, 154. See also emotions
Moses, Michael Valdez, 72
Mouvement Révolutionnaire National pour le Développement de la Démocratie (MRND), 107
Mubarak, Hosni, 15

Mueller, John, 72, 85
Mugesera, Léon, 107–10, 118, 120

Nahimana, Prosecutor v., 111–12
nationalism: as a creative force, 95–96; and economic hardship, 115, 183n65; elites' mobilization of, 116–19; and football matches, 116. See also Yugoslavia
National Security Strategy (NSS), 83, 84
National Socialism, 56, 173n45
national unity, 12, 43, 136, 140–42, 143, 146–47, 149–50
Nazism, 56
nesting, 20–21
networks. See social networks
neuropsychology, 46
neuroscience, 2, 3, 152–53, 157; and creativity, 49–50; and emotional recognition, 16, 25–27; and memory, 49; nonconscious attention, 3, 34; and primitive emotional contagion, 24–25; and racial difference, 81–82; and simulation, 10, 16, 25–27, 41, 50, 153; social neuroscience, 3, 50, 163n3; and tone of voice, 110, 120, 159
neurosociology, 3, 50, 112, 140, 153, 163n3
New York Times, 87, 125–26
Nietzsche, Friedrich Wilhelm, 164n10
9/11, 4, 30; analogy to Pearl Harbor, 68–69, 71–73, 75, 91; anger after, 11–12, 15, 42, 67–68, 69, 70, 71, 75, 85–86, 91; and the anthrax attacks, 73–76; and anti-Muslim/anti-Arab sentiment, 58, 63; circulations of affect after, 70–81; and creation of Islamic terrorist identity, 11, 45, 48, 69, 76–81, 82, 155; effect on norms, 81–85; emotions of perpetrators, 157; emotions surrounding, 67–85, 91–92; fear after, 11–12, 15, 32, 67–69, 70, 71, 75, 85, 91, 92; global emotion after, 37; and hate crimes, 4, 5; hatred after, 67–68; and the media, 5, 70–71; and Muslim/Arab stereotypes, 11, 45, 69, 76–81, 155; and political speeches, 63, 70, 77, 84; and racial profiling, 4, 5, 11, 69, 79–81; social context of, 68–70, 91
Noon, David Hoogland, 73
norms: and circulations of affect, 16, 42; constructivism on, 10, 59, 63, 84–85, 152, 160; and emotions, 10, 33, 42, 47,

norms (*cont.*)
    158–59; grafting of, 158, 189n4; and
    legal exceptions, 82–85, 92; and the Ma-
    drid bombings, 92; 9/11 effect on, 76,
    81–85; and social interactions, 60; and
    war, 160–61
NSS. See *National Security Strategy* (NSS)
nuclear proliferation, 159

ontological security, 169n75
Onuf, Nicholas, 53
Osiel, Mark, 129, 145, 146

Palestine, 34, 47, 76
Parsons, Talcott, 33, 47, 52
Partido Popular (PP), 86–89, 178n63
passion, 17, 40, 52, 130
Patriot Act, 79
patriotism, 92
Pearl Harbor, 60, 68–69, 71–73, 75, 85, 91
Pearl Harbor (film), 72
Petersen, Roger Dale, 57
political action, 17, 32–34, 38, 76
political protests, 4, 5, 16, 63, 87, 91–92,
    94, 96, 114–16, 152
political rallies, 62, 94, 96, 113–14, 115,
    152, 184n74
political speeches: ambiguity in, 95, 108–9,
    112, 120; and circulations of affect, 16;
    emotions used in, 34; after 9/11, 63, 70,
    77, 84; in Rwanda, 4, 94, 95, 107–10,
    120, 182n43; and social interactions,
    112–13, 152; in Yugoslavia, 4, 95,
    117–19, 120. See also discourse; tone
    of speech
Pouliot, Vincent, 48, 53, 139, 165n22
PP. See Partido Popular (PP)
practices. See social practices
Price, Richard, 189n4
pride, 21, 28, 44, 51
Principles of Psychology, The (James), 19–20
print media, 30, 70; in Rwanda, 110; in
    Yugoslavia, 101–2
Prosecutor v. Akayesu, 99, 131
Prosecutor v. Nahimana, 111–12
prosody, 64, 110, 111, 120. See also tone
    of speech
psychology: of emotions, 17–20, 25, 43,
    153; of memory, 49, 104; sociological,
    35. See also social psychology
Pupavac, Vanessa, 127

race: racial difference, 81–82; racial dis-
    crimination, 81–82; racial profiling, 4,
    5, 11, 48, 69, 79–81, 89; racial stereo-
    types, 11, 45, 50, 69, 76–81, 155
radio broadcasts, 4, 5, 30, 31, 63, 94, 95,
    96, 110–12, 113
Radio et Télévision Libres des Milles Col-
    lines (RTLM), 110–12
Ražnatavić, Željko, 116
rape, 99, 124, 131–32, 138, 186n25–26
rationality, 151–52
realism, 18, 36, 84–85
reburials: in Rwanda, 140; in Yugoslavia, 4,
    94, 96, 101–6
reconciliation, 135–37, 145, 149
repair. See social repair
repetition, 45, 48, 154
repression, 104, 126
resentment, 2, 19, 43, 147, 154
revenge. See vengeance
Ribot, Théodule, 40, 46, 49, 157
rituals: after 9/11, 70; commemoration,
    16, 62; interaction, 22, 29, 32, 33, 44,
    47–48, 165n21; reburial, 4, 94, 96,
    101–6, 140
Rosenberg, Emily, 72
RPF. See Rwandan Patriotic Front (RPF)
RTLM. See Radio et Télévision Libres des
    Milles Collines (RTLM)
rules, 59
rumor, 95, 141
Rushdie, Salman, 36
Russia, 37
Rwanda: anger in, 63, 145; categorization
    of Tutsis, 98–99, 108–9, 150, 155,
    180n10–11; economic and cultural
    change in, 97; fear in, 18, 37, 96–99,
    108, 110, 111, 119, 156, 180n7; gacaca
    courts, 125, 143–48, 189n74; hatred in,
    6, 18, 31, 63, 93–94, 111, 156; Hutu
    Power movement, 97; identity in, 37,
    98–99, 108–9, 140–42, 147, 155; incite-
    ment to genocide, 12, 106–12; memory
    in, 138, 141–42; Mouvement Révolu-
    tionnaire National pour le Développe-
    ment de la Démocratie (MRND), 107;
    national unity in, 140–42, 143, 146–47,
    149–50; norms in, 158; political speeches
    in, 4, 94, 107–10, 120, 182n43; radio
    broadcasts in, 4, 5, 31, 63, 94, 95, 110–
    12, 113; reburials in, 140; Rwandan

Patriotic Front (RPF), 97, 98, 107, 142, 143, 146; sexuality in, 98–99; social repair in, 137–39, 142, 144, 146, 147; transitional justice in, 12, 63, 130–34, 137–39, 143–48; war rape, 99, 124, 131–32, 138, 186n25–26; women in, 98–99, 131–32, 137–38. *See also* International Criminal Tribunal for Rwanda (ICTR)

Rwandan Patriotic Front (RPF), 97, 98, 107, 142, 143, 146

sadness, 19
Sarat, Austin, 130, 145
Save Darfur movement, 49, 156, 158
Schacter, Daniel, 49, 104–5
Schatzki, Theodore, 41
Scheff, Thomas J., 28
Searle, John, 59, 173n49
security dilemma, 18, 101, 151
September 11. *See* 9/11
sexuality, 98–99, 124. *See also* women in Rwanda
shame, 28
simulation, 10, 25–27, 41, 50
60 Minutes, 80
social context, 124–25
social interactions: and circulations of affect, 1–2, 4, 10, 21–22, 38, 39, 40, 41, 62, 64–65, 94, 119, 121, 148, 153, 160; and communications technologies, 5, 6, 16, 28–31; and communities, 155; and contagion, 2, 40, 44, 45, 49–51; and copresence, 5, 10, 28–30; and creativity, 47–48; and discourse, 160, 168n67; and emergence, 60; and emotions, 1, 3, 4, 8, 123–24; interaction rituals, 22, 29, 32, 33, 44, 47–48, 165n21; memory as a product of, 105–6; and racial profiling, 79–81; serial participation in, 31; and social repair, 139–40; and symbols, 73, 75; and transitional justice, 146; and trust, 139–40; vs. social practices, 165n22. *See also* political protests; political rallies; political speeches
socialization, 3, 16, 32–34, 39, 59–60, 152
social networks, 22, 30, 36, 54, 138, 161, 166n29, 180n5; and communications, 5, 6, 9, 30, 71, 87, 88, 156; and person-to-person networks, 87, 88, 92; transnational, 11, 55, 85. *See also* actor-network-theory; assemblages; terrorism

social neuroscience. *See* neurosociology
social norms. *See* norms
social practices, 37, 41, 48, 53, 165n22
social psychology: and contagion, 10, 27–28, 29, 40, 42, 43–44, 115, 157; and flexibility of emotions, 2; and primitive emotional contagion, 24; and social sharing, 71. *See also* psychology
social repair, 137–42, 144, 146, 147, 148, 149–50; vs. reconciliation, 137
sociology, 16, 22, 161. *See also* neurosociology
South Africa: Human Rights Violations Committee (HRVC), 135, 186n37; national unity in, 43, 136, 140, 149–50; racial identity in, 141; transitional justice in, 12, 135–36, 140, 158; Truth and Reconciliation Commission (TRC), 33, 125, 135–36, 140
Spain: Madrid bombings, 4, 11–12, 62, 69–70, 86–90, 91–92; Partido Popular (PP), 86–89, 178n63
speech, tone of. *See* tone of speech
speeches, political. *See* political speeches
spillover, 43. *See also* contagion
states, 34–36
status reports, 25, 166n37
Straus, Scott, 37, 94, 99, 111, 181n15
strikes, 39, 63, 94, 96, 114, 115, 116
Sunstein, Cass, 159
symbols. *See* emotional symbols
sympathy, 39

Taliban, 83, 91
Tarde, Gabriel, 22, 23, 30, 35, 45, 54, 166n26; and levels of analysis, 35, 54; and "the public," 30; and "sociological psychology," 35
Taylor, Charles, 22, 52
television broadcasts, 5, 30, 96, 113, 115
terrorism: and anger, 85–90; and collective agency, 36, 37; complexity of, 161; European views on, 89; and revenge, 61. *See also* Madrid bombings; 9/11
Tito, Josip Broz, 99–100, 101, 103
tone of speech, 31, 95, 109–10, 111–12, 118, 120, 159. *See also* prosody
torture, 34, 82–83, 92
transitional justice: and anger, 148; and collective agency, 37; and emotions, 124–50, 185n3; and forgiveness, 12,

transitional justice (*cont.*)
128, 135–36, 145, 147, 150, 186n37; gacaca courts, 125, 143–48, 189n74; and hatred, 19, 93, 123, 125–29, 148; and memory, 135–36; popular partici- pation in, 144; public relations in, 131; and reconciliation, 135–37, 145; and revenge, 126, 127–28; in Rwanda, 12, 63, 125, 130–34, 137–39, 143–48; and social repair, 137–42, 144, 146, 147, 148, 149–50; in South Africa, 12, 135– 36, 140, 158; trials as public rituals, 16, 129–34, 143–48; truth commissions, 12, 33, 125, 128, 135–37; war crimes trials, 129, 130–34, 185n22; witnesses in, 131–32, 135; in Yugoslavia, 130–31, 134, 185n22. *See also* International Criminal Tribunal for former Yugoslavia (ICTY); International Criminal Tribunal for Rwanda (ICTR); South Africa Truth and Reconciliation Commission (TRC)
TRC. *See* South Africa Truth and Reconcilia- tion Commission (TRC)
trust, 2, 13, 40, 44, 47, 138, 139–40, 146, 147, 185n3, 187n53
truth commissions, 12, 33, 125, 128, 135–37, 140
Tudjman, Franjo, 101, 116
Turner, Jonathan H., 29
Tutu, Desmond, 136

UN. *See* United Nations (UN)
Unger, Roberto, 137
United Nations (UN), 33–34, 35–36, 78, 90, 106, 133. *See also* International Criminal Tribunal for former Yugoslavia (ICTY); International Criminal Tribunal for Rwanda (ICTR)
United States, 47, 133, 145, 158. *See also* 9/11; Pearl Harbor

vengeance, 61, 67, 90, 91, 126, 127–28, 145–46, 147

Verdery, Katherine, 102, 103–4, 105
Vietnam War, 73

war, 160–61. *See also* Iraq War; World War II
war crimes trials, 129, 130–34, 185n22
Washington Post, 74
Wendt, Alexander E., 53–54, 169n84, 173n49
Wight, Colin, 53–54
will, 171n29
Willis, Susan, 74
Wilmer, Franke, 180n2
Wilson, Richard, 136
witnesses, 131–32, 135
Wittgenstein, Ludwig, 29
women in Rwanda, 98–99, 131–32, 137–38
workers' strikes. *See* strikes
World War II: memory of, 72–73, 103–6, 182n32; Pearl Harbor, 60, 68–69, 71– 73, 75, 85, 91; reburial of war dead, 94, 96, 101–6

Yugoslavia: ethnic cleansing in, 100; and ethnic homogeneity, 34; ethnic identity in, 8, 119; fear in, 99–101; football matches in, 116; hatred in, 6, 18, 94; Jasenovac, 101–2; manipulation of popular emotion by elites, 95, 116–19; memories in, 45, 103–6, 118, 182n32; nationalism in, 12, 116–19, 156; norms in, 158; political protests in, 4, 5, 94, 96, 114–16; political rallies in, 94, 96, 113–14, 115, 184n74; political speeches in, 4, 117–19, 120; reburials in, 4, 94, 96, 101–6; strikes in, 39, 94, 96, 114, 115, 116; television broadcasts in, 5, 96, 113, 115; transitional justice in, 130– 31, 134, 185n22; unemployment in, 60. *See also* International Criminal Tribunal for former Yugoslavia (ICTY)

Zapatero, José Rodríguez, 87, 89–90
Zillmann, Dolf, 44, 168n63